NIETZSCHE: AN INTRODUCTION

Cultural Memory
in
the
Present

Mieke Bal and Hent de Vries, Editors

NIETZSCHE

An Introduction

Gianni Vattimo

Translated by Nicholas Martin

STANFORD UNIVERSITY PRESS
STANFORD, CALIFORNIA 2001

Stanford University Press
Stanford, California

© 1985 Editori Laterza
This translation © 2002 The Athlone Press
First published in Italy as *Introduzione a Nietzsche* by
Editori Laterza, 1985

Originating publisher of the English edition: The Athlone Press
First published in the U.S.A. by Stanford University Press, 2002
Printed in Great Britain on acid-free, archival-quality paper.

Cloth ISBN 0-8047-3798-3
Paper ISBN 0-8047-3799-1

Last figure below indicated the year of this printing:
10   09   08   07   06   05   04   03   02   01

Typeset by CentraServe, Saffron Walden, Essex
Printed and bound in Great Britain

Contents

Contents

Publisher's Note

Readers unfamiliar with the main events of Nietzsche's life and the sequence of his works may find it helpful to refer first to Section IV, which provides a factual chronology.

Abbreviations

Quotations in the text from Nietzsche's works are translations from the standard German edition (*Nietzsche: Werke. Kritische Gesamtausgabe*, edited by Giorgio Colli and Mazzino Montinari (Berlin and New York, 1967ff)). The abbreviations used refer to the following texts in the volumes indicated:

AC	*The Antichrist*: VI.3
BGE	*Beyond Good and Evil*: VI.2
BT	*The Birth of Tragedy*: III.1
D	*Daybreak*: V.1
EH	*Ecce Homo*: VI.3
GM	*On the Genealogy of Morals*: VI.2
GS	*The Gay Science*: V.2
HAH I	*Human, All Too Human*, Volume One: IV.2
N	*Nachlass* (posthumously published notes fragments)
TI	*Twilight of the Idols*: VI.3
TL	*On Truth and Lies in an Extra-Moral Sense*: III.2
UM	*Untimely Meditations*: III.1 (UM I–UM III); IV.1 (UM IV)

Abbreviations

WS   *Human, All Too Human*, Volume IIii (The
Wanderer and his Shadow): IV.3

Z   *Thus Spake Zarathustra*: VI.1 (Z I–Z IV)

The abbreviations are usually followed by two numerals: the first refers to the chapter or aphorism (which are the same in all editions); the second refers to the correponding page number in the relevant volume of Colli and Montinari's edition shown above. In the case of the *Untimely Meditations*, an additional Roman numeral (from I to IV) indicates which of the essays is being referred to. The same principle applies to the four parts of *Thus Spake Zarathustra*. In the case of works in which the section numbering is not continuous (*Thus Spake Zarathustra* and *Twilight of the Idols*), the chapter number is given first in small Roman numerals, followed by the section number – e.g. Z IV, iii, §2 refers to the second section of the third chapter of Part Four of *Thus Spake Zarathustra*.

References to Nietzsche's *Nachlass* (his posthumously published notes and fragments) follow Colli and Montinari's notation, whereby each fragment is given two numerals. So, for example, N June – July 1879, IV.3, 437, 40[7], refers to fragment number 40[7] of that period, on page 437 of volume IV.3.

I. From Philology to Philosophy

1. HOW NIETZSCHE IS TO BE READ

Nietzsche research has produced a whole variety of perspectives and conclusions, which are set out in the concluding chapter on the history of Nietzsche reception. The greatest influence on Nietzsche research in the last few decades, however, has been that of Martin Heidegger, whose two-volume study was written between 1936 and 1946, but not published until 1961.[1] It brought about a sea-change in Nietzsche interpretation. In Heidegger's view, Nietzsche should be related to Aristotle.[2] In other words, he should not be regarded as an essentially metaphysical thinker. Heidegger rightly considered Nietzsche to be not merely a philosopher but also a philosopher in the technical sense of the word, because the oldest and most fundamental problem of philosophy was the central focus of Nietzsche's attention, namely the question of Being.

Looking back to the earlier history of Nietzsche's impact in Europe, in the last years of the nineteenth century and the first decades of the twentieth century, it

is not hard to see how revolutionary Heidegger's interpretation was. For early Nietzsche reception was indeed
'literary' and 'culturally critical', more concerned with
his place in the history of ideology than with his work
as philosophy in the narrower sense (see ch. V). And, at
first sight, Nietzsche's texts – with the possible exception
of some of his late works and those posthumous fragments which were first published as *The Will to Power*
(see ch. III and Bibliography) – do appear to prove
Heidegger wrong and Nietzsche's early interpreters
right. Both the predominant form of these texts – the
aphoristic form – and their contents (the critique of
morality, of religious ideas, of prejudices as a whole, as
well as their 'cultural criticism') can scarcely serve to
justify a strictly ontological and metaphysical approach
of the kind Heidegger pursues. Wilhelm Dilthey's evaluation of Nietzsche's work, set out in *The Essence of
Philosophy* (1907), seems much more acceptable. It should
be noted in passing that Heidegger owes more to this
text than he openly admits. Dilthey's book characterizes
the philosophy of the second half of the nineteenth
century as a 'philosophy of life'. Admittedly, Dilthey
does not mean by this any vitalist metaphysics of the
kind that soon appropriated this concept, but rather a
reflexion on existence, which renounces any 'scientific'
claim to validate or ground it. Dilthey groups Nietzsche
together with Carlyle, Emerson, Ruskin, Tolstoy and
Maeterlinck, whose counterparts in other eras of European cultural history were men such as Marcus Aurelius
and Montaigne. In other words, he brackets Nietzsche

with philosophical writers who inhabited a climate created by, among others, Schopenhauer.

> This genre of writing is related to the classical art of
> the Sophists and the Rhetoricians, which Plato ban-
> ished so emphatically from the realm of philosophy, in
> the sense that persuasion supplants methodical proof
> [. . .] Their eye remains fixed on the problem of life,
> but they despair of solving it by means of a universally
> valid metaphysics or a theory of how the world hangs
> together; life should be interpreted from it – this is
> the great thought which connects these philosophers
> of life with the world's experience and literature.[3]

Their explanation of life is not 'methodical', it is expres-
sive and suggestive. Dilthey's thesis which, in opposition
to Heidegger's metaphysical approach, appears to justify
a primarily literary consideration of Nietzsche's work,
also provides the precondition for relating these contrast-
ing attitudes to each other; because, even for Heidegger,
Nietzsche is admittedly a metaphysical thinker who
must be read with reference to the problem of Being,
but he is at the same time the last thinker in the history
of metaphysics, in whom metaphysics reaches the end of
the line. We may therefore legitimately assume that this
'end' invests both the content and the style of his thought
with a special particularity. Perhaps it was precisely this
which Dilthey had in mind when he characterized
Nietzsche's philosophy as a 'philosophy of life'. Indeed
for Dilthey, too, this philosophy is tied to the final

3

moments of 'metaphysics', those great metaphysical systems which, according to him, crop up periodically in the history of Western thought.

It is not, of course, our concern to synthesize the interpretative thesis/antithesis (Dilthey/Heidegger), which is of exemplary significance for the whole history of Nietzsche's influence. The reason we refer to it is because we wish to indicate that it is entirely fruitful to read Nietzsche as Heidegger wishes to, as above all a philosopher in the full sense of the term. At the same time, however, we are seeking to locate the particularity of Nietzsche's situation (as the thinker who 'rounds off' metaphysics) precisely in his practice of philosophy as 'literature' or a 'philosophy of life', in a very much more profound sense than Heidegger's interpretation wished to concede. Paradoxically, what Heidegger does not recognize in Nietzsche, and which crystallizes the peculiar connection between the idea of the end of metaphysics and the notion of poetry and literature, is precisely the way Nietzsche practises philosophy. For the latter develops in large measure as a dialogue between thought and literature in a way which Dilthey, perhaps without hesitation, would have consigned to the same 'category' as he consigns Nietzsche. It is already clear that we are dealing here not merely with a reading of Nietzsche but also of Heidegger and, in a more general sense, with a reading of the philosophy of the era which can be regarded, and which both Dilthey and Heidegger (in different ways) regard, in every sense as the 'end of metaphysics'.

From Philology to Philosophy

In what follows we wish to limit ourselves to trying to set out Nietzsche's thought in context. Although we cannot explore all the theoretical implications of his thought, we cannot shirk the task of locating it within the horizon of those more general philosophical problems which have been raised by his most influential interpreters. In short, we will broadly follow Heidegger's interpretation (though in a way that goes beyond his intentions) and attempt to show how philosophy as practised by Nietzsche, in line with the proper task of metaphysics, arrives at specifically ontological conclusions, namely statements about the meaning of Being. But the path it takes in the process, which is not accidental or arbitrary, extends from cultural criticism and 'moralistic' reflexions through the analysis of prejudices, to a psychological observation and self-observation; in other words, through all the staging-posts which make Nietzsche a 'philosopher of life' in Dilthey's sense. To put it another way: our reading of Nietzsche is part of a 'hermeneutic ontology', though this thesis cannot be expanded upon here.[4] The entirely open problem of the place Nietzsche occupies in the framework of contemporary philosophy (which is dismissed more with sheer rhetoric than with substantive argument), in other words which philosophical current or school he should be assigned to, can be solved if we grant Nietzsche a significant role in that philosophical strand which begins with Schleiermacher, develops through Dilthey and German Historicism, and continues through to Heidegger and post-Heideggerian hermeneutics (i.e. to

Gadamer, Ricoeur and Pareyson, to name only the most important figures). Unlike other generally acknowledged currents of thought such as phenomenology, for example, or existentialism or neo-positivism, this philosophical 'school' does not possess a strong, unified character and does not figure as such in histories of philosophy. One reason for this is presumably that it is only since Heidegger that hermeneutics has been recognized as a philosophical approach rather than a technical discipline. Another reason is that precisely because of its innovativeness, compared to other philosophical schools of the past, this current can never present itself (not even given a different and more mature approach to history of philosophy) in as unified a fashion as these other philosophical schools, with respect to its methods, propositions and conclusions.

From this angle Nietzsche is a more than emblematic figure, for nothing is more difficult than showing that any contemporary philosophical 'school' takes it lead from him, even though his influence is pervasive and very much alive. It is likely that the study of Nietzsche's philosophy will lead to a more precise definition of the strangely unified character of 'hermeneutics' as a philosophical strand in nineteenth- and twentieth-century culture. At the beginning of this account of Nietzsche's works, the concepts 'hermeneutics' and 'hermeneutic ontology' should be taken to mean only that peculiar link he establishes between 'cultural criticism', a philosophy of life and the consideration of decadence on the one hand – in other words, thought focused on existence in its concreteness and historicity – and the renewed attempt to tackle the problems of Truth and Being on the other. Viewed from the angle of this hermeneutic thought at least, which Nietzsche's works expressly take up and discuss, the grasping of this link (i.e. the hermeneutic ontology), which for the time being we have merely suggested as a hypothesis, is at the centre of current philosophical problems and forms the basis of the particular theoretical relevance of Nietzsche's thought.

2. FROM PHILOLOGY TO PHILOSOPHY AS CULTURAL CRITICISM

a) Dionysus, the Tragic, and Decadence
In order to grasp Nietzsche's thought and its importance to a hermeneutic 'solution' of the problems of philosophy, it is necessary to return to those pointers given by Dilthey in *The Essence of Philosophy*. It is not primarily a question here of grasping the peculiar link between philosophy and 'literature' in Nietzsche's work. More fundamental than this link is the thing that brings Nietzsche's philosophy closer to Dilthey's and connects it to the thought of the early twentieth century. This is the relationship between philosophy and philology, which characterizes the first phase of Nietzsche's work and is maintained in various guises throughout the whole course of his development as a thinker. This relationship makes it possible to grasp more clearly Nietzsche's

position in the area surrounding hermeneutics and to move him closer to Dilthey and the philosophical problems of academic history in the early twentieth century, although his ideas appear extraordinary, indeed revolutionary, and completely incompatible with contemporary academic history. As has been true of all of the more significant philosophy of the twentieth century, the starting-point of Nietzsche's project lies in reflexions on the 'human sciences'; or, to put it in more general terms, on historiography and the knowledge man has of himself. The task now is to consider his early works in this light.

Nietzsche's early philosophy took shape during his time as a university professor in Basle and its characteristic features reveal both his philological training and his youthful admiration of, above all, Schopenhauer and Wagner. This early philosophy contains a series of topics which recede or lose importance in later elaborations. Nevertheless, it is legitimate to say that the young Nietzsche had a philosophy. For though it lacks any systematic coherence (out of which Nietzsche would later develop a particular style of thought), and though some of its aspects contradict one another, it does contain one central, original and characteristic concept which can serve as a guiding thread for a reading of Nietzsche's œuvre. This is the binary opposition of the Apollonian and the Dionysian, which initially developed in connection with the problem of the birth and demise of Greek tragedy, but gathered around itself all the essential aspects of Nietzsche's early cultural criticism, namely the metaphysics of the artist, the doctrine of language, and the polemics against historicism. Moreover, this binary opposition paved the way for the later development of his philosophy.

When Nietzsche entered the scene at Basle in 1869 with his inaugural lecture 'Homer and Classical Philology' (II.1, 247–69) and his lectures in 1870 on 'The Greek Music-Drama' (III.2, 3–22) and 'Socrates and Tragedy' (III.2, 23–41), he showed he did not think that his work as a philologist was consonant with established academic philology. Instead, he drew closer to philosophy, or at least to his Schopenhauerian understanding of it. What is more, it is very clear that he had experienced doubts about his vocation as a philologist even before he was called to Basle. Since 1868 he had been turning his attention, together with Rohde, to the study of texts from the natural sciences, chemistry being one example.[5] And the letters to Rohde in his first years in Basle are clear evidence of these doubts. Consequently, Nietzsche lived 'in a high-spirited alienation' from philology, 'which one cannot imagine being worse' (Letters, II.1, 90). What were the causes of this early inner distancing from philology, a subject Nietzsche had chosen after abandoning the idea of devoting himself to theology towards the end of his second semester at Bonn in 1865? Had he never taken the idea seriously, merely accepting it at the beginning of his studies for the sake of appearances, in order to satisfy the expectations of his mother and sister?[6] If the rejection of theology presented an outward problem in his relations with his family, the inner 'distancing' from philology proved very much more complex. It is crucial that we do not to present this 'distancing' in such a way that it might appear that Nietzsche was devoting himself to his work as a professor of Greek in Basle for purely mercenary or self-serving reasons, even though he found this work generally unbearable. For, at that time, Nietzsche had no doubts about his calling as a teacher; and, after a theological career had been ruled out as a professional alternative, he viewed a training in classical philology as the foundation of his own education, and that of others. It was, however, subject to two kinds of doubt. First, these doubts appeared in a radical manner owing to his repeatedly stated intention of turning to the natural sciences (which he did in Basle, at least in his reading). In the process Nietzsche was hinting at, or mythicizing, a possible shift of emphasis in his *education*, without at this time defining his position more precisely, as he was to do in his writings after *Human, All Too Human*. There was a second, related motivation behind the inner distancing from philology, namely the unbearable nature of *academic* philology. This motivation appeared, on the hand, to be narrowly conceived; in his opinion, the study of antiquity had become a purely antiquarian activity which led to the creation of an unbridgeable gap between the philologist and the objects of his study. In other words, it created a gulf between the beauty of the Greek world and the inevitable spiritual deformation of those researchers who were supposed to remind us of it.[7] But on the other hand, this motivation was formulated in more general terms. From this second perspective, classical philology appeared to Nietzsche to be a betrayal of the classical spirit, in the sense that philology was no longer capable of regarding antiquity as a model worth imitating, seeing it instead as no more than an accumulation of (arte)facts for academic investigation. This perspective clearly involved a wider judgment of a society whose relation to antiquity had been reduced to, at best, a profession and, at worst, mere philological donkey work; it also implied stupefaction at a situation in which the classical model could have sunk to being nothing more than an object of scholarly inquiry. Nietzsche's dissatisfaction with philology thus begins with the criticism that it is a profession and that its goal is no more than the positivistic and 'objective' investigation of antiquity.[8] This dissatisfaction then becomes, first, a critique of an age which is capable of establishing a relation to antiquity only in this way and which shuts itself off from any deeper understanding of antiquity as a *model*; and, secondly, a critique of the means by which this image of antiquity is disseminated to that age and ultimately brought down to its level. This concern with how the classical legacy is handed down to us moderns emerges persistently in the young Nietzsche's philological writings. This is true both of his investigation into Diogenes Laertius's sources, which he completed in 1868 in Leipzig and in which he demonstrated in what ways the image of ancient philosophy that Diogenes handed down arose, and of his inaugural lecture at

11

Basle entitled 'Homer and Classical Philology', which traces the history of an historico-philological image of antiquity over time. Even his studies of 'The Greek Music-Drama', 'The Birth of the Tragic Idea' (III.2, 71–91) and 'The Dionysian World-View' (III.2, 43–69) (which are taken up and elaborated upon in *The Birth of Tragedy*) are, it has to be said, works dealing with clearly defined 'objects' of philological study, yet they aim, above and beyond these 'objects', at an understanding of how they have been handed down in and through European cultural traditions.

In those early years in Basle, Nietzsche characterized philosophy as the totality of such problems, which are admittedly centred on philology, but which also go beyond its boundaries as an academic discipline (as well as beyond the more general boundaries of examining the past) in favour of a critique of contemporary culture. Even his encounter with Schopenhauer, whose work *The World as Will and Representation* he read in 1865, did not lead him from philology to philosophy, if one understands the latter to mean metaphysics, the study of Being or anything of that kind. Instead it made him rethink his attitude to philology, and this is particularly evident in his first philosophically orientated work, *The Birth of Tragedy out of the Spirit of Music*, which was published in December 1871. One of the main attractions of this unparalleled work lies in its peculiar fusion of philology and philosophy. The scope and impact of this work have no equal, not even in the great philosophizing of philologists in the Romantic period, to which

Nietzsche himself refers – Creuzer's, for example, or the Schlegel brothers'.⁹ *The Birth of Tragedy* is at once a re-interpretation of ancient Greece, a philosophical and aesthetic revolution, a critique of contemporary culture, and a programme to revitalize it. The work revolves around the discovery of two concepts, the Apollonian and the Dionysian, though admittedly this can be seen as a 'discovery' only in the sense that Nietzsche conferred a fresh significance upon these already well-worn concepts.¹⁰

The prevailing image of Greece in the European tradition was dominated by notions of harmony, beauty, balance and proportion, in other words by all those features which were held to be *classical*. According to Nietzsche, this image concentrated on a particular moment in Greek history, namely fifth-century Athens, as well as on particular art forms, above all architecture and sculpture. The prime contributor to this stereotyping of our image of Greece had been Christianity, through which our knowledge of ancient culture had been filtered. Christianity's role in determining this tradition was so marked that, in the notes Nietzsche made for the draft of a fifth *Untimely Meditation*, it sometimes appears that, with the waning or disappearance of Christian faith in the modern age, any possibility of gaining access to classical antiquity is also disappearing. If Christianity clung to antiquity's classical features, then these were already signs of decadence because they no longer corresponded to a living historical moment in the fullest sense. The living roots, the fundaments of the

Olympian 'magic mountain' (BT §3, 31), which lie hidden (or disappear from view) in the classical form of antique culture, emerge as soon as one refers to those elements of the ancient tradition which have remained marginal to that tradition. Among the arts, the marginal element is not so much architecture and sculpture as music, and beyond the arts, it is not so much literary and philosophical texts as elements of folk wisdom, which are hard to discern in the beautiful images of Winckelmann's heroes. The wisdom of Silenus, for example, a mythological figure deeply rooted in Greek folk traditions, who is half-man, half-animal and the teacher of Dionysus. According to Silenus, the best thing for man would be not to be born at all or, failing that, to die as soon as possible. This saying reveals a conception of human existence which eludes any 'classical' interpretation. The classicism of Winckelmann, Schiller and Hegel had advanced the view that the Greeks had been capable of producing beautiful works of art, for the simple reason that they themselves were beautiful, harmonious and serene. However, if we place the tragic myths and, moreover, the evidence we have of the spread of orgiastic cults in the Greek world alongside such 'marginal' fragments (which were nevertheless firmly rooted in folk wisdom), then 'we must take down, stone by stone, as it were, the elaborate construction of Apollonian culture' (BT §3, 30) to discover beneath it a different principle – the Dionysian.[11] The Apollonian and the Dionysian, according to Nietzsche, represent a duality which profoundly defined the Greek spirit.

> The Greeks knew and felt the terrors and horrors of existence: in order to be able to live at all they had to interpose the radiant dream-birth of the Olympians between themselves and those horrors. That terrible mistrust of the Titanic forces of nature [...] – the Greeks repeatedly overcame all this, or at least veiled and concealed it, with the artistic *middle world* of the Olympians. (BT §3, 31f.)[12]

The Olympian gods were the means by which the Greeks made existence bearable, whose fragility they had experienced, whose painful intertwining of life and death they knew, and which, owing to their desperate sensitivity, they felt and suffered deeply. 'Thus the gods provide a justification for the life of man by living it themselves' (BT §3, 32); because they live it in bright sunlight and beyond the terrifying threat of death. Even nature produces an illusion like this to achieve its aims (cf. BT §3, 33). In the Olympian gods, men could 'see themselves in a higher sphere, without this contemplation seeming either a command or a reproach' (BT §3 33f.) – unlike the normative metaphysical sense of the world of Platonic ideas.

The world of the Olympian gods is a world produced by the Apollonian drive. On the other hand, the experience of chaos, the loss of all clear forms in the ceaseless flux of life, which is itself death, corresponds to the Dionysian drive. In the same way that the Apollonian drive attempts to produce definable images, harmonious and reliable forms which bestow security, the Dionysian drive possesses not only a sensitivity to the chaos of every existence but also urges us to dive into this chaos, to withdraw from the *principium individuationis*.

Together with many other explicit indications in *The Birth of Tragedy*, the allusion to the *principium individuationis* shows how dependent Nietzsche's arguments are on Schopenhauer's metaphysics, even if, as he remarks in the foreword to the new edition of 1886, he was working against asceticism and consequently against Schopenhauer's Platonism in this work which is, after all, written in Schopenhauerian language. Nietzsche's Apollonian world of Greek gods is admittedly a totality of all Will-less representations, in line with Schopenhauer's *Ideas*; but the relation of the Olympian gods to the dark ground of the primal Oneness is not, as it is for Schopenhauer, a mere antithesis. For Schopenhauer, the figures of art (which represent the Ideas) find shelter from the Will which forms the irrational essence of the world. For Nietzsche, on the other hand, the figures of the Olympian gods in *The Birth of Tragedy* (and other later concepts) can only attain their significance as liberators from guilt if they remain *in contact with* the Dionysian, in other words with the world of chaos, from which they are helping us to escape. In the passage where Nietzsche comments on Wagner's opera *Tristan and Isolde*, in which he sees the spiritual

16

rebirth of Greek tragedy, he states: 'Dionysus speaks the language of Apollo, but Apollo ultimately speaks the language of Dionysus' (BT §21, 136). Nietzsche is also certainly not writing in the spirit of Schopenhauer when he speaks of the horror that consumes a person when he sees the *principium individuationis* disintegrating. According to Nietzsche we must add to this Schopenhauerian sense of horror, 'the blissful ecstasy which, prompted by the same fragmentation of the *principium individuationis*, rises up from man's innermost core, indeed from nature' (BT §1, 24). We feel this ecstasy because:

> [n]ot only is the bond between man and man sealed y the Dionysian magic: alienated, hostile or subju-gated nature, too, celebrates her reconciliation with her prodigal son, man [...] Now the slave is a free man, now all the rigid and hostile boundaries that distress, despotism or 'impudent fashion' have erected between man and man break down. (BT §1, 25)

Ultimately, this relation of the Apollonian and the Dionysian reaches as far the relation of forces in each individual human being. Nietzsche compares it at the beginning of the work to the states of dreaming (Apol-lonian) and intoxication (Dionysian). In the develop-ment of a culture, the relation plays the same role as the duality of the sexes plays in preserving the species. The whole of human culture is the fruit of the dialecti-cal play of these two drives, which, more narrowly defined, also operate as artistic drives (cf. BT §2, 26), in

17

the face of which the artist is only active as imitator. The Apollonian and the Dionysian therefore define not only a theory of civilization and culture but also of art. The relation between artistic creation and the origin of the gods, above all in Greek mythology, had of course been a favourite topos of Romantic thought. By proposing an 'aesthetic' which was simultaneously and above all a general theory of culture, Nietzsche was obviously referring to these precursors. In the narrower framework of a theory of art, it allowed the Apollonian-Dionysian duality, the different phases in the development of Greek art, to be read in terms of the struggle between Dionysian and Apollonian drives. This struggle also unfolded as the conflict between different peoples during the succession of invasions and peace agreements which determined the history of ancient Greece. So Doric art can only be read as the result of a defence by the Apollonian against attacks which were real attacks by invading peoples, attacks by the Dionysian and orgiastic cults of barbarians. In this way, 'earlier [ancient] Greek history falls into four major artistic stages in the battle between these two hostile principles' (BT §4, 38) Nietzsche shows:

> how the Homeric world developed out of the 'bronze age', with its Titanic struggles and its stern folk philosophy, under the constraints of the Apollonian drive to beauty; how this naïve magnificence was engulfed once more by the encroaching Dionysian flood, and how, in the face of this new power, the

Apollonian rose to the rigid majesty of Doric art and the Doric world-view.

The different art-forms are also connected with the predominance of one or other of these impulses, though these connections cannot be strictly schematized. If music is predominantly a Dionysian art-form, then sculpture, architecture and the epic are Apollonian. The Doric world is not the apogee of Greek culture, however, neither from the point of view of civilization nor in terms of artistic maturity. The apogee is represented by Attic tragedy which is the perfect synthesis of the two impulses (BT §4, 38). As far as its origin is concerned, Nietzsche takes up an established notion, namely that tragedy emerged from the tragic chorus (cf. BT §7, 48); but he presents a new interpretation of this notion by linking it to the concepts of the Apollonian and the Dionysian. The chorus from which tragedy sprang was the chorus of satyrs, the sacred procession, whose participants metamorphosed into 'invented *natural beings*', 'yet this is not a world randomly imagined to fit between heaven and earth, rather it is a world both real and believable, as Olympus with its inhabitants was for the believing Hellenes' (BT §7, 51). In the condition of heightened excitement dominating the procession of dancing and singing satyrs, man, restored to the state of a natural being, glimpses the mystery of the primal One-ness and, in the grip of horror and ecstasy, calls forth delirious visions. In this Dionysian excitement the satyr chorus undergoes 'the primal *dramatic*

19

phenomenon [...]: seeing oneself transformed and acting as though one had truly entered another body, another character' (BT §8, 57). An essential aspect of Nietzsche's anti-Platonism can also be detected in this observation; for the shattering of individual identity, the absorption of the Self into the Other, and the loss of self-continuity were the decisive reasons for Plato's rejection of dramatic art. Nietzsche saw in them its origin, and his evaluation of this origin is diametrically opposed to Plato's. He even stresses the social preconditions of the drama:

> the dithyrambic chorus is a chorus of people transformed, whose civic past and social status are completely forgotten: they have become the timeless worshippers of their god, beyond all social contingencies [...] In this enchanted state the Dionysian reveller sees himself as a satyr [as the satyr procession was originally held in honour of Dionysus, G.V.], *and it is as a satyr that he looks upon the god*: i.e. in his transformation he sees a new vision outside himself, the Apollonian complement of his state. With this new vision the drama is complete. (BT §8, 57f.)

We must therefore see Greek tragedy 'as the Dionysian chorus, continuously discharging itself in an Apollonian world of images' (BT §8, 58). Nietzsche's explanations of these matters took the form primarily of philological hypotheses about the origins of Greek tragedy, and as such were discussed and criticized by contemporary philologists, most notably Wilamowitz-Moellendorff.[13] However, in spite of not laying claim to 'historiographical' soundness or to empirical testability, the true significance of these hypotheses is that they provided fresh access to classical antiquity while simultaneously offering a radical critique of the present. For, more generally speaking, Nietzsche laid the foundations here of his interpretation-based 'ontology' which is developed later in his mature works and in the notes contained in *The Will to Power*. The interplay of the Apollonian and the Dionysian, and the ambiguous sense of tragedy as a liberation both *from* and *towards* the Dionysian in the beautiful image of the Apollonian,[14] remain decisive elements throughout Nietzsche's later philosophical development and form the basis of his theoretical importance today.

Nietzsche's starting-point for a theory and critique of culture in *The Birth of Tragedy* is the problem of how and why Attic tragedy died. Unlike other ancient genres, which died a 'natural' death (in other words, were superseded and left no void behind them), tragedy died by her own hand (cf. BT §11, 71). The prime mover in this suicide was Euripides who 'brought the spectator on to the stage' and thereby set in motion a process eventually finished off by New Attic Comedy, in which 'the degenerate figure of tragedy' lived on (BT §11, 72). Euripides transformed tragic myth into a series of probable and necessary connections, into essentially realistic plots.

We may ask whether the casting of Euripides in this

villainous role in the development of Greek tragedy is historically accurate.[15] Yet Nietzsche was concerned with more than pinning the responsibility on Euripides; he wanted to unmask the person who had really inspired tragedy's suicide. Euripides recast tragic myth in realistic and rational terms in order to satisfy the demands of one particular spectator – Socrates. Socrates had established a rational view in Greek thought of the world and human life, according to which the just person can come to no harm in either this world or the Beyond. The realism of Euripidean tragedy is a consequence of Socrates's theoretical optimism, because he wanted to see the rational structure of life represented on the stage. Because this aroused no emotions (not least because, by introducing a prologue explaining the action before it started, Euripides robbed tragedy of any 'epic tension' and 'exciting uncertainty' (BT §12, 81)), the whole action had to be played out in great scenes of rhetorical lyricism, creating feelings of pathos in the spectator, feelings which could now no longer be achieved in any other way. And because everything had to proceed according to a pre-ordained, rational scheme, it was easy to understand the need for a *deus ex machina*. The action that occurred between prologue and epilogue, which are both epic phenomena, happened in a dramatic and lyrical *present*. The tragic synthesis of the epic and the lyric, of music and the representation of an action, of the Apollonian and the Dionysian, had disappeared. But this had not happened as a result of an inner dynamic within this new literary form, but rather as a means of conforming to the new intellectual demands connected with the triumphalism of Socrates's theoretical optimism, in other words with the rise of classical Greek philosophy.

If the universe has a rational structure, as Socrates believed and taught, then tragedy has no meaning any more, and not only in the limited sense which holds that in a rationally ordered world there can be no uncertainty, excitement, tension or ambiguity. The opposition between the Socratic and the Tragic [Apollonian/Dionysian] sheds light on what Nietzsche was actually pursuing with the concepts Apollonian and Dionysian, and on what he was to later to define as the Platonism of all European culture, which he wished to overcome. The Apollonian images of the Olympian gods, and then Attic tragedy, were forms of existential redemption, which did not in any way imply hypostasizing essences or metaphysical structures. These forms arose, as Nietzsche later declared in and after *Human, All Too Human*, from a need for calm, from the need to make life's chaos bearable in a particular way, the need to come to terms with the ceaseless cycle of birth and death. Yet according to Nietzsche, seeking metaphysical consolation in essences and the rational structure of the universe was characteristic of an enfeebled and decadent culture. When Nietzsche writes that 'it is only as *an aesthetic phenomenon* that existence and the world are eternally *justified*' (BT §5, 43) he is seeking nothing less than an alternative to metaphysics – what he terms Socratism or Platonism. In whatever guise, metaphysics strives for reassurance in essential structures, in a 'perfect world' which, unlike the world of the Olympian gods, is in opposition to the world of experience, to which it appears as 'either a command or a reproach' (BT §3, 34). The contemplation of this 'perfect world' produces feelings of melancholy, which is the stuff of the decadence associated with Socratic and Platonic/Christian rationalism.

In the works that followed *The Birth of Tragedy*, Nietzsche explored the implications of decadence in connection with the Socratic rationalism that found expression in metaphysics, ethics, and the 'Christian' culture of the West. *The Birth of Tragedy* was concerned with negatively delimiting Socratism. Socratism was a phenomenon which had closed off a tragic view of human existence, both in the sense of myth and mystery and in the sense of an aesthetic justification of existence which, however unclearly, escaped a metaphysical grounding. Nietzsche referred to Socratism, while conscious of its inadequacy, which had come clearly and distinctly to the fore during the last crisis of metaphysics, in the thought of Kant and Schopenhauer, and in which a thoroughly Dionysian wisdom had been expressed (cf. BT §19, 124). A return to tragic culture was therefore possible, which Nietzsche hoped, at least in those early years, would spring from Richard Wagner's music-dramas. Launched upon the world by Socratic rationalism, and

spurred on by its powerful illusion, science[16] is rush-
ing irresistibly to its limits, where the optimism
essential to logic collapses. For the periphery of the
circle of science has an infinite number of points, and
while it is as yet impossible to tell how the circle
could ever be fully measured, the noble and gifted
man, even before the mid-point of his life, inevitably
reaches that peripheral boundary, where he finds
himself staring into the ineffable. If he sees here, to
his horror, how logic twists itself around against
these limits and finally bites its own tail, there dawns
a new form of knowledge, *tragic knowledge*, which
needs art as both protection and remedy, if we are to
bear it. (BT §15, 97)

As this quotation reveals, the return of tragic culture
is not simply the return of myth. It is instead the need
for rationality inherent in scientific thinking taken
to an extreme, which, by a 'logic' which anticipates
that of the 'Death of God' in *The Gay Science*, flips
over (by virtue of its very need for security) into that
brand of desperate scepticism characteristic of Kant's
and, later, Schopenhauer's teachings. Admittedly, we
should note here an ambiguity and misunderstanding of
himself on the part of the young Nietzsche. The consequence of his enthusiasm for Wagner, which dominates
the whole text on tragedy, was that it appeared to be a
sermon prophesying the return of myth, and indeed in
large parts that is what it probably was. However, the

25

passages dealing with the 'Dionysian wisdom' of Kantian philosophy (for instance, the passage just quoted) allow us to identify another possible solution to the problem of a return of tragic culture, a solution which does not imply an irrationalist remythologization *à la* Wagner. Nietzsche searches for this other solution, beginning with *Human, All Too Human*, in which some of the fundamental tenets of *The Birth of Tragedy* are retained, but admittedly freed from the faith in Wagner that had determined his first years in Basle.

The paradoxical mixture of Kant and Wagner in the closing passages of *The Birth of Tragedy* is only *one* aspect of the more general difficulty of establishing just what Nietzsche had in mind when he talked of a return of tragic culture. Though they do not offer conclusive solutions to this problem, the other texts of the same period do provide some clues. The texts in question are the posthumously published *On Truth and Lies in an Extra-Moral Sense* (TL, III.2, 367–84), in which Nietzsche attempts to form, but does not complete, a specifically 'philosophical' theory, and the second and third *Untimely Meditations*. His distancing of himself from Wagner, which was completed in *Human, All Too Human*, but already adumbrated in the fourth *Untimely Meditation* and in the notes of the same period, can be accounted for primarily in psychological and personal terms.[17] The break with Wagner becomes understandable when we consider that although Nietzsche had not renounced, at least not expressly, his dream of a reborn tragic culture, he no longer envisaged it in connection with a phenomenon like Wagner's music, nor perhaps with any art. It would, however, be mistaken to assume that Nietzsche's unease with an 'aesthetic' solution had even the remotest connection with Hegel's notion of the 'death of art'. Nietzsche's dissatisfaction with an aesthetic solution to the problem of decadence cannot be interpreted as though art were something merely 'temporary' for him, though one or two of his texts can be interpreted in this way (cf. 'The Art of Works of Art' [GS §89, 122]). In general, Nietzsche does not believe that a renewal of tragic culture can be brought about by a kind of aesthetic liberation of our whole existence, if this were to spell the end of art as a separate domain. In *Human, All Too Human*, his dissatisfaction with an aesthetic solution to the problem of decadence is instead associated with a psycho-historical 'untimeliness' (or ill-fittedness) of art to modern man, for whom freedom of the spirit and the Dionysian impulse tend to unfold in science rather than art.

Art in the early works on the other hand, from *The Birth of Tragedy* to the *Untimely Meditations* and the posthumously published *On Truth and Lies in an Extra-Moral Sense*, appears to justify existence in its entirety, even (and perhaps above all) in the framework of a Socratic culture. One of the fascinating but also disturbing peculiarities of *On Truth and Lies in an Extra-Moral Sense* is the way in which Nietzsche shows how socially-established language with its rules and cognitive functions originates as a random fixing and hardening of a particular system of metaphors which, from the perspective

27

of *On the Genealogy of Morals* at least, is tied to relations of power within society. One particular system of metaphors, then, which like every other system of metaphors is arbitrary and freely invented, has established itself as the sole, governing system. The world may only be described using that system. Every language is metaphorical in origin, referring to things by what seem initially to be random sounds which, as they stand, have nothing to do with the things they purport to represent. Society comes into being when *one* system of metaphors wins through against the others and becomes the publicly prescribed and accepted way of characterizing things metaphorically (i.e. lying). From this moment on, all other systems of metaphor, past and future, are relegated to the level of 'art' and are hence recognizable as lies. This 'genetic', if idealized account of language does not, however, lead Nietzsche to idealize a capacity to invent metaphors freely, which would become lost by being canonized in a single system. On the contrary: 'in this conceptual game of dice [...] "Truth" uses each die as it is marked' (TL §1, 376). In other words, in a hierarchical order of abstract concepts which are remote not just from things, but also from the intuitions of the individual players. It is here that man differs from animals, who remain submerged in the flow of their perceptual images. In order to justify his own rational humanity, which rests on the ability 'to lie in a universally binding manner' (TL §1, 375), man must forget 'that he is a subject, an *artistically creative* subject' (TL §1, 377). But at no point in this text does Nietzsche insist on the need to recreate a world where metaphors can be freely and creatively invented, a world without canonical rules and, ultimately, without society or mankind. One of the reasons why he left the essay unfinished and never published lies presumably in his own uncertainty and in the problematic nature of his conclusions. In one sense, there are good reasons to connect *On Truth and Lies* with the arguments in *The Birth of Tragedy* concerning the rebirth of tragic culture by reclaiming the Dionysian element suppressed by Socratism, and consequently by redeploying free artistic creativity as the 'mastery of art over life' (TL §2, 383). In another sense, however, the hardening of a system of metaphors into a canonical language of truth is basically nothing more than a continuation of the tendency towards 'lies', towards the establishment of names and descriptions, images and metaphors, at the expense of that 'reality' of things, in which an original impulse towards creating metaphors persists. There must be a contradiction when Nietzsche condemns abstraction and the rule-bound, conceptual nature of everyday language in the name of a greater 'faithfulness to reality' which can be had by freely creating metaphors. Moreover, the motivation to lie and create illusions is rooted in a need for security, which in the 'state of nature' asserts itself in ceaseless fighting between individuals and between their private metaphors. Society, by contrast, reacts to the same need by institutionalizing rules, which enables lying to become universal and binding. Many passages in this short treatise reveal that Nietzsche did not in fact underestimate the emancipatory significance for mankind of the emergence of a regulated language and a universal system of metaphors. Admittedly, he writes: 'The intellect, that master of disguise, remains free and relieved of its usual servitude' for as long as it jumbles metaphors 'with creative contentment' and displaces 'the boundary stones of abstraction'. But Nietzsche is here describing the joys of the slave during the Saturnalia, during a fleeting suspension of the usual rules, when 'he can deceive without doing *harm*' (TL §3, 382).

As this text is more philosophically ambitious (in systematic terms), the problematic nature of the conclusions drawn in *The Birth of Tragedy* surfaces here again, but in a more complex fashion. How is one supposed to imagine the rebirth of a tragic culture? Is it really a case of recreating Greekness, of reasserting the 'mastery of art over life' (TL §2, 383)? And, in the light of *On Truth and Lies*, does this not carry with it the risk of a regression to the 'state of nature', in which the price of artistic freedom is extreme danger and insecurity? Or is the rebirth of the tragic through art's fictions reserved for that 'excitement' when the intellect celebrates its Saturnalia without doing *harm*, when it remains tied to the preconditions of security, out of which the system of abstractions arose and because of which that system is maintained?

b) *The Untimely Thinker*

In the early Basle years, Nietzsche's thought appeared to be moving in the very direction just outlined. *Human,*

All Too Human, with which the second, mature phase of his philosophy begins (and in which his distance from Wagner and Schopenhauer is made clear) does not therefore represent any sudden and unforeseen shift. In that text he speaks of a culturally specific 'double-brain'. Every higher culture must give man 'as it were two brain-ventricles, one for the perceptions of science, the other for those of non-science: lying beside each other, not confused together, separable, capable of being shut off; this is a demand of health' (HAH I, §251, 213). This view, in a less explicit form, had already been advanced in *On Truth and Lies*.

Consequently, the rebirth of a tragic culture, which was in Nietzsche's mind in his early writings, should happen in the form of a 'revolution', in which art assumes a decisive role. While this revolution is not sufficiently defined in *The Birth of Tragedy*, in the works immediately following that text it appears tied to the function of a *critique* of culture. This critical view of culture, as opposed to civilization characterized by Socratic decadence, did not, however, lead to the idea of revolutionary upheaval. Rather, it sought to define itself in different conceptual terms, and therein lay the task of the *Untimely Meditations*. The concept of the untimely, stressed in the title, points to the problematic nature of this relationship. The untimely thinker, which is how Nietzsche viewed himself, does not work directly towards the establishment of another culture, in which his arguments might become 'timely'; rather, he is working 'against my age, and thereby influencing

my age, and hopefully for the benefit of a future age'
(UM II, Foreword, 243). Yet Nietzsche is not at all
certain that a future age will alter the position of the
man of culture vis-à-vis society: in the second *Untimely
Meditation* as well as, above all, in that manifesto on the
relations between culture and society (the third Meditation *Schopenhauer as Educator*), the terms 'culture' and
'civilization' appear as radical alternatives. Nietzsche
expressly opposes the terms in his late notes (cf. N
1888–89, VIII, 3, 16[10], 281f.). He uses them in the
same way as German cultural criticism was to use them
at the beginning of the twentieth century.[18] Both the
second and the third *Untimely Meditations* end, not with
a proposed *civilization* which would stand in opposition
to our own, familiar, decadent one, but rather with a
call to the forces of culture, which represent 'critical'
moments *within* this civilization. It is these 'suprahistor-
ical' or eternal forces that are discussed at the close
of the second *Untimely Meditation* (UM II, §10, 327).
They are also embodied in the figures of the saint, the
artist and the philosopher in *Schopenhauer as Educator*.
Together with Wagner's art (from which Nietzsche later
distanced himself), these figures represented the only
possibilities of a rebirth of tragic culture in the contemporary world. In all of them admittedly the 'metaphysics
of the artist', as sketched in the *The Birth of Tragedy* is
to the fore, but this metaphysics is also simultaneously
beginning to disintegrate and disappear. The second and
third *Untimely Meditations* are important to the young
Nietzsche's work, less for their theoretical 'constructions'

than for the following two aspects: on the one hand, they come close to dissolving the original conception of a 'metaphysics of the artist' by showing that this metaphysic can only develop in a theory of *culture* as criticism rather than as an alternative to *civilization*. On the other hand, these two texts make clear the aims of this criticism by laying the foundations for the development of Nietzsche's mature thought in a 'deconstructive' sense.

The second *Untimely Meditation* of 1874 (*On the Uses and Disadvantages of History for Life*) is particularly fascinating even though it throws up more problems and poses more questions than it solves or answers – even more so perhaps than Nietzsche's other writings. Its fascination can be gauged above all from its influence on European thought of the twentieth century. One need only think of Martin Heidegger and Walter Benjamin.[19] In this text Nietzsche is concerned with a critique of historicism ['Historismus'] which could in no way be described as a marginal phenomenon; for it is evident that the great philosophy of this century often tackles historicism in a polemical manner. Viewed within the context of Nietzsche's works, the problem with the second *Untimely Meditation* is that only with difficulty can it be conceived as either the culmination of earlier developments or as the precursor of later ideas (the doctrine of Eternal Recurrence, for example), with which it nevertheless has to be connected. It seems at least as likely that, in the works which followed, Nietzsche gradually retracted the anti-historicist ideas of the *Untimely Meditation* on history. It is possible that he went so far down this road that the claim in one of his confused letters from Turin of 5 or 6 January 1889 ('basically I am every name in history') can be interpreted as the logical conclusion of his quest to re-adopt the historicism that had been the target of his polemic in 1874.

Independent of these developments, which will be discussed later, the second *Untimely Meditation* appears to be the first fundamental critique of one of the predominant intellectual tendencies in nineteenth-century culture, in addition to scientific positivism which Nietzsche had already attacked in *The Birth of Tragedy*. It was not so much historicism in its metaphysical, Hegelian form that was characteristic of nineteenth-century education, but rather in its historiographical form. Nietzsche's starting-point was that a person or a culture who/which was fully conscious of the historical dimension of his/its actions would not possess either the motivation or the capacity to produce anything new. Indeed, something is historical in the sense that is 'produced' by something that has been and makes way for something to come. Every point on a line which can be determined only by its relation to other points on that line is historical therefore. While this relation constitutes the point, it also simultaneously dissolves it. If historical knowledge dominates an individual or (as in the case of the nineteenth century) a culture, then that individual's or culture's creative powers diminish. For it seems pointless and fruitless to devote oneself to sketching that which sooner or later must disappear in the unstoppable flow of history. Nietzsche describes this state of mind as the historical sickness.

As in Hegel's case, this historical sickness is connected with the development of the Christian world-view. The *memento mori* of medieval religiosity was made concrete in nineteenth-century historiography in the diffuse awareness of being late-comers (epigones) who did not believe there could be anything new under the sun and who thought instead that everything was being ceaselessly born and destroyed (cf. UM II, §8, 301f.). According to Nietzsche, Hegel's belief in Providence was nothing more than a transformation of this epigonal consciousness into the claim that we are not at the end but at the culmination of the historical process. This process now appears as a rationally determinable sequence of events, in the spirit of Socrates who had opened the possibility of observing the world and history as a rational whole. What is more, the process appears definitively (in accordance with Benjamin's definition which invokes Nietzsche) to be 'history written by the victors'.[20] The sceptical, epigonal awareness and the Hegelian, positivist, evolutionist claim (of nineteenth-century Europeans) to be at the culmination of history mingle indistinguishably in the consciousness of that century. An important factor behind the triumph of this intellectual disposition was the enormous growth of positivist knowledge about the past during the nineteenth century. More material about the past was available to people of the time than they could possibly take in or digest. The material lay heavily on their stomachs and led to that 'lack of style' which essentially constituted their decadence. When a person cannot absorb or digest historical knowledge, the inner and outer selves are no longer in harmony. The forms which the people of the nineteenth century imposed on their artistic productions, by borrowing these forms from the past (which was treated as a kind of storeroom or a set of theatrical props), no longer had any organic, necessary connection with their inner selves. An excess of historical knowledge and material leads to an inability to produce new forms and to the even worse 'cure' for this evil and incapacity, namely historical eclecticism.

But it was not only an excess of historiography that contributed to bringing this situation about. The pre-dominance of history teaching in the educational system also had a direct impact on the education and training of the workforce:

> men have to be adjusted to the purposes of the age in order to be ready for employment as soon as possible; they must labour in the factories of the general good before they are mature, indeed so that they shall not become mature – for this would be a luxury which would deprive the 'labour market' of a great deal of its workforce [. . .] The young man is harried through all the millennia: youths who under-stand nothing of war, diplomacy, commerce are thought fit to be introduced to political history. But

just as the young man races through history, so do we moderns race through art galleries and listen to concerts. (UM II, §7, 295)

Alongside these tasks designed for the rapid training of the workforce, historiography also develops something spectacular which provides repeated stimuli for the modern character weakened by an excess of historical consciousness.

Modern man, Nietzsche writes, 'continually allows his historical artists to prepare a world exhibition for him; he has become a hedonistic, strolling spectator [. . .] The war is not even over and already it is transposed into a hundred thousand printed pages and set before the jaded palates of the history-eaters as the latest delicacy' (UM II, §5, 275). Nietzsche here foresees a characteristic feature of twentieth-century mass culture.

These then are the types of damage that an excess of historiography inflicts on a society. Indeed, Life requires some 'forgetting', a delimited horizon, a degree of unconsciousness. However, this should not be taken to imply that an awareness of the past has no use at all for Life. This usefulness appears in the three 'positive' ways of studying history that Nietzsche suggests: 'monumental', 'antiquarian' and 'critical' historiography. It should be noted that none of these three modes of studying history is consonant with the dominant approach to historiography in the nineteenth century. For none of them seeks a 'logical course of events' in the past which, once identified, would serve to justify

37

the present, educate the workforce or cultivate that sense of the unstoppable flow of all things human (the *memento mori*).

> History belongs to the living man in three respects: it belongs to him as a being who acts and strives, as a being who preserves and reveres, as a being who suffers and seeks deliverance. (UM II, §2, 254)

The three approaches to the past useful to Life are based on these three demands. They are also accompanied by dangers which are to be combated by limiting each of the three modes with the aid of the other two. But alongside these three non-harmful historiographical modes (which form the basis of Nietzsche's later 're-adoption' of historicism, to which we have already referred), contemporary culture can only hope to recover from the historical sickness and decadence with the help of the supra-historical or eternal powers of art and religion (cf. UM II, §10, 362ff.). The recourse to these powers is, however, not made theoretically explicit in Nietzsche's text. It is a mere appeal. Decadence on the other hand is to be firmly relinquished by cultivating a vital relationship – be it monumental, antiquarian or critical – with the past, which is intended to contribute to the growth of the individual instead of to reducing him to a factory worker or a consumer of gala perform-ances. Yet in view of the clarity and directness of the text's destructive animus, its constructive aspects appear to be, at best, a collection of largely undefined demands.

The third *Untimely Meditation*, *Schopenhauer as Educator* (which appeared towards the end of 1874), also conceives of a critical culture rather than one expressly understood as an alternative ideal to *civilization*. As the title suggests, it is not a synopsis of Schopenhauer's philosophy. Instead, Schopenhauer is presented as a thinker and as an exemplary intellectual figure of Nietzsche's own age. Schopenhauer is viewed primarily as standing in opposition to academic functionaries, those salaried university professors who are not allowed to teach any philosophy that might rock the ship of state. But philosophy worthy of the name must necessarily be critical of institutions. At any rate, it does not produce citizens who cravenly acquiesce in the aims of the state. Consequently, the only 'philosophy' permitted in the universities is the history of philosophy which creates boredom and dissatisfaction among the students and lacks any real educational purpose, which is to criticize the *status quo*. The Schopenhauer essay thus extends to a general account of culture's relation to institutions, not just to the state but also to the economic and academic worlds, which together belong to the enemies of culture. In this way the essay comes close to the outlook of Jacob Burckhardt whom Nietzsche knew personally in Basle and who doubtless influenced him.[21] It is clear, though, that Nietzsche's stance in this text is connected with the premises of *The Birth of Tragedy*; it simultaneously realizes the claims of the latter and of the second *Untimely Meditation* on history. More explicitly than the work on *The Uses and Disadvantages*

of History, the essay on *Schopenhauer as Educator* emphasizes that, to Nietzsche, the rebirth of a tragic culture
has something to do both with a rebirth of art (and
probably myth and religion too) and with an increased
capacity to *criticize* the *status quo*. As Nietzsche's glori-
fication of the figure of the philosopher (together with
that of the artist and the saint) shows, this critique
reveals itself as a reverent quest for *truth*, though not
truth as it is understood by the scientist. For the
philosopher is separated from the scientist by his ability
(which Nietzsche regards as his essential characteristic)
not to limit himself to narrow specialization but instead
to have an 'intuition of the whole', a kind of knowing
'wisdom' that fixes its gaze on the whole of existence.

If it is the critical element that is crucially important
to the rebirth of tragic culture, then the ideal of such a
rebirth is no longer that of Dionysian-Apollonian beauty
as described in the second section of *On Truth and
Lies*. . . . The third *Untimely Meditation* characterizes
what men call 'beauty' as 'a gentle evening-weariness'.
It rests on the faces of those who have experienced a
'great *enlightenment* as to the character of existence' (UM
III, §5, 376). This beauty, which is certainly not the
beauty of life overflowing from a rediscovered Dionysian
element, is also not the beauty of the nostalgic look
backwards. The following passage in the third *Untimely
Meditation* is revealing in this respect:

> There are three images of man which our age has set
> up one after the other and which will no doubt long

inspire mortals to a transfiguration of their own lives: they are the man of Rousseau, the man of Goethe and finally the man of Schopenhauer. (UM III, §4, 365)

The first appeals to our impulsive nature; he wants to burst every fetter and chain and spur us on to revolution. The man of Goethe, by contrast, 'hates all violence, all sudden change – but that means he hates: all action; and so the world-liberator Faust becomes, as it were, only a world-traveller' (UM III, §4, 366). He is 'the contemplative man in the grand style, who can avoid languishing on earth only by bringing together for his nourishment everything great and memorable that has ever existed or still exists and hence lives' (ibid., 366f.). If Rousseau's man is always in danger of becoming a 'Catiline', then Goethe's man is in danger of becoming a 'philistine' (ibid., 367). '*The Schopenhauerian man*', on the other hand, '*voluntarily takes upon himself the suffering involved in being truthful*' (ibid.). He can quite legitimately be described as a critical spirit who forces himself to 'know everything' like the man of Goethe, but with a heroic love of truth which also forces him to sacrifice himself.

Here too, as was the case at the end of *The Birth of Tragedy* and of the second *Untimely Meditation*, the 'positive' ideal is not systematically defined despite appearing ascetically and heroically charged. Alongside Nietzsche's emphatic opposing of philosophy to any form of institutionalization and the polemic against science as the business of specialists with no comprehensive world-view, there are nevertheless traces here of the respect for science that will be in much greater evidence in *Human, All Too Human*. In contrast to the emptiness, dogmatism and obscurantism of academic philosophy, Nietzsche asserts: 'It is indisputable that the individual disciplines are now pursued more logically, cautiously, modestly, inventively, in short more philosophically, than is the case with so-called philosophers' (UM III, §8, 416). Though this is no more than a hint, Nietzsche seems to have noticed that the opponents that (good as well as bad) philosophy has to reckon with are the natural sciences and history. Despite all his reservations about these disciplines, Nietzsche engages with them seriously during the creative period which begins with *Human, All Too Human*. They interest him as forms of knowledge and because of their implications for the organization of society, and he is prepared to redefine his own understanding of philosophy's tasks in relation to both these areas.

II. The Deconstruction of Metaphysics

1. ART AND SCIENCE IN *HUMAN, ALL TOO HUMAN*

We have already pointed out that, particularly since 1961 when Heidegger's book on Nietzsche was published, Nietzsche research has concentrated on the late work as well as on those posthumously published fragments which Nietzsche himself, at least for a time, had wanted to gather together in a work entitled *The Will to Power*. These writings proclaim Nietzsche's great ontological ideas, which Heidegger characterizes as the centrepiece of Nietzsche's work.[1] But a certain distancing from Heidegger's interpretation has caused the Nietzsche literature of recent years to view the problems in a different light. For Nietzsche's philosophical ideas (even those that particularly interested Heidegger) make sense, as we shall see, in the light partly of Nietzsche's intellectual biography and partly of that picture of him that we as readers can only form against the background of his 'cultural criticism'. Nietzsche develops this cultural criticism in the works that are usually classed as part of his 'middle period' (see Chapter III below). The 'philological' beginnings of Nietzsche's career did not in fact unfold only, or even primarily, on 'methodical' territory. Even when the late Nietzsche states that he is 'philosophizing with the hammer', we can hear echoes of his philological training. For the process does not involve smashing idols but rather putting them to the test, teasing them out, as it were, and using the hammer as a tuning fork (TI VI, §3, Foreword, 51). Nietzsche's philological training left its mark above all in the close connection between his philosophical ideas and his cultural criticism. This connection – which might well be described as the characteristic feature of a large part of our own century's philosophy and in particular of its hermeneutic thinking – finds its peculiar expression in the idea of *nihilism*, which is one of Nietzsche's later 'metaphysical' conceptions and simultaneously represents an unmistakeable interpretative model in the history of European thought. Nietzsche's works from his last years in Basle and first years of wanderings as a 'pensioner' – in other words from the first volume of *Human, All Too Human* until he began work on *Zarathustra* (1878–82) – are concerned, in a peculiarly dense linking of philosophical interpretations, with both the gradual development of ontological ideas and cultural criticism. We can therefore say with good reason that the prevailing concentration on Nietzsche's late writings may well be excessive and runs the danger of missing many of the particularities of Nietzsche's philosophy, which consist in the inexhaustible connection between reflexions on the development of European culture and reflection on Being. This link between philosophy and cultural criticism was clearly present in Nietzsche's early works, as can be seen in the dualism of the Dionysian and the Apollonian in *The Birth of Tragedy*. But in the works of his middle period Nietzsche's philosophy acquires a content that was lacking in the earlier writings, or at least was barely visible. For the latter reveal a total dependence on Schopenhauer's metaphysics as well as an unresolved disparity between irreconcilable positions.[2] *Human, All Too Human* clearly marks the transition to a new creative phase, and Nietzsche's final break with Wagner in that work is symptomatic of this shift.

What immediately impressed Wagner about this work, and what immediately strikes the reader today when comparing it to his previous works, is Nietzsche's new attitude to art. There are admittedly, as we have seen, adumbrations of this attitude in the earlier works, written during his first years in Basle. But these adumbrations are marginal, and even the third *Untimely Meditation* thinks of science as one of the great enemies of any true culture. In *Human, All Too Human*, on the other hand, the picture appears to be reversed. There is no suggestion here of 'the metaphysics of the artist' and what is more no hope that art can lead us out of decadence. Indeed, the very notion of decadence is problematized in this text, as is the global condemnation of modern civilization. In *Human, All Too Human*, the first edition of which (1878) is dedicated to Voltaire,

45

Nietzsche demonstrates a generally 'Enlightened' approach, although on closer inspection it is clear that he distances himself from the Enlightenment particularly with regard to the belief in 'progress'.

Factors which contributed decisively to this new attitude included Nietzsche's new acquaintances, the reading he had done during the Basle years, and his experience of Wagner's music. This experience is set out comprehensively, and not entirely without critical barbs, in the fourth *Untimely Meditation* (*Richard Wagner in Bayreuth*) which appeared in 1876. As a result of his relationship with Wagner and his acolytes Nietzsche realized that the project to give new birth to tragic culture on the basis of Wagner's operatic practice was hopeless. Nietzsche's experience of the Bayreuth Festival, which Wagner created in 1876 to stage his operas more effectively, revealed to him the limits of this undertaking conceived (by Wagner) as an 'aesthetic revolution'.[3] Yet his experience of 'true Wagnerianism', with all its personal, and more than personal aspects was only one element in his coming of age in those Basle years. Other (and perhaps even more important) influences were his new friendships and cultural interests – for example, his close connection with the historian and theologian Franz Overbeck, his closest and most loyal friend right up until his mental breakdown. It was Overbeck who went to Turin in January 1889 and brought the sick Nietzsche back to Switzerland. A further point to note is Nietzsche's personal acquaintance with Jacob Burckhardt who undoubtedly had a decisive influence both on the ideas of the second *Untimely Meditation* and on Nietzsche's retraction of the hopes for the rebirth of tragic culture. Nietzsche also had occasion in Basle to deepen his knowledge of the natural sciences by reading relevant texts. His biographers have documented his lively interest in scientific writings at that time. Between 1873 and 1874 he borrowed Boscovich's *Naturphilosophie* [*Natural Philosophy*] several times, as well as histories of chemistry and treatises in physics. Moreover, as early as 1872 he read Johann Karl Friedrich Zöllner's book of 1871, *Über die Natur der Kometen. Beiträge zur Geschichte und Theorie der Erkenntnis* [*On the Nature of Comets: Contributions to the History and Theory of Knowledge*], as well as the writings of Ludwig Rütimeyer, a neo-Lamarckian palaeontologist, who also taught at the University of Basle.[4] Also important to Nietzsche's thought from *Human, All Too Human* onwards was the reading he did that revealed an interest in a 'positive' analysis of man and culture. It included Edward Burnett Tylor's *Primitive Culture: Researches into the Development of Mythology, Philosophy, Religion, Art and Custom* (one of the works which inaugurated cultural anthropology at the end of the nineteenth century and which Nietzsche read in 1875, four years after its publication) as well as the works of the great French *moralistes*, Montaigne, La Rochefoucauld, Chamfort, Fontenelle and Pascal.[5]

These influences found their outlet, in various guises, in Nietzsche's texts of the period 1878–82: *Human, All Too Human*, *Daybreak*, and *The Gay Science*. Roughly, this period can be summarized as the one in which Nietzsche puts an end to the notion of the 'artist's metaphysics', problematizes the concept of decadence and develops a new understanding of the relations between art, science and culture, and renounces the ideal of a rebirth of tragic culture.

As Nietzsche writes in *Human, All Too Human*, art has the disadvantage that it represents a 'superseded' phase in the education of mankind. This education is conceived as a process of enlightenment, in which science now plays the dominant role:

> *Art as necromancer.* – Among the subsidiary duties of art is that of conserving, and no doubt also of taking extinguished, faded ideas and restoring to them a little colour: when it performs this task, it winds a band around different ages and makes the spirits that inform them return. It is only a phantom life that here arises, to be sure, such as appears about graves, or like the return of the beloved dead in dreams; but the old emotions are again aroused, if only for a few moments, and the heart beats to a rhythm it had forgotten. On account of this useful function of art one must overlook it in the artist himself if he does not stand in the foremost ranks of the Enlightenment and the progressive *masculinization* of man: he has remained a child or a youth all his life, stuck at the point where he was first assailed by his creative urge; feelings belonging to the first stages of life are, however, admitted to be closer to those of

earlier times than to those of the present century. Unwittingly, his task becomes that of making mankind childlike; this is his glory and his limitation. (HAH I, §147, 144f.)

The preceding aphorism (§146) similarly ascribes 'a weaker morality' to the artist's knowledge of truth than the thinker's. In order to preserve the presuppositions of his art, he is obliged to interpret life in essentially mythical terms, in other words he has to cling to its emotional side, to the sense of the symbolical, and be open to the fantastic. If he refuses to abandon this view of life, it becomes to him 'more important than the scientific devotion to the true in any form, however plainly this may appear' (HAH I, §146, 144). This regressive attitude on the part of the artist does not depend so much, or not exclusively, upon the fact that art must necessarily conceal the truth of things by means of the 'symbolical'. Rather, it can be traced to the fact that, in order to function, art needs a particular world and a particular culture. For the ages and conditions in which art flourishes most vigorously are those characterized by violent emotions and a belief in gods and spirits not shared by science (HAH I, §159, 151). What makes art untimely (and Nietzsche is almost certainly thinking of Wagner's art here) is not so much its abstract opposition to science as a truer and more extensive knowledge, but rather the change in society's underlying conditions. As a result of this change, which is connected with the triumphal advance of science, the situation arises where art appears to be a thing of the past. A passage in the second volume of *Human, All Too Human* (*The Wanderer and his Shadow* §170) entitled 'Art in the age of labour' also discusses this change in society. In it Nietzsche discusses 'the most general circumstance through which the relationship of art to life has been altered' (WS §170, 261). It can be traced to the advent of a social structure based upon work, in which art is reserved for 'leisure time' which is also the time of tiredness and distraction. As a result, art has to become coarser and reduce itself to the level of the common people. In order to arouse the attention of an audience which can spare it only the evening hours, even grand art has resort to 'narcotics, intoxicants, convulsives, paroxysms of tears' (ibid., 261f.). Many of these terms surface in Nietzsche's later writings as criticisms of Wagner's operas.

Even if it makes no great difference to the outcome of his reflexions, it is nevertheless worth noting that Nietzsche does not come down on the side of science for purely epistemological reasons – in which case the job of science would be to know things and that of art to symbolize and imagine them. Viewed under the heading of 'cultural criticism' we may say: in order to affect the human spirit, art needs a world that is no longer our own. If it wishes to stay alive in our world, it must invoke the past and create artificially those preconditions which gave it relevance in other epochs. These preconditions cannot be described in terms of the greater or lesser objectivity of art's knowledge but

rather in terms of the force of its passions, the changea-
bility of its moods, and its childlike vehemence and
unreasonableness (cf. HAH I, §151).

Consequently, Nietzsche assesses even science in
Human, All Too Human not as objective knowledge of
reality; he evaluates it on the basis of the intellectual
attitudes that accompany it. Science is the foundation of
a more mature and ultimately less intemperate and less
violent culture. Nowhere in *Human, All Too Human*
does Nietzsche ascribe to science the ability to furnish
us with an objective knowledge of things. Aphorism 19,
for example, describes the errors and arbitrary assumptions on which counting and calculating (and hence the
mathematical structure of the natural sciences) are
based. However, the validity of scientific assumptions is
not thereby cast into doubt because the errors on which
our calculations rest remain more or less constant.
Nietzsche appeals to Kant here, whom he interprets in
a radically phenomenological manner by drastically
reducing the transcendental structures to a 'summation
of a host of errors of the understanding' (HAH I, §19,
37). Our picture of the world (the picture with which
science also operates) is founded on these errors:

That which we now call the world is the outcome of
a host of errors and fantasies which have gradually
arisen and grown entwined with another in the
course of the overall evolution of the organic being
[. . .] Rigorous science is capable of detaching us from
this ideational world only to a limited extent – and

51

more is certainly not desirable – inasmuch as it is incapable of making any essential inroad into the power of habits of feeling acquired in primeval times. (HAH I, §16, 33)

Science cannot lead us beyond the phenomenal realm to the 'thing in itself' ('Ding an sich'), a notion which Nietzsche believes, for precisely this reason and in opposition to Schopenhauer and Kant, to be 'worthy of Homeric laughter' (HAH I, §16, 34). Science can only 'illuminate, quite gradually and step-by-step, the history of the genesis of this world as idea – and, for brief moments at least, lift us up out of the whole process' (HAH I, §16, 33f.).

So if science therefore moves only in the realm of representations, in other words within those errors consolidated by human history, its difference from art is not to be found in its greater objectivity and truth. Even in *Human, All Too Human*, and more clearly still in *Daybreak* and *The Gay Science*, science appears instead as a model and methodological ideal. It is regarded as an activity that can bring about a certain mental attitude which Nietzsche values independent of its knowledge-related results in the narrower sense. What he writes in aphorisms 501 and 547 of *Daybreak* is probably also true of the scientific man, namely that, for us and future generations, knowledge is no longer to be thought of something to which we should be committed for the salvation of our souls. The way is thereby clear for a great collective effort on the part of

science and for noticing small things and nuances – i.e.
for all those phenomena on which the development of
the specialized sciences depends. '"What do I matter!"
– stands over the door of the thinker of the future' (D
§547, 322). The belief, dear to past ages, in the immor-
tality of the soul made the eternal salvation of the soul
dependent on recognizing the truth of things. Today,
however, where that belief has been overcome, the
riddle of reality may not be solved precipitately by any
belief. Mankind as a whole can 'now fix its eyes on
tasks of a vastness that would to earlier ages have
seemed madness and a trifling with Heaven and Hell'
(D §501, 298).

The last part of the first volume of *Human, All Too
Human* (in particular aphorism 635) also belongs to this
horizon of thoughts and expectations. It becomes clear
here that Nietzsche does not expect a truer picture of
the world from science, but rather a model way of
thinking which is not fanatical and proceeds methodically, soberly and 'objectively' in the sense that it
remains capable of making judgments outside the
immediate pressure of interests and passions. He characterizes this way of thinking as that of a 'free spirit'.

All this, however, renders the talk of art as a
phenomenon of the past a little ambiguous and brings
movement in to the 'Enlightenment' theory of knowledge Nietzsche presents in these works. Its ambiguity
can be demonstrated with reference to a series of themes
which crop up in *Human, All Too Human* and which
play a greater role in the later writings. In fact, he

shows how art and science are not different from each other because the former is a pure play of the imagination while the other is cold knowledge of things in themselves. Rather, the difference lies far more in the greater freedom, equanimity and sobriety with which the scientific man approaches the world. Yet these aspects are also important to the aesthetic approach. For example, at the end of aphorism 16 of *Human, All Too Human* Nietzsche states that science cannot free itself from the world of appearances, which is the result of a long history of errors that have become second nature to humans. It can only help us for brief periods to 'lift us up out of the entire proceeding' and help us to the discovery 'that the thing in itself is worthy of Homeric laughter'. This laughter of the kind that can momentarily raise itself above all those errors, from which the world of our appearances arises, is the same kind that is discussed later in aphorism 213. In that passage the laughter is occasioned by art's ability to make us enjoy nonsense for brief moments when art suspends the iron laws of our usual apprehension of the world. From this viewpoint we can understand Nietzsche's claim that 'the scientific man is the further evolution of the artistic' (HAH I, §222, 188), even if in the context of this aphorism the idea is deliberately expressed in narrower terms: art, Nietzsche writes there, has taught us 'to take pleasure in life and to regard human life as a piece of nature, as the object of regular evolution, without being too violently involved in it' (HAH I, §222, 187). Precisely this attitude is evident in the scientific man's need for knowledge. In a more developed form the interest and the pleasure comes to life in him, which art has taught us over the centuries, namely to observe life in all its forms. With this interest and pleasure we counter the development of errors, from which the world of appearances arises, in those moments when we raise ourselves above them. This long education through art has prepared the ground for science and the free spirit, and both must therefore be grateful to art.

Our Ultimate Gratitude to Art. – If we had not approved of the arts and invented this sort of cult of the untrue, the insight into the general untruth and falsity of things now given us by science – and insight into delusion and error as conditions of intelligent and sentient existence – would be quite unbearable. *Honesty* would have disgust and suicide in its train. Now, however, our honesty has a counterpoise which helps us to escape such consequences; – namely, art, as the *good* will to illusion. We do not always restrain our eyes from rounding off and perfecting in imagination: and then it is no longer the eternal imperfection that we carry over the river of becoming – for we think we carry a *goddess*, and are proud and artless in rendering this service. As an aesthetic phenomenon existence is still *bearable* to us; and through art, eye and hand and above all the good conscience are given to us, *to be able* to make such a phenomenon out of ourselves. We must rest from ourselves occasionally by contemplating and

55

looking down upon ourselves, and by laughing *at* or weeping *over* ourselves from an artistic remoteness: we must discover the *hero*, and likewise the *fool*, that is hidden in our passion for knowledge; we must now and then be joyful in our folly, that we may continue to be joyful in our wisdom! And just because we are heavy and serious men in our ultimate depth, and are more weights than men, there is nothing that does us so much good as the *fool's cap and bells*: we need them in the presence of ourselves – we need all arrogant, soaring, dancing, mocking, childish and blessed art, in order not to lose *the free dominion over things* which our ideal demands of us. It would be *backsliding* for us, with our susceptible integrity, to lapse entirely into morality, and actually become virtuous monsters and scarecrows, on account of the over-strict requirements which we here lay down for ourselves. We ought also *to be able* to stand *above* morality, and not only stand with the painful stiffness of someone who every moment fears to slip and fall, but we should also be able to soar and play above it! How could we dispense with art for that purpose, how could we dispense with the fool? – And as long as you are still *ashamed* of yourselves in any way, you still do not belong to us! (GS §107, 140f.)

Among others, a theme emerges here that was already of central significance in *The Birth of Tragedy*:

the notion that art is the only force that can make life bearable. Yet here the meaning of the theme is quite different. It is not a question here of following Schopenhauer, of fleeing from the chaos of the will into a world of forms, which is removed from the struggle for life that dominates the world of appearances. It is instead a question of making bearable the knowledge that those errors on which life and knowledge are founded are unavoidable, and of acknowledging that this is the sole source of the beauty and richness of our existence. The 'positivity' of those artistic representations discussed in *The Birth of Tragedy* is now granted to the *whole* world of appearances and not merely the world of art. Paradoxically, this generalizing of appearances ('that the thing in itself is worthy of Homeric laughter') leads to an alliance between science and art. Science has the twin tasks of apprehending the world of appearances methodically and grasping the way this world constitutes itself, including being aware of its errors. Art, on the other hand, has the job of keeping the hero and the fool within us alive and of helping science to make bearable the consciousness of our unavoidable errors. This consciousness of error separates Nietzsche's conception of science from that of positivism. Rather than concentrating on the individual results of our knowledge, it sets out the meaning of science for human progress. For precisely this reason science is maturer than art because it is art's heir and extension. The relationship of science and art, as Nietzsche conceives of it in *Human, All Too Human* and the other works of that time (1878–82), appears in the image of the 'double-brain'. According to him:

> a higher culture must give to man a double-brain, as it were two brain-ventricles, one for the perceptions of science, the other for those of non-science: lying beside one another, not confused together, separable, capable of being shut off; this is a demand of health. In one domain lies the power-source, in the other the regulator: it must be heated with illusions, one-sidednesses, passions; the evil and perilous consequences of overheating must be obviated with the aid of the knowledge furnished by science. (HAH I, §251, 213)

Here, as in the texts quoted above, we are not dealing with a separation of domains or differing 'species' or 'types'. In a mature person's attitude to the world, art and science complement each other. If, from the point of view of their simultaneity and actuality, they appear as power-source and regulator respectively, their profound connection emerges in their shared origin where we see that science is only a later, more mature development of that drive to which art owes its existence. As will become clear very shortly, the structural viewpoint has incomparably less significance for Nietzsche than a genealogical or genetic one.

2. THE SELF-SUBLIMATION OF MORALITY

Even if, as we have seen, the opposition of art and science in *Human, All Too Human* is not as complete and radical as it may appear at first sight, Nietzsche no longer hopes for the rebirth of a tragic culture founded on art and, to a certain extent, a regeneration of myth. Of the three figures Nietzsche had named in *Schopenhauer as Educator* as possible 'redeemers' of culture, the saint and the artist now take a definite backseat, while the philosopher (working in the spirit and with the methods of the scientist) begins to occupy a central position. If Nietzsche intends with *Human, All Too Human* a certain return to the tragic age of the Greeks, he wishes in the process to draw up a 'chemistry of concepts and sensations', as he terms it in the title of the work's first aphorism. For him, philosophical problems 'once again pose the same form of question as they did two thousand years ago: how can something originate in its opposite, for example rationality in irrationality, the sentient in the dead, logic in unlogic, disinterested contemplation in covetous desire, altruism in egoism, truth in error' (HAH I, §1, 19)? The earliest philosophers had attempted to define this even before the advent of metaphysics, by inquiring into the basic elements of things, an inquiry which could explain their difference and variety in terms of the composition of these elements. Metaphysics, which then established

59

itself in European culture, denied that a thing could be derived from its opposite. It assumed, for example, that values judged to be 'higher' could only come from above or from a mysterious 'thing in itself'.

> Historical philosophy, on the other hand, which can no longer be separated from natural science, the youngest of all philosophical methods, has discovered in individual cases (and this will probably be the result in every case) that there are no opposites, except in the customary exaggeration of popular or metaphysical interpretations [...] according to this explanation there exists, strictly speaking, neither an unegoistic action nor completely disinterested; both are only sublimations, in which the basic element seems almost to have dispersed and reveals itself only under the most painstaking observation. (HAH I, §1, 19f.)

'Historical' philosophy, working with the methods of 'chemistry', is the discipline which, as Nietzsche points out in aphorism 16 of *Human, All Too Human*, 'can, quite gradually and step by step, illuminate the history of the genesis of this world as idea' and 'for brief periods at any rate, lift us up out of the entire proceeding' (HAH I, §16, 33f.). Even if it is only the subtitle *Daybreak* that explicitly mentions 'moral prejudices', the concern of the whole chemical 'deconstruction'[6] in these works is, above all, morality. This is understood in a global sense as the subjugation of life by those supposedly transcendent values which, however, have their roots in life itself. The errors of metaphysics and religion belong in this broadly conceived notion of morality; even art appears – as already shown in *Human, All Too Human* – intimately bound up with that world of morality which is to be deconstructed.

The use of the category of morality to characterize all 'higher' spiritual forms does not only result, however, from a broad and undefined use of this concept. To Nietzsche, there lies at the root of all prejudices, even those of religion and metaphysics, the problem of man's 'practical' relationship with the world, and in this sense everything spiritual has to do with morality as it is practised. Besides, this reducing and unifying is a both a prerequisite and the result of the 'chemical' analysis conducted in *Human, All Too Human* and the other works of that period. Nietzsche's analyses, which are often carried out using very diverse materials, show that, in his opinion, truth itself is nothing more than a kind of prop for, and amplification of, a certain form of life. The opening aphorism of *Human, All Too Human* takes the first step and makes clear the general direction of Nietzsche's critique of morality. Everything that declares itself superior and transcendent, in other words everything we deem valuable, is nothing more than a product of the sublimation of 'human, all too human' factors; and not in the sense that moral values and the actions that result from them are only conscious lies on the part of those who preach them and act accordingly. Instead, errors come to light in them, to which one can subscribe in all good faith (cf. D §103, 89f.). As a system of prescriptions, as a complex of actions and codes of behaviour inspired by values, and finally as a world-view, morality is built on 'errors'. Here the results of Nietzsche's 'chemical' analysis reveal themselves, namely that it is precisely these errors that have bestowed richness and depth on the world and human existence.

Morality's first and fundamental error consists in the belief that there can be *moral acts*. For this presupposes above all that the subject has sufficient awareness of what his actions are. Even Schopenhauer, who taught us to see the world of representations as the 'veil of Maja', as a totality of appearances which conceal an invisible and unrepresentable 'thing in itself', believed that actions could be appropriately recognized and assessed. Yet what holds for the world of appearances, for external things, also holds for the inner world of the subject. The fact is that the intellectual awareness of an action and even of the value it possesses for us is never sufficient to carry it out. Our experience shows us that unambiguously. When we act there are thus other factors in play which cannot be the object of our knowledge.

We have expended so much effort learning that external things are not as they appear to us – very well! the same is true of the inner world! Moral actions are in reality 'something other than that' –

more we cannot say: and all actions are essentially unknown. (D §116, 107)

If this phenomenalist remark casts doubt on every possible judgment, it cannot apply to the dominance of morality, for even Christian ethics accepts in principle the idea that there is no final arbiter of actions – except God. The remaining aspects of Nietzsche's critique of morality cannot be tied into a systematic whole, but are instead put together in a somewhat disordered manner, even if they touch upon further important aspects of moral errors. For an action cannot be evaluated not only because it cannot be known, but also because the very possibility of moral evaluation implies that an action is freely chosen, which is not the case or at least cannot be proved. Nietzsche's denial of free will, which occurs frequently in the texts of this period, follows to some extent logically from his denial of the knowability of action. If not even the agent has a clear awareness of the motives behind his action, then his decision to perform that action will never be wholly full and free. By the same token, if action in its variegated aspects escapes the control and awareness of the subject, then this is only a consequence of the fact that it does in fact escape him. There are elements at work in the actions of a man, which elude his awareness because they lie outside his control and vice-versa (cf. HAH I, §107, 101ff.).

'Historical philosophy', which reconstructs the history

of moral sensations, exposes morality as an error – this is the theme of the second part of *Human, All Too Human* which ends with the aphorism (107) we have already quoted. According to Nietzsche, this history shows that man is motivated 'by the drive to preservation or, more precisely, by the intention to achieve pleasure and avoid displeasure' (HAH I, §99, 93). It would be right to object here that this proposition possibly goes against the principle that actions are unknowable; for it appears to imply a thoroughly knowable motive for action, namely 'the drive to preservation' or 'the intention to achieve pleasure and avoid displeasure'. It is hard to resolve or refute this 'contradiction' in Nietzsche's philosophy. In his subsequent investigation of individual phenomena, both 'the drive to preservation' and 'the intention to achieve pleasure and avoid displeasure' remain so formal (almost 'transcendental') that they cannot be filled with any specific content. Therefore they, too, remain fundamentally unknowable. But then it would be a question of determining to what degree the unknowability of actions for an agent (from which the impossibility of free will and thus moral determinism would follow) implies a second-degree unknowability, as it were, which prevents the philosopher from talking about morality. We can therefore admit that there is a problem here that affects the coherence and consistency of Nietzsche's thought, while stressing that the scope of this problem should not be overestimated.

Determinism does not by any means represent the

culmination of Nietzsche's critique of morality. As the critique develops, it becomes ever clearer what is at stake here, according to Nietzsche's conception of 'science'. Science's problem is not to free itself from the world of appearances in order to arrive at an ultimate principle (which might include a 'true' account of the mechanisms of action), but to arrive at a viewpoint overlooking the whole process by which appearances constitute themselves and develop. With regard to this programme, Nietzsche's thought, however great its contradictions may be, undeniably possesses coherence and consistency. To detect something like a 'drive to preservation' or 'the intention to achieve pleasure' at the root of morality is not the same as identifying the source of a moral value in stable, *fixed* structures of Being – in other words, in those structures which since time immemorial have provided traditional, metaphysical or religious, morality with a justification for its prescriptive systems. The 'drive to preservation' and 'the intention to achieve pleasure' are malleable forces which permit us to view morality as a diachronic process. Above all, however, they open up the possibility of viewing moral values as phenomena that have 'become'. And this is precisely the fact that a 'chemistry' (of knowledge of the variety of human cultures), informed by an 'historical philosophy', cannot forego. In *Human, All Too Human*, 'science' rests on the effort to reconstruct the process, indeed the varied processes which have led to the establishment and development of a moral world with all its nuances and deceptions – Nietzsche found the

French moralists' depiction of these masterful. This reconstruction proceeds solely on the basis of 'the drive to preservation' and 'the intention to achieve pleasure and avoid displeasure'. In this sense, and in this sense alone, even Nietzsche requires a unifying principle for science. However, this principle does not function as a foundation, on which something is 'grounded' and which hence consoles us because it provides a plausible confirmation of how things 'really' are. Instead, it operates as the starting-point of a process which only reveals itself in its variety and growing richness to those who move with it (D §44, 47f.).

Starting from the single principle of preservation and pleasure, the moral world shapes itself through a multiplicity of mechanisms, which Nietzsche describes in his aphorisms from new and ever-changing perspectives. Sublimation is the means by which we can move from the 'drive to preservation', the 'intention to achieve pleasure' and the avoidance to pain to heroism, self-sacrifice and altruism, in short to all those actions that seemed miraculous to Schopenhauer because they are 'impossible and yet real'. This sublimation is possible due to a 'self-division of man', who, in order to to be able to pursue his goals of self-preservation and pleasure more effectively, constitutes these as autonomous objects independent of himself.

Morality as the self-division of man. – A good author whose heart is really in his subject wishes that someone would come and annihilate him by presenting the same subject with greater clarity and resolving all the questions it contains. A girl in love wishes the faithfulness and devotion of her love could be tested by the faithlessness of the man she loves. A soldier wishes he could die on the battlefield for his victorious fatherland; for his supreme desire is victorious in the victory of his fatherland. A mother gives her child that of which she deprives herself: sleep, the best nourishment, if necessary her health, her strength. – But are these all selfless states of mind? Are these moral deeds *miracles* because they are, in Schopenhauer's words, 'impossible and yet real'? Is it not clear that, in all these cases, man loves *something of himself*, an idea, a desire, an offspring, more than *something else of himself*, that he thus *divides* his nature and sacrifices one part of it to the other? Is it something *essentially* different when some obstinate man says: 'I would rather be shot down than move an inch out of that fellow's way'? – The *inclination to something* (wish, impulse, desire) is the present in all the above instances; to give in to it, with all the consequences, is in any event not 'unegoistic'. – In morality man treats himself not as *individuum* but as *dividuum*. (HAH I, §57, 74)

Yet this split, which also reveals one root of religious feeling,[7] and to which all the later complications of morality that we would call sado-masochistic can be traced, is not the only mechanism Nietzsche detects in the constitution of values. The temporal piling up and layering of experiences and habits is just as important to the constitution of the self as a multitude of individuals who behave as strangers towards one another when it comes to morality. These experiences and habits were once useful to the individual or species in the struggle for survival, and although they have now lost this function they have nevertheless been preserved. The basic mechanism at work here is the same one Nietzsche had described as the origin of language from metaphors in *On Truth and Lies*. An individual forgets either that something is only a part of him (this is clear from the 'self-division' cases mentioned above) or that certain actions recommended by morality are demanded only by a purpose. In Kant's terminology, they are only 'hypothetical imperatives'.

> *The significance of forgetting for the moral sensation. –* The same actions that in primitive society seem to have been performed first with a view to common *utility* have been performed by later generations for other motives: out of fear or reverence for those who demanded and recommended them, or out of habit because one had seen them done all around one from childhood on, or from benevolence because their performance everywhere produced joy and concurring faces, or from vanity because they were praised. Such actions, whose basic motive, that of utility, has been *forgotten*, are then called *moral* actions: not because, for instance, they are performed out of those *other* motives, but because they are *not* performed

from any conscious reason of utility. – Where does it come from, this *hatred* of utility which becomes visible *here*, where all praiseworthy behaviour formally excludes behaviour with a view to utility? – It is evident that society, the hearth of all morality and all eulogy of moral behaviour, has had to struggle too long and too hard against the self-interest and self-will of the individual not at last to rate *any other* motive morally higher than utility. Thus it comes to appear that morality has *not* grown out of utility; while it is originally social utility, which had great difficulty asserting itself against all the individual private utilities and making itself more highly respected. (WS §40, 208f.)

However, corresponding to that which was said about the in no way unambiguous and certainly not reductionist principle of preservation and pleasure-seeking, it must be remembered that the moral world is also multi-coloured. For it encompasses religion and metaphysics in addition, which in their turn represent 'worlds' of values opposed or reacting to the world of everyday experience. The moral world also has other wellsprings apart from the self-division of the 'I' and the layerings of hypothetical imperatives whose origin in utility was later forgotten. An essential aspect of the principle of preservation and pleasure-seeking is the need for security and reliability, which is a contributory factor in the emergence of the basic tenets of metaphysics. Science develops from these, as the example of causality shows. *Human, All Too Human* traces the two basic concepts of metaphysics (the ideas of substance and free will) back to the sensations of pleasure and pain. These are the elementary sensations which regulate a living organism's contact with the world around it (cf. HAH I, §18, 34ff.). Abstract and generalizing thought, as well as the effort to see things 'objectively', also correspond to this same need for security:

> For this reason the animals learn to master themselves and alter their form, so that many, for example, adapt their colouring to the colour of their surroundings [. . .] Thus the individual hides himself in the general concept 'man', or in society [. . .] Even the sense for truth, which is basically the sense for security, man has in common with the animals: one does not want to deceive oneself, does not want to mislead oneself, one listens mistrustfully to the promptings of one's own passions, one restrains oneself and lies in wait for oneself; the animal understands all this just as man does, with it too self-control springs from the sense of what is real (out of prudence). It likewise observes the effects it has on the perceptions of other animals and from this learns to look back upon itself, to take itself 'objectively'. (D §26, 32f.)

The demand to grasp the *essence* of things and states of affairs also corresponds to the idea of 'objective' knowledge. The illusion of comprehending timeless essences

70

and eternal structures bestows a feeling of security because it proceeds from a kind of fixed point where one can position oneself (cf. WS §16, 188f.).

At the root of the other form of moral error, represented by religion, is not merely the need to arrive at a fixed point, a point where essences are separated from incidentals, but the need to reach a stability superior to man, which hence offers higher guarantees: 'one *confirms* an opinion in one's own estimation when one feels it to be a revelation, one thereby deletes its hypothetical nature, one removes it from criticism, indeed from all doubt, one makes it sacred' (D §62, 58). Over and above this, for the primitive mind which is incapable of seeing natural events as the product of individual causes, the first form of security consists in seeing everything that happens as the manifestation of a, of *the* divine will, with which one can in some way form a relationship (cf. HAH I, §111, 112–16).

If all these mechanisms can in large part be traced back to a drive for preservation, there are others which seem to have a closer connection with pleasure-seeking. Nietzsche defines this as a 'feeling of one's own power, of one's own strong arousal' (HAH I, §104, 99). This second motive of the processes of sublimation leads to a new series of more varied and still less well-defined moral phenomena, in which morality, metaphysics, religion and art no longer act as safety devices in an initial coming to terms with the world, but as pleasure sources in a staging and dramatizing of the inner life.

The most usual means the ascetic and saint employs to make his life nonetheless bearable and enjoyable consists in occasionally waging war and in the alternation of victory and defeat. For this he needs an opponent and he finds him in the so-called 'enemy within'. Specifically, he exploits his compulsive vanity, his thirst for honour and domination, then his sensual desires, in an attempt to see his life as a prolonged battle and himself as a battlefield. (HAH I, §141, 134; cf. GS §353, 271f.)

A dramatization of the inner life has, moreover, serious negative consequences that are inseparable from the moral mechanisms: 'How much needless cruelty and torture of animals has issued from the religions which invented sin!' (D §53, 53).

The work to deconstruct the results of morality, metaphysics and religion ultimately dissolves that place containing possible safety devices, namely a human's inner self. Consciousness is an area where different 'parts' of the self do battle – not that one can say which of these different selves is the authentic one. Once the belief in the ultimate immediacy and unity of the self was undermined, everything that man characterized with this name appeared doubtful. The self is now only the stage on which the drama of a moral life unfolds, where different and opposing impulses fight it out. The battles of conflicting motives, which we take to be the maturation of *our* moral choices, lead to a situation where 'we finally choose the most powerful of them – as we say (in truth, however, [...] the most powerful chooses us)' (HAH I, §107, 102). The presence of moral imperatives in us, which divides our personality, is but a trace of the various layers of our culture (cf. the already quoted aphorism WS §40). Even the image of oneself, which one uses as the criterion and reference point of one's own self, is mostly governed by others:

> Whatever they may think and say about their 'egoism', the great majority nonetheless do nothing for their ego their whole life long: what they do is done for the phantom of their ego which has formed in the heads of those around them and has been communicated to them. (D §105, 90f.)

In this way, the supposed immediacy and 'final validity' of consciousness, upon which all morality is founded, becomes untenable. Even consciousness is a 'construct' and a product, and hence no final arbiter – compare the passage in *The Gay Science* where Nietzsche develops a still more complex argument which reinvokes many of his points against the 'final validity' of consciousness in a moral sense (GS §335, 240–4).

We can conclude from all of this that Nietzsche's chemical work does not reach a result commensurate with its method. It does not close with the establishment of the ultimate elements and simple components of the various forms of morality. Neither consciousness nor the self, which were supposed to be the 'subject' of the

drive to preservation and of pleasure-seeking, are ultimate, immediate, simple elements. Nietzsche's 'chemistry' reveals itself more as a method which allows him
to reconstruct 'historically' the 'becoming' of morality,
metaphysics and religion. On the basis of the results of
this analysis, such a reconstruction represents their sole
sense. The aphorism we have already quoted from
Daybreak (*Origin and significance* [D §44, 47f.]) points to
this. Nietzsche's 'chemistry' does not lead to original
elements; instead these are revealed time and again as
already 'assembled'. But the assembly and transformation processes, the richness of colours and nuances
which go to make up the spiritual life of humanity –
from the errors of morality, metaphysics and religion to
the productions of a religious asceticism – can only be
understood if one applies the method of a 'chemical'
analysis, and returns to its perenially problematic roots
– admittedly, this brings with it a particular form of
production, in which one lifts oneself above the entire
proceeding. Nietzsche characterizes the dissolution of
the idea of fundamentals, of a first principle, in the
course of the very process which is attempting to return
to such a principle, the *self-sublimation of morality*. In
the 1886 preface he transfers this task to *Daybreak*. Yet
it is not imposed from the outside, in other words it
does not result from new positions Nietzsche had
adopted in the intervening period (1881–86). Rather, it
remains faithful to the results of the work that was
begun with the 'chemical' analysis in *Human All Too
Human*.

The self-sublimation of morality refers to the process whereby 'faith in morality is withdrawn – but why? *Out of morality!*' (D, Preface §4, 8). On the basis of the very commitment to truth which metaphysical and then Christian morality has always preached, the 'realities', in which this morality has always believed (God, virtue, truth, justice, brotherly love), are exposed as untenable errors. As it says in a lengthy aphorism in *The Gay Science*, because '*we, too, are still pious*' we are governed by the belief that:

> even we knowledge-seekers of today, we the godless and anti-metaphysical, still take our *fire* from the conflagration ignited by a belief dating back millennia, that Christian belief which was also Plato's belief, that God is the truth, that truth is divine.... But what if this itself becomes ever more untrustworthy, what if nothing proves to be divine any more, unless it be error, blindness, lies; – what if God Himself turns out to be our most enduring lie? (GS §344, 256, 259)

We have now reached the point in the self-sublimation of morality which leads to the proposition: 'God is dead'. This proposition is first proclaimed in *The Gay Science* (GS §108, 145 and §125, 158ff.). God has been slain by religious men out of piety and devotion (cf. GS §357, 282).[8] The self-sublimation of morality and the death of God display early characteristics of the process Nietzsche was later to summarize on one page of

Twilight of the Idols under the heading 'How the "Real World" at last Became a Myth' (TI iv, 74; cf. further discussion below p. 77f.).

Nietzsche sees a connection between the process in question here and a kind of inner logic at work in moral-metaphysical discourse.The process does, however, also have an 'outer' basis in the way the general conditions have changed on account of the discipline introduced by morality, and they have changed so much that ultimately morality becomes redundant and its superfluousness becomes apparent. For this reason amongst others, the pronouncement 'God is dead' is not, in Nietzsche's case, simply a metaphysical denial of His existence. For it is not a statement concerning the 'true structure' of reality, in which God does not exist while people believe that He does. Instead, conditions have altered and have rendered a fable superfluous, which in other ages was useful and decisively important. The new conditions make other 'fables' possible, indeed they make possible a more explicit and self-conscious 'yarn spinning' (cf. GS §54, 90f. which deals with 'continuing the dream' despite our 'consciousness of appearance'). The self-sublimation of morality has the outward goal of reducing existential insecurity within society or in an environment created by the division of labour and technological development. 'The ultimate decisions (concerning so-called eternal questions) lose their importance when the character of life in society is *less violent*. One thinks how rare it is for a person today to have anything to do with them' (N June – July 1879,

IV.3, 437, 40[7]). Today, 'metaphysics and philosophy are attempts to take *violent* control of the most fruitful areas' (N June – July 1879, IV.3, 441, 40[21]). As has been shown, the origin of belief in God, in a substance, or in free will, or indeed in the imperative of truth, generally depends closely on violence and insecurity – this belief is rooted in the need to protect oneself in the struggle for life against the deceptions and self-deceptions emanating from the passions. In a still later fragment Nietzsche writes:

> We have a different view of 'certainty'. Because it is fear that has been cultivated in man the longest and because bearable existence began with the 'sense of security', this continues to have an effect on thinkers. But as soon as the outer 'dangerousness' of existence recedes there emerges a desire for insecurity, for limitless lines of horizon. The happiness of the great explorers in the striving for certainty could now metamorphose into the happiness of demonstrating uncertainty and risk everywhere. Equally, the timidity of an earlier existence is the reason why the philosophers stress preservation (of the ego or the species) so emphatically and grasp it as a principle; while in fact we continue to play a lottery game against this principle. (N 1884, VII.2, 221f., 26[280])

Even if the freedom to play with appearances is preserved in art as festive moments (for example, the 'Saturnalia' mentioned in HAH I, §213, 176), and if the artist awakens in us 'the *hero* as well as the *fool*', we are today in a different position from earlier gener-ations, as far as life's seriousness is concerned, thanks to the greater security that the organization of society has gradually vouchsafed to us through a science founded on a moral-metaphysical basis. Even if the belief in mankind's necessary progress, as a metaphysical dogma, cannot be accepted, we can testify from our experience to the possibility of such progress; it shows itself not least in the improvement in life's material conditions (cf. HAH I, §24, 41). And under these (at least rela-tively) secure new conditions, the possibility of a new form of human existence grows and takes shape, which Nietzsche dubs the self-sublimation of morality, the death of God, or even (at the end of *Human, All Too Human*) a '*philosophy of the morning*' (HAH I, §638, 375).

3. PHILOSOPHY OF THE MORNING

This expression, which occurs in the beautiful final aphorism of *Human, All Too Human*, appears to suggest something purely 'climatic', but certainly a metaphor, a decorative image which is to be 'translated' into some-thing with more conceptual substance. Clearly, this image represents a symmetrical opposite to Hegel's image of philosophy as the 'Owl of Minerva', and Nietzsche probably wanted to bring out this opposition. Yet this metaphor cannot be traced back entirely to a concrete meaning; for in Nietzsche's works of this period (1878–82) – and still more so in the later writings – allusions to these 'climatic' moments are so numerous that they appear to refer to something more meaningful than merely a search for literary effect. A 'good temperament', health and convalescence are often mentioned in such a way that the reader gains the impression from these texts more of an indeterminate 'intellectual atmosphere' than of a metaphorically expressed academic institution. This impression corresponds fairly precisely to the actual conditions: the culturally critical and demystifying philosophy which Nietzsche developed in his 'middle period' is a philosophy relatively 'free' of positive theorizing. In fact, it lacks those 'results' which would be obtained from going beyond the setting out of an 'intellectual attitude'. What result can an unmasking project produce, which, to judge from the examples of the self-sublimation of morality and the death of God, ultimately unmasks itself by revealing that its own motive is a dogmatic impulse towards truth? Yet only – but really only? – to a future humanity whose virtue and sickness will be 'the historical sense' (GS §337, 244). The spirit of the future human, which Nietzsche prepares with his philosophy, will be nothing other than feeling the whole past history of mankind 'to be *his own history*' (ibid., 245). Knowing how to bear the weight of this past, and knowing how to feel oneself the heir to its burdensome obligation, means:

[burdening] one's soul with all of this – the oldest, the newest, losses, hopes, conquests, and the victories of humanity; if one could finally contain all this in one soul and crowd it into a single feeling – this would surely have to produce a happiness that man has not yet known: the happiness of a god full of power and love, full of tears, and full of laughter. (ibid.)

What in the second *Untimely Meditation* was purely a sickness (the intolerable burden of a past which rendered humans incapable of creating their own history) becomes here the dominant characteristic of a future humanity. One might think that is not really a *volte-face* since Nietzsche clings fast to the demand that one must take upon oneself the whole history of humanity and experience it as *one's own history*. It is, however, another way of relating to history than when it is experienced as the historical sickness (which is characterized by the burden of an undigested and unassimilated past). Yet here, in contrast to the second *Untimely Meditation*, such an assimilation of history no longer appears impossible. It is achieved through the 'scientific' work of tracing anew the course of human history through humanity's 'errors'. Nietzsche shows this in *Human, All Too Human* (whose text is incidentally the first and most appropriate realization of a 'historical philosophy') by placing individual aphorisms at 'strategic' points – as well as the closing aphorism already cited, we can point to aphorism 292 at the end of the fifth part, aphorism 34 at the end of the first, aphorism 223 at the end of the fourth, and aphorism 107 at the end of the second. At these points we are reminded of the liberating significance of assimilating past human history in this way, a history which is always a history of 'errors'. However, the liberation does not consist in refuting these errors. One aphorism in the *The Gay Science* relates that the history of the origin and value of moral sensations certainly does not amount to a justification of them but, equally, does not lead to their refutation (cf. GS §346, 261–3). To renounce superstition and to recognize errors as errors are only a first step:

> *A few rungs back down.* – One, certainly very high level of culture has been reached when a man emerges from superstitious and religious notions and fears and no longer believes in the choir invisible, for example, or in original sin, and no longer speaks of the salvation of souls; if he is at this level of liberation he still has, with the greatest exertion of his mind, to overcome metaphysics. *Then*, however, a *retrograde step* is required: he has to grasp the historical justification that resides in such ideas, likewise the psychological; he has to recognize that they are most responsible for the advancement of mankind and that without such a retrograde step he will deprive himself of the best that mankind has hitherto produced. – With regard to philosophical metaphysics, I see more and more who have reached the negative goal (that all positive

81

metaphysics is an error), but still only a few who are climbing back down a few rungs; for one may well want to peer over the topmost rung of the ladder, but one should not want to stand on it. The most enlightened only get as far as freeing themselves from metaphysics and then looking back down it: whereas here too, as in the hippodrome, it is necessary to round the bend once you have reached the end of the straight. (HAH I, §20, 37f.)

Nietzsche characterizes this attitude (which is beyond refutation and rejection) as 'a good temperament' that is required by the new thinking. For it has 'nothing of snarling and sullenness about it – those familiar tedious qualities of old dogs and men who have long lain fettered' (HAH I, §34, 51; cf WS §350, 340).

Perhaps one should term this attitude 'contemplative' for it is directed at the history of those errors which have constituted human culture and which have lent the human world richness and depth. Yet this contemplation is not necessarily immobile and passive. A 'free spirit' can only develop this attitude if he has the courage to risk adventure and uncertainty – let us not forget, however, that these have only been made possible by the less violent conditions in which we exist. In present-day society, a free spirit nevertheless often takes up a marginal position, where the singularity of genius meets illness (cf. HAH I, §§234–6, 199–202, where genius is discussed above all).

The entirely non-systematic definition of the free

spirit sketched by Nietzsche is also unable to provide
the concept of the 'philosophy of the morning' with any
positive theoretical content. So it remains the definition
of an attitude, a spiritual climate, not of a philosophical
'doctrine' in the strict sense. Nietzsche's explanations
seem on the whole to be an effort to prompt men to
adopt a different outlook, one that is not based on
particular philosophical propositions but rather on part-
ing company with attitudes inherited from the past. His
very critique of the errors of metaphysics has led
Nietzsche to mistrust global 'visions of the world' and
universal philosophical propositions. A free spirit therefore inhabits *'the closest things of all'* and lives on the
'surface' (cf. WS §6, 180 and GS §256, 195). In a certain
sense, therefore, the impression is justified that more
so than in his youth (when he was working more or
less on the basis of Schopenhauerian metaphysics),
Nietzsche's philosophy in this second period (1878–82)
is devoid of a theoretical 'content'. Yet it is not a
case, as one might expect, that 'literary' intentions
predominate in his texts (along the lines of Dilthey's
idea of a 'philosophy of life', to which we referred
at the beginning of our discussion). It is also not
the case that Nietzsche is concerned simply (as some
twentieth-century thinkers, notably Wittgenstein, have
been) with reducing philosophy to a 'therapy' – linguistic and attitudinal, even though this conception of
philosophy is certainly present in his work. Despite
considerable interpretative difficulties, it is important to
understand how to a certain extent (and connected with

this apparent and also real 'emptiness' of Nietzsche's philosophical arguments in these writings) ontological positions are already beginning to mature, which do not represent a 'leap' out (or away) from his work as cultural critic and 'historical philosopher'. In this second period (and more explicitly in the late writings) there is already a philosophical conception of Being, an 'ontology', which in its particular form can only be understood within a specific conception of cultural history (without being in either form or content a 'philosophy of history' in the Hegelian mould). On the contrary, one can say quite the reverse, namely that the ontological 'propositions' which Nietzsche develops in his final period (and from which Heidegger's reading draws inspiration) are in principle no different from the cultural criticism in *Human, All Too Human* and indeed represent its continuation.

This is particularly evident in one of the main ideas of the late Nietzsche's ontology, namely the idea of the Eternal Recurrence of the Same, which unlike others (the Will to Power, for example, the Übermensch, or nihilism) is already announced in *The Gay Science*, the last text of Nietzsche's second period. In the penultimate aphorism of Book Four (§341),[9] the idea of Eternal Recurrence (which was later to have multifarious meanings imposed upon it, some of them traditionally 'metaphysical') has the same meaning as the ideas of other texts, in which the new attitude to life which Nietzsche wishes to promote is being described and which he characterizes from time to time as the philosophy of the morning. An example is that aphorism from *Human, All Too Human* referred to above (§107). If one places this passage alongside aphorism 341 of *The Gay Science*, it may perhaps become clear that Eternal Recurrence is merely another way of formulating that unconditional endorsement of life which constitutes the philosophy of the morning.

The 'Annunciation' of the Death of God is characteristic of the connection that emerges in the writings of the second period between cultural criticism and the working-out of ontological ideas. As was indicated above, the 'Death of God' (the summation of what Nietzsche terms the self-sublimation of morality) is not a metaphysical pronouncement on the non-existence of a God. It should instead be taken literally as the announcement of an *event*. To announce an event does not mean, however, that one is 'proving' anything. Nor does it mean, strictly speaking, that one is seeking any agreement for the announcement (which could only be sought on the basis of a historico-metaphysical belief in the rationality of the event). Yet announcing an event, allied to describing its immediate circumstances (in this case, a reconstruction of morality's errors and eventual self-sublimation), cannot avoid provoking other events in its turn. And this is precisely what *The Gay Science* also says of the thought of eternal recurrence: 'If this thought took hold of you, it would transform you as you are [...] it would lie upon your actions as the greatest weight' (GS §341, 250).

As we intend to show, the philosophical ideas of

85

Nietzsche's late period are, as a whole, a mixture of the factual and the hypothetical. This is directly connected with the radical nature of the self-sublimation of morality that Nietzsche described in his second period. 'God is dead' is an idea which is no different from a culturally critical statement. It is an 'historical' assertion yet because of its radical historicity presupposes no acknowledgment of any necessary, historical rationality. The observation that God is dead does admittedly sets in train a whole series of possible effects, consequences and metamorphoses. An example of this is the question with which the reflections on Eternal Recurrence is introduced: 'What, if [. . .]' (ibid.) Looked at from this point of view, Nietzsche's philosophy can rightly be termed experimental thinking[10] which holds to the 'discovery' – but perhaps only to the suspicion – that belief in the truth is only a belief. As long as nothing 'occurs' that can prove the opposite the only way open is to experiment: 'What, if . . .'

III. The Philosophy of Zarathustra

1. MORNING AND NOONTIDE

Nietzsche's works are commonly divided into three periods: a) the early works; b) the genealogical and deconstructive thought from *Human, All Too Human* to *The Gay Science*; c) the philosophy of Eternal Recurrence that begins with *Zarathustra*. This division is, of course, only schematic and should therefore not be given undue weight. It is nevertheless largely accepted, implicitly or explicitly, in the secondary literature. Two possible alternatives to this division present themselves. They are either to treat his whole mature thought from *Human, All Too Human* to the late writings as essentially a unity, or to make a distinction between the philosophy presented in *Zarathustra* and that of the later works. The latter are on the whole dominated by the (ultimately abandoned) project to write a great, systematic work with the title *The Will to Power*[1] – this was in any event one of the titles which cropped up more frequently than others in Nietzsche's plans of that time.

Even those like C. P. Janz, the author of the latest (and most comprehensive) Nietzsche biography,[2] who view the thought of the mature Nietzsche as unified, nevertheless recognize that *Zarathustra* came into being after a turning-point that Nietzsche himself understood was decisive – and not only in the autobiographical reconstruction of his own works, which he undertook in that text written in those final months in Turin, *Ecce Homo*, whose messianic and exultant tones appear to herald the imminent onset of madness. In the chapter 'Thus Spake Zarathustra' Nietzsche recounts how, in August 1881, the fundamental conception of that work (the thought of Eternal Recurrence) came to him. It happened on a walk by Lake Silvaplana in the Oberengadine ('6,000 feet beyond man and time'), in other words close to Sils-Maria where, from now on, he would spend his summers. This entire passage, together with the succeeding paragraphs and chapters demonstrate that Nietzsche ascribed to this event a shattering significance, not only for himself and his work but also for the whole history of humanity. From here on there is a consequential development in his thought, concentrated on the programme for a 'Transvaluation of All Values', which is simultaneously a programme for the planned, systematic work which he wished, at least for a time, to call *The Will to Power*. The decisive importance of this 1881 turning-point is not simply a matter of retrospective reconstruction in *Ecce Homo*, however. On 14 August 1881 Nietzsche wrote a letter from Sils-Maria to Heinrich Köselitz, who became better known under his pseudonym Peter Gast.[3] This letter demonstrates that even at this point Nietzsche was aware that something new was about to happen in his thinking. He wrote: 'Thoughts have soared over my horizon, the like of which I have never seen, – I won't let them utter a sound and I will, for my part, keep an unshakeable silence on the subject [. . .] The intensities of my emotions make me shudder and laugh.'[4] Nietzsche's ideas were so new and shocking, even to himself, that he resolved not to speak about them. *Ecce Homo* describes the period immediately following this until February 1883, during which Part One of *Thus Spake Zarathustra* appeared, as an interim period of 'becoming' that was only interrupted by the first proclamations of the new doctrine in *The Gay Science* – where there is not merely that first mention of Eternal Recurrence at the end of Book Four but also, in aphorism 342, the first mention of Zarathustra.

On the level of theoretical content, then, the turning-point for Nietzsche is the 'discovery' of Eternal Recurrence, and on the level of his works this turning-point is marked by *Zarathustra*. In purely stylistic terms, too, *Zarathustra* signifies a revolution in the development of Nietzsche's works because it is not written in any of the forms he had hitherto employed, namely the essay, the treatise, or the aphoristic style. It is also not poetry in the strict sense. Instead, it is a kind of long prose poem, whose most obvious model would appear to be the New Testament. *Zarathustra* is similarly set out in verses, in which the didactic and cultic aims of the text are expressed.

Nietzsche's choice of this new literary form can clearly

not be explained by the new doctrine of Eternal Recurrence. It is more the case that both the idea of Eternal Recurrence and the 'prophetic' form of *Zarathustra* stem from a common root. For the idea of the Eternal Recurrence of the Same, which serves as a theoretical leitmotif in *Zarathustra* and subsequent works, coincides with a new conviction on Nietzsche's part of what his mission is. As we shall see, the second great theme of *Zarathustra* (the doctrine of the 'Übermensch') intends a radical re-formation of humanity. What is new about the writings of the third period, and of which we are made aware principally by Nietzsche himself, is a series of new theoretical ideas (above all the idea of Eternal Recurrence) together with Nietzsche's new understanding of a thinker's task. The choice of the 'prophetic' form in *Zarathustra* indicates that Nietzsche felt more decisively and more radically than in the period of his deconstructive and genealogical works that he had now been entrusted with an epoch-making task. Admittedly, those works also adopt a critical distance from the whole European tradition of morality and metaphysics; but from *Zarathustra* onwards the novel aspect is the conviction that, on the basis of this distancing, a radical transformation of culture and civilization can and must be brought about. It would be fruitless to attempt to establish whether the new theoretical ideas produced the new 'prophetic' attitude or vice-versa. What is certain, however, is that in view of the broadly political function that Nietzsche now ascribes to his thought, the great new ideas of his philosophy acquire decisive importance; and this is true not so much of their theoretical content but rather in terms of Nietzsche's formulation of a draft 'system', even if this is unlikely to be fully realized. For a certain degree of 'system' seems indispensable to a philosophy that insists on its 'applicability' and wishes to becomes the principle of a new humanity.

All of Nietzsche's late work is characterized as much by his excessive interest in achieving an historical 'effect' as it is by the great ontological ideas connected with the idea of Eternal Recurrence. This accounts for (without, admittedly, being able to solve) many of the ambiguities, contradictions and self-misunderstandings that mark, or mar, the writings from 1883 to 1889. The 'political' ravings which characterize the last notes in Turin just before the onset of mental illness (and which were probably already influenced by the illness) should be viewed in this light. This excessive interest in achieving an historical 'effect' is a thread running through the mature Nietzsche's thought. From *Zarathustra* onwards he regards the philosopher as a legislator, an inventor of values that are to underpin a new sense of history. In a note of 1883 he writes: 'It is not enough to devise a doctrine: one must also change men violently so that they accept it! – Zarathustra has finally understood this' (N 1883, VII.1, 545, 16[60]).

In our opinion, Nietzsche's eager interest in historico-political efficacity is responsible for the ambiguities and self-misunderstandings that mark his late thought. This can be cited as a justification of many characteristic peculiarities of the works written in that period. On the other hand, as Janz has recently demonstrated, the depictions of Zarathustra's relationship with his pupils have to be taken more literally. The highs and lows of this relationship, the disappointments and anger of the master, his ironical attitude towards 'higher men' but also his recurring need to turn to them, to gravitate towards friends, and the feeling of growing loneliness (which dominates Part Four above all) all illustrate on the level of a 'prophetic' fiction something that motivates Nietzsche himself, and show how aware he was of the historic destiny of his teaching during the years of working on the four parts of *Zarathustra*.[5]

As well as explaining Nietzsche's efforts to devise a system and write a central work, his concerns about the historical efficacy of his philosophy also account for his interests and for the targets of his polemics during those years. For instance, the insistence and violence of the anti-Christian polemics that culminate in *The Antichrist* appear scarcely justified, if viewed in a purely theoretical light. Significantly, Nietzsche regards *The Antichrist*, written in the last months of his conscious life, as the concluding part of the *Transvaluation of all Values* (his planned central work).[6] In *The Antichrist*, as in earlier works of this final period, the influences of Nietzsche's extensive reading are clearly apparent. Nietzsche had gathered information on the history of the origins of Christianity, the history of Islam, as well as psychology and anthropology. On a theoretical level, however, it is hard to discern what a work like *The Antichrist* adds to

Nietzsche's previous writings. The importance which he himself ascribes to the work is clearly connected with worries about his own historical impact because he is now concerned not only to criticize the errors of morality and religion but also to issue decrees for a new humanity. In polemical fashion, Nietzsche compares himself with the world of ideas and institutions which has shaped and moulded European modernity, namely the world of Christianity. He does this to such an extent, with such polemical incisiveness and such a wealth of historical arguments that the justification for it would seem to be less theoretical than political.

With regard to the Will to Power, Colli and Montinari have presented an interesting hypothesis linked to this problem of historical impact or effect:

Exoteric – esoteric
1. – everything is Will against Will
2. There is no Will at all
1. Causality
2. There is no such thing as cause-effect.
(N Summer 1886 – Autumn 1887, VIII.1, 191, 5[9])

The Will (and hence also the Will to Power, the magic formula that has divided interpreters for over a century) could in Nietzsche's eyes be nothing other than exoteric: i.e. the popular expression of his thought which, on the esoteric level, would be the exact opposite, namely the theoretical knowledge that 'there is no Will at all'. Needless to say, Nietzsche's need for an exoteric expression of his own thought, according to this hypothesis, arose as a result of his tireless artistic and political labours, which seek to excite, shake up and fascinate his readers in order to achieve an historic impact. Although it would appear reductive to want to see all the problems thrown up by the Will to Power resolved by the distinction between the exoteric and the esoteric, it remains the case that, in general, the ambiguities in the late Nietzsche's thought are connected with worries about his historical efficacy and therefore also indirectly with other problems, one of which is the necessity of formulating his doctrine exoterically. Yet these are ambiguities which Nietzsche by no means 'controls', as would be necessary were they only popular 'disguises' of his thought for the masses. They are, instead, ambiguities into which he himself falls, precisely because he is concerned about the historical effects (for the masses, too) that he is attempting to bring about.

In any event, the central role ascribed by Colli and Montinari's hypothesis to the distinction between the exoteric and the esoteric in Nietzsche's late writings confirms that one of the dominant features of these late works is a concern with the historico-political realm.

A further aspect of Nietzsche's texts from 1883 to 1889, which various interpreters have pointed out, must also be viewed in this context, namely, a certain 'regressive' tendency in his thought. He takes up once again themes of his early writings, such as the anti-historicism of the second *Untimely Meditation*, a theme which returns in many later passages (above all in *Beyond*

Good and Evil), an ironical attitude to science, and even that hope of a general renewal of culture which had dominated *The Birth of Tragedy*.[7]

In *Zarathustra* there are new stylistic elements, and 'external' factors also play a role; for example, the new significance and historical scope which Nietzsche ascribes to his own thought and which can perhaps be understood as an 'ideological' reaction to his growing loneliness or else as a psychological compensation for his isolation as a wandering intellectual. The theoretical content (which will be examined in detail below) also reveals that the change and the particularities of this final period are in tune with his previous development. When compared to the 'philosophy of the morning', on which the works of the second period turn, there are two characteristic new developments in the texts from *Zarathustra* to the posthumous fragments of *The Will to Power*. First, Nietzsche insists with fresh emphasis on a *decision* (we think here of the two central sections in Part Three of *Zarathustra*, 'The Convalescent' and 'Of the Vision and the Riddle'). Secondly, it becomes clear that his critique of the subject is more radical. One can see that, on the theoretical level, the element of 'decision' is more closely connected with Nietzsche's effort to bring about cultural renewal whereas the critique of the subject, with its theoretically radical implications, is more closely linked to the idea of Eternal Recurrence. At the same time, though, the two themes (that of 'decision' and that of the disintegration of the subject) can both be viewed as aspects of the idea of Eternal Recurrence. We must nevertheless emphasize a tension which ultimately remains unresolved and to which Nietzsche's thought falls victim more thoroughly than it does to madness. It is the tension between the element of 'decision' (and thus also of a historical renewal and the birth of the 'Übermensch') and the element of the subject's disintegration (the consequence of the radical acknowledgment of Eternal Recurrence). Even at first sight one can understand that the programme for a renewal of humanity on the basis of a doctrine such as the Eternal Recurrence of the Same will not be easily accomplished. Admittedly, the latter does make it abundantly clear that the only way to make this 'leap' to the 'Übermensch' will consist in changing the way we experience time – here, too, Nietzsche can be seen returning to the themes of his early works, because reflections on history familiar to us from the second *Untimely Meditation* are reappearing. But if Eternal Recurrence represents an 'objective' circularity of time, as Nietzsche is at pains to show, or if (following Karl Löwith's interpretation) Eternal Recurrence means the radical reduction of linear, 'historical' time to cyclical, 'natural' time,[8] it is hard to see how the programme of 'renewal' which Nietzsche intends to bring about with his writings could be founded upon this kind of demolition of history.

These tensions and contradictions become denser still in the image of the 'noontide', which henceforths supplants the image of the 'philosophy of the

morning' in Nietzsche's texts.[9] 'But some time', he
writes in *On the Genealogy of Morals* (1887), in a
stronger age than this rotten, self-doubting present,
he must come to us, the *redeeming* man of great love
and contempt, the creative spirit [. . .] This man of
the future will redeem us not only from the ideal
held up until now but also from the things *that had
to grow out of it*, from the great nausea, from the will
to nothingness, from nihilism – this stroke of noon
and great decision. (GM II, §24, 352)

If the noontide is being proclaimed here through the
tolling of bells which are calling for a great decision, it
appears in the chapter entitled 'At Noontide' in Part
Four of *Zarathustra* as 'the secret, solemn hour when no
shepherd plays his flute', in other words as a moment
of perfect silence. 'What? Has the world not just
become perfect? Round and ripe?' Nevertheless, these
pages of *Zarathustra* demonstrate very well the tensions
that lie concealed in the noontide image. Zarathustra
wishes to remain still and motionless, enjoying the
happiness of noontide, revelling in the feeling of calm,
melancholy and richness which this hour brings him:
'Like a ship that has entered its calmest bay [. . .] Like
such a weary ship [. . .] thus do I now rest close to the
earth, faithful, trusting, expectant, fastened to it by the
finest threads.' But Zarathustra's 'soul' wants to sing,
to move. 'Up! (he said to himself) up, you sleeper!
You noontide sleeper! Come on, look lively, old legs! It
is time and past time, you still have a fair way to go'

(Z IV x, 339f.). Even though the noontide appears to Nietzsche-Zarathustra as the perfect hour, the moment of total rest and perfect stasis, it contains the problem of having to make a decision, which must necessarily lead to movement, which in turn will disturb the noontide perfection. It means having to set off towards a downfall; perhaps not towards death (as Löwith suggests in his wonderful commentary on this text)[10] but rather towards the unavoidable disintegration of the subject, which is the consequence of the idea of Eternal Recurrence, if thought through radically enough.

If only in the form of a brief introduction, we have made clear the problems running through the third period of Nietzsche's philosophy. Though we are unable to discern a solution in this period, these problems invest Nietzsche's thought with (an otherwise inexplicable) contemporary relevance. The linking of critical reflection on culture with a working out of a new group of ontological themes (taken up in the concept of nihilism) presents itself here in a new configuration. This nihilism can be summed up as the gradual draining away of vital necessity from metaphysical and moral ideas during the civilizing of humanity; God 'dies' and as a result Being itself draws closer to Nothingness. In this new configuration it is not a question any longer of a philosophy of the morning, of a mere critical, genealogical survey of the past, or even of a grateful, nostalgic enjoyment of those 'errors' which have enriched and deepened human experience. In view of Nietzsche's concentration on the idea of the Eternal Recurrence of the Same, we are justified in arguing that the philosophy of the morning may be approaching hitherto unknown tensions and find itself exposed to profound instability. It is hard to say whether this instability and these tensions are necessary implications of the theory. Why can Zarathustra find no peace at noon, why can he not, armed with that attitude which combines gratitude, fatigue and melancholy, simply enjoy and contemplate the sense and non-sense of the world, the rounded perfection of everything? Are his gratitude, fatigue and melancholy not connected with that path he has had to tread? Do they not in their tension remain tied to a temporal dimension that, from now on, will perhaps have been overcome? Why does the philosophy of the morning not represent the culmination of Nietzsche's thought? We know from Zarathustra's discourses that, on the one hand, the attainment of this state (a complete suspension of time) is accompanied, as we shall see, by a decision, in other words by a sharp *leap* in time. On the other hand, the attainment of the 'circularity' of time leads (perhaps in a theoretically more relevant and radical form) to 'disintegrative' effects on the notion of subjectivity, which may render impossible the state of perfect contemplation which Zarathustra experiences (but cannot retain) at noontide.

It must be said that these problems do not only affect the inner development of Nietzsche's thought. If, as Löwith has claimed, the philosophy of Eternal Recurrence is supposed to be an 'anti-Christian repetition of antiquity on the pinnacle of modernity' – as the title of the fourth chapter of his book terms it, then its success or failure and its associated motivations turn on our relationship with modernity, on the latter's relationship with antiquity, and on the significance of Christianity, in other words on those questions with which modern philosophy has been dealing at least since the Romantic period. Löwith advances the view that Nietzsche's failure to hold fast to a philosophy of the morning, and simultaneously to find a theoretically coherent alternative to it, is due to the fact that Nietzsche is too deeply rooted in the Christian, modern tradition. According to Löwith, Nietzsche can conceive of the idea of Eternal Recurrence (i.e. the regaining of a Greek, naturalistic understanding of life) only as the result of a framework fraught with tension, as a redemption that must be *attained*. By this means, man is supposed to be made eternal once and for all – his 'natural' mortality, on which the naturalism of antiquity was based – will be removed from him.[11] As we can see, we are dealing here with that contradiction to which we have already referred between Eternal Recurrence and decision. Yet the problem thrown up by Löwith raises other questions, as well as doubts concerning the terms which Löwith uses to deal with it. For example, is the positing of a radical opposition between a 'naturalistic' antiquity, which clings to the image of a circle in its conception of time, and a Christian, historicist modernity, which has a linear conception of time moving towards a *telos*, not itself entirely a product of the modern consciousness? And is it not the case that this modern consciousness fails to resolve Nietzsche's problem (i.e. the opposition of history and nature, of decision and Eternal Recurrence) precisely because it persists in viewing it as that 'mythical' opposition which, it is fair to say, was invented by Classicism and Romanticism. When one starts to take this problem seriously, one is beginning perhaps to move closer to Martin Heidegger's understanding of Nietzsche. According to Heidegger, the distinction between 'antiquity' and Christian modernity plays no role in Nietzsche's thought. Instead, both notions orientate themselves along the guiding thread of what Heidegger terms 'metaphysics'.[12] Only against this background, according to Heidegger, can Nietzsche's reflections be properly understood.

This gives some idea of the problems that arise when reading Nietzsche.This is true above all of his late philosophy with its multifarious implications and of the interpretations which these have given rise to. Perhaps Nietzsche was not over-exaggerating when he entitled one chapter of *Ecce Homo* 'Why I am a Destiny'. For the 'transition' from the philosophy of the morning to Zarathustra's 'noontide' involves more than Nietzsche's intellectual biography. For the purposes of the present study, it seems sensible to investigate the key concepts in Nietzsche's thought and their relation to one another in those late texts, written between 1883 and 1889.

2. NIHILISM, ETERNAL RECURRENCE, DECISION

Thus Spake Zarathustra, the work in which Nietzsche's new philosophy begins (and which had already been announced in the closing aphorisms of the first edition of *The Gay Science*) starts where the road that had been mapped out by the 'philosophy of the morning' ended. That at least is how it is presented later in a chapter of *Twilight of the Idols*, in which the individual stages, not of Nietzsche's thought but of European philosophy (as Nietzsche reconstructs them), which led to *Zarathustra* are taken up again:

> *How the 'Real World' at last Became a Myth*
> *History of an Error*
> 1. The real world, in reach of the wise, the pious, the virtuous man – he lives in it, *he is it*.
> (Oldest form of the idea, relatively clever, simple, convincing. Rewriting of the proposition 'I, Plato, *am* the truth'.)
> 2. The real world, out of reach for the moment, but promised to the wise, the pious, the virtuous man ('to the repentant sinner').
> (Progress of the idea: it becomes more refined, more enticing, more incomprehensible – *it becomes woman*, it becomes Christian . . .)
> 3. The real world, unattainable, undemonstrable,

cannot be promised, but already thought of as a consolation, an obligation, an imperative.

(Fundamentally the same old sun, but shining through fog and scepticism; the idea grown sublime, pale, northern, Königsbergian [i.e. Kantian].)

4. The real world – unattainable? Unattained, at any rate. And if unattained also *unknown*. Consequently also not consoling, not redeeming, with no power to impose duties: how could we have a duty towards something unknown? . . .

(The grey of dawn. First yawnings of reason. Cock-crow of positivism.)

5. The 'real world' – an idea that has outlived its usefulness, it is no longer even a duty – an idea grown useless, superfluous, *consequently* a refuted idea: let us abolish it!

(Broad daylight; breakfast; return of *bon sens* and cheerful serenity; Plato blushes with shame; all free spirits run amok.)

6. We have abolished the real world: what world remained? the apparent world perhaps? . . . But no! *With the real world we also abolished the apparent world!*

(Noon; moment of the shortest shadow; end of the longest error; zenith of mankind; INCIPIT ZARA-THUSTRA.) (TI iv, 74f.)

In paragraph 5 of this section, the philosophy of the morning is described as that phase in which we have

liberated ourselves from the 'real world', from metaphysical structures and from God. There is, however, a
further step: with the real world, the apparent world
was also abolished, thereby bringing about the noontide,
the shadowless hour, the hour when Zarathustra's
teaching begins. Is it possible, following Nietzsche's
reconstruction on this page of *Twilight of the Idols*, to
find the distinctions between the 'thought of noontide'
and the 'philosophy of the morning' readopted and
justified in the removal of the apparent *and* the real
worlds? Zarathustra's teaching (and hence the late
Nietzsche's thought) appears simply to draw the consequences from the situation that with the real world we
have also abolished the apparent world. Among these
consequences we must clearly number Zarathustra's
most shattering and profound thought: the idea of
Eternal Recurrence.

How, though, is the idea of Eternal Recurrence
linked to the 'unmaskings' which Nietzsche undertook
in the works of his second creative period (1878–82). As
can be easily seen, some constitutive elements of this
idea are already present in the 'unmasking' texts from
Human, All Too Human onwards. The latter, for
example, spoke of the attitude of a knowing man, the
man of good temperament, who looks upon himself
and the world without praise or blame (HAH I, §34,
50). Elsewhere in the text the same attitude is described
as the 'teaching imparted by art to take pleasure in life
and to regard human life as a piece of nature' and to
educate ourselves to the thought that 'life, however it

may be, is good' (HAH I, §222, 187). The same feelings dominate the passage in which Nietzsche first announces the idea of Eternal Recurrence, namely the penultimate aphorism of the first edition of *The Gay Science* in 1882:

The greatest weight – What if, some day or night a demon were to creep after you into your loneliest loneliness and say to you: 'This life as you now live it and have lived it, you will have to live once more and innumerable times over; and there will be nothing new in it, rather every pain and every joy and every thought and sigh and everything unutterably small or great in your life will return to you, all in the same succession and sequence – even this spider and this moonlight between the trees, and even this moment and I myself. The endless hourglass of existence is turned upside down over and over again, and you with it, speck of dust!' Would you not throw yourself down and gnash your teeth and curse the demon who spoke thus? Or have you once experienced a tremendous moment when you would have answered him: 'You are a god and never have I heard anything more divine!' If this thought took hold of you, it would transform you as you are, or perhaps crush you; the question for each and every thing, 'Do you desire this once more and innumerable times more?' would lie upon your actions as the greatest weight. Or how well disposed would you have to become to yourself and to life *to demand*

105

nothing more fervently than this ultimate, eternal confirmation and seal? (GS §341, 250)

When Nietzsche first 'discovered' the idea of Eternal Recurrence in the summer of 1881 in Sils-Maria he was deeply interested in Spinoza,[13] and it is Spinoza we should be thinking of when reading many of Nietzsche's passages, not least the ones just quoted from *Human, All Too Human* and *The Gay Science*. If Nietzsche's own declarations are to be believed, he had only a very superficial knowledge of Spinoza's works before 1881.[14] Yet in the same way as Spinoza's *amor dei intellectualis* was founded upon a fully worked out metaphysical doctrine (the ethics of *more geometrico demonstrata*), so perhaps Nietzsche, too, was thinking in 1881 of Eternal Recurrence as a doctrine which might give more substance to what, in *Human, All Too Human*, had appeared as simply a 'good temperament'. In general, it can be established that the idea of Eternal Recurrence in Nietzsche's work is a systematization, though not a classical 'foundation', of the nihilism inherent in the philosophy of the morning. This philosophy has indeed abolished the real world and led to a freedom of the spirit in the face of those errors on which life necessarily builds. However, Nietzsche seems to believe that still greater problems arise when the apparent world is abolished along with the real one; because the apparent world also loses its own (but as always 'inferior') lightness and freedom which it acquired from its opposition to the real world. The attitude of the man who raises himself up for a moment above the whole process, who revels 'as though at a spectacle' (HAH I, §34, 50) in the errors that have given our world its depth, richness and colour, cannot be viewed as any kind of culmination. One cannot therefore stop at 'historical philosophy' and genealogical thinking. Whether or not one finds the transition from Nietzsche's second to his third period (from 'morning' to 'noontide') legitimate, it does in fact correspond to the requirement to reach, with the aid of the doctrine of Eternal Recurrence, a unified systematization and radicalization of the nihilism already arrived at in the philosophy of the morning.

One might well ascribe a *moral* meaning to the passage just quoted from *The Gay Science* (§341). On the other hand, however, and inextricably linked to this 'moral' interpretation, it can also be understood *cosmologically*. As an ethical hypothesis, the idea of Eternal Recurrence can mean only this: if we thought it possible that each moment of our lives could become eternal and repeat itself endlessly, we would have acquired an excellent evaluative criterion for our actions, for only an entirely happy being would desire this endless repetition. Set against this, however, there is the broader sense that the idea of Eternal Recurrence assumes in connection with the concept of nihilism. Only in a world no longer conceived within the framework of linear temporality would such perfect happiness be possible. Linear temporality – conceived as past, present and future, none of which can be repeated – amounts to the idea that each moment acquires its meaning only in relation to other moments on the temporal axis, as the second *Untimely Meditation* had shown. On the temporal axis each moment appears like a son devouring his father (i.e. the preceding moment) only then to suffer the same fate himself. There can be no true happiness in this construction – which elsewhere I have termed the 'oedipal' structure of time[5] – because no lived moment carries within itself the fullness of its own import. If this is so, it becomes clear why Eternal Recurrence must have a 'cosmological' dimension. For it is not simply a question of devising moments in our existence that are so fulfilled and dense that their eternal recurrence would be desired; rather, moments of this kind are only possible if we alter our attitude radically so as to suppress the distinction between the real and the apparent worlds, together with all that this implies. And the most important of these implications is the 'oedipal' structure of time. Eternal Recurrence can only be desired by happy people, yet a happy person can only exist in a world quite differently conceived. And this means that the doctrine of Eternal Recurrence has to have a 'cos-mological' dimension.

Yet is the removal of the opposition between the real and the apparent worlds, and of all the moral and metaphysical structures derived from this opposition (among them the oedipal structure of time where no moment ever contains its real significance), necessarily an affirmation of the idea of Eternal Recurrence? This question is simply a reformulation of that other question

The Philosophy of Zarathustra

we encountered in our discussion of the problems associated with the transition from the philosophy of the morning to that of 'noontide'; in other words, the question of whether this transition is required by forces internal to the theory or whether it is occasioned by external forces, such as Nietzsche's practical, political interest, which make him (in his eyes) search for 'more effective' formulations of his own thought. Nietzsche, it appears, could have confined himself to the theory that with the dissolution of metaphysics – and the sense of linear temporality connected with it – there can now be a happy humanity for the first time, no longer intimidated by the separation of the experience of an event from its meaning – a characteristic of life in a world determined by morality and metaphysics. Why did he instead feel the need once again to give this notion a kind of 'metaphysical' foundation and develop a theory that time is 'objectively' circular? If one follows Löwith's views, which we have already had occasion to quote several times, then the classical philologist Nietzsche's admiration for ancient Greece plays a part here. According to Löwith, Nietzsche wanted to return to a Greek, indeed to a pre-Socratic view of the world, as opposed to the Judaeo-Christian view that sees time as punctuated by unrepeatable moments: the Creation, sin, Redemption, the end of the world ...

Whatever the reasons behind and the consequences of this motive may have been, the fact is that in both the published writings and the notes of this last period Nietzsche attempts again and again to ground the

109

doctrine of Eternal Recurrence cosmologically. The
most conclusive argument in favour of this attempt can
be found in a note of autumn 1881, whose terminology
will be repeated with slight variations in many later
texts (cf. N 1888, VIII.3, 167, 14[188]). In the 1881 note
Nietzsche writes:

> The measure of the power of the universe is *fixed* not
> 'infinite': let us be on our guard against such concep-
> tual excesses! Consequently the number of situations,
> changes of state, combinations and developments of
> this power is admittedly enormously large and prac-
> tically 'immeasurable' but in any event it is also fixed
> and not infinite. The time in which the universe
> exerts its power is, however, infinite [. . .] before this
> moment an infinity has elapsed, i.e. all possible states
> of affairs must already have happened. Consequently
> the present state of affairs must be a repeat, and so
> must the one which gave birth to it be a repeat, and
> the one which arises from it, and so on forwards
> and backwards! [. . .] (N Spring – Autumn 1881, V.2,
> 421, 11[202])

Since Georg Simmel's time many interpreters have
made strenuous efforts to refute this argument in detail,
while others have simultaneously tried to *disprove* the
theory of Eternal Recurrence.[16] In scientific circles in
Nietzsche's time, the theory was, however, not at all
unusual[17] and this may perhaps explain why Nietzsche
might have thought that a 'scientific' version of his

doctrine in tune with contemporary thought would be generally beneficial to his philosophy; at this point we should remember the hypothesis mentioned above concerning the exoteric character of many aspects of Nietzsche's philosophy. In fact, the greater difficulties lie not with the possibility and validity of a 'scientific' proof of Eternal Recurrence but rather with the reconcilability of such a proof with Nietzsche's other tenets.

Is there any sense in arguing – on the basis of the real world's 'becoming a myth' (in the writings of his second period) and of the 'perspectivism' in the late texts – that Nietzsche could have given his philosophy a 'descriptive' foundation? In the context of the idea of Eternal Recurrence, one of the late Nietzsche's characteristic tenets is this: 'there are no facts, only interpretations' (N Autumn 1885 – Autumn 1887, VIII.1, 323, 7[60]). But, in that case, the circular structure of cosmic becoming is also not a fact. Nietzsche, who frequently comes back to 'cosmological' arguments in order to prove Eternal Recurrence, is quite possibly well aware of these difficulties. Indeed, in a note from the time of *The Gay Science* he seriously ponders whether the idea of Eternal Recurrence is perhaps only something probable or even something merely possible. Yet even then this thought would have the power to transform us in the same way that down the centuries fear and the mere possibility of Eternal Damnation have done (cf. N Spring 1881 – Summer 1882, V.2, 421f., 11[203]).

It is clear that the large number of notes dealing with

the cosmological nature of Eternal Recurrence is no proof that Nietzsche regarded this aspect of his theory as its strong and decisive suit. It is more likely that he had the feeling that he could not clarify the link between this aspect and the ethical significance of his doctrine – and, for precisely this reason, felt he had to keep returning to it. For even to him the ethical significance of Eternal Recurrence remained the most important thing about it. For instance, it dominates the great discourses of Zarathustra that deal with the doctrine of Eternal Recurrence, above all 'Of the Vision and the Riddle' in Part Three. Its length and complexity preclude a detailed commentary here, but it contains some of the most important passages in the whole work.[18] In this discourse Zarathustra tells of his walk over a lonely mountain path, accompanied by the 'Spirit of Gravity', who is 'half dwarf, half mole; crippled, crippling'. This spirit is his 'devil and arch-enemy' who pours a 'dwarf-like' version of Eternal Recurrence into Zarathustra's brain:

> 'O Zarathustra,' he murmured mockingly, syllable by syllable, 'you stone of wisdom! You have thrown yourself high, but every stone thrown must – fall!' [After a while they came to a gateway.]
> 'Behold this gateway, dwarf!' I went on: 'it has two aspects. Two paths join here: no-one has ever reached their end.
> 'This long lane behind us: it goes on for an eternity.

And that long lane ahead of us – that is another eternity.

'They are in opposition to each other, these paths; they abut on each other: and it is here at this gateway that they come together. The name of the gateway is written above it: "Moment".

But if one were to follow them farther and ever farther and farther: do you think, dwarf, that these paths would be in eternal opposition?'

'Everything straight is a lie,' murmured the dwarf contemptuously. All truth is crooked, time itself is a circle.'

'Spirit of Gravity!' I said angrily, 'do not treat this too lightly!' (Z III, ii, §2, 195f.)

A little later Zarathustra hears a dog howling and, as if in a dream, finds himself transported to another landscape:

Suddenly I was standing between wild cliffs, alone, desolate in the most desolate moonlight.

But there a man was lying! [. . .]

I saw a young shepherd writhing, choking, convulsing, his face distorted; and a heavy black snake was hanging out of his mouth. [. . .]

My hands tugged and tugged at the snake – in vain! They could not wrest the snake from the shepherd's throat. Then a voice cried from me: 'Bite! Bite!' [. . .]

The shepherd, however, bit as my cry had advised

113

him; and his bite was good! He spat the snake's head far away – and leaped up.

No longer a shepherd, no longer a man – a being transformed, surrounded by light, *laughing*! Never yet on earth had anyone laughed as he laughed! (Z III, ii, §2, 197f.)

Much of this chapter remains puzzling, and even Zarathustra presents it as a riddle. What is clear at least is that here the 'cosmological' version of Eternal Recurrence (the assertion that 'everything straight is a lie' and 'crooked is the path of eternity') is rejected, if not as false then as a too superficial view of things. In a mysterious way, the image of the shepherd who has to bite off the snake's head (a symbol of circularity and of the ring eternally returning to itself) ties the idea of Eternal Recurrence to a *decision* which man has to make and which is his only means of transforming himself. The chapter entitled 'The Convalescent' in Part Three of *Zarathustra* confirms this interrelation between Eternal Recurrence and decision. In that chapter, the 'light' version of Eternal Recurrence is presented by Zarathustra's animals, the eagle and the snake:

'O Zarathustra,' said the animals then, 'all things themselves dance for such as think as we: they come and offer their hand and laugh and flee – and return.
'Everything goes, everything returns; the wheel of Being rolls eternally' [. . .]
'Being begins in every instant; the ball There rolls

around every Here. The middle is everywhere. Crooked is the path of eternity.'

'O you buffoons and barrel-organs!' answered Zarathustra and smiled again; 'how well you know what had to be fulfilled in seven days:

'and how that monster crept into my throat and choked me!

'But I bit its head off and spat it away.

And you – have already made a hurdy-gurdy song of it?' (Z III, xiii, §2, 268f.)

In this chapter, too, there is much that is puzzling – let it be said once and for all that it must have been puzzling to Nietzsche, too, since the 'prophetic' form of *Zarathustra* does not only go back to stylistic considerations alone but is also connected with the relative 'unthinkableness' of its content. The fundamental contradiction is, however, clear. What both the animals' 'hurdy-gurdy song' and the 'Spirit of Gravity' in the other chapter lack is something that has to do with decision. This is made much clearer here than in the chapter 'Of the Vision and the Riddle', since in his attitude to the idea of Eternal Recurrence Zarathustra is here expressly equating himself with the shepherd who had to bite off the snake's head.

3. REDEMPTION FROM TIME

As we have shown, Nietzsche is interested in presenting the idea of Eternal Recurrence as both an ethical and a cosmological tenet. Indeed, the essential feature of this doctrine seems to lie here and it is the reason why he regards it as a decisive, shattering and fateful idea which in its historic scope unites, radicalizes and, in a certain sense, 'concretizes' the ideas of his earlier works, the notions of genealogy and nihilism, and the entire philosophy of the morning. Clearly it would not have such weight, were it merely a 'heuristic' fiction or an aid to evaluating life – 'how well disposed would you have to become to yourself and to life [...]' (GS §341, 250). There must be much more contained in the idea of Eternal Recurrence, if it is to function as a decisive thought that will transform man. And it is precisely this that Nietzsche is attempting when he presents his 'cosmological' arguments. The state of happiness in which man can will the Eternal Recurrence of the Same will only be possible if our perception that time is linear structure is done away with.

'Redemption', which is the subject of a great discourse in Part Two of *Zarathustra*, is thought of as redemption from the 'spirit of revenge' which has dominated man until now; because the man of the Platonic-Christian tradition is a prisoner of the linear structure of time. The misery of contemporary man is described in terms that echo the modern conception of alienation following the disintegration of man from his supposedly harmonious state in Greek antiquity. Specifically, they echo the sixth of Schiller's *Letters on the Aesthetic Education of Man*, as well as thoughts advanced later by Hegel and Marx:

> But it is the least serious thing to me, since I have been among men, to see that this one lacks an eye and that one an ear and a third lacks a leg, and there are others who have lost their tongue or their nose or their head.
> I see and have seen worse things and many of them so monstrous that I should not wish to speak of all of them; but of some of them I should not wish to be silent: and they are, men who lack everything except one thing, of which they have too much – men who are no more than a great eye or a great belly or something else great – I call such men inverse cripples [. . .]
> Truly, my friends, I walk among men as among the fragments and limbs of men! [. . .]
> And when my eye flees from the present to the past, it always finds the same thing: fragments and limbs and crass coincidences – but no men! (Z III, xx, 173ff.)

This fragment is modern man. Yet he is fragmented in another and more subtle sense; for he is the man crushed under the huge rock of the past and its 'It was', against which the will is powerless and which imposes

117

on itself (and others) all those sufferings which constitute the cruelties of morality, religion and asceticism:

> It [the will] is sullenly wrathful that time does not
> run back; 'That which was' – that is the name of the
> stone which it cannot roll away [. . .]
> This, yes, this alone is *revenge* itself: the will's antip-
> athy towards time and time's 'It was.' [. . .]
> *The spirit of revenge*: my friends, that, until now, has
> been mankind's chief concern; and where there was
> suffering, there was always supposed to be suffering
> [. . .]
> And then cloud upon cloud rolled over the spirit:
> until at last madness preached: 'Everything passes
> away, therefore everything deserves to pass away!'
> [. . .]
> All 'It was' is a fragment, a riddle, a dreadful
> coincidence – until the creative will says to it: 'But I
> willed it thus!' [. . .]
> The will that is the Will to Power must will some-
> thing higher than reconciliation – but how shall that
> happen? Who has taught it to will backwards too?
> (Z III, xx, 176f.)

Redemption can only be obtained if we transform
radically the way we experience time. This transformation cannot, however, be an *amor fati* that amounts to
nothing more than acknowledging things as they are.
Fate, to Nietzsche, is never something that simply
happens but is instead a unity of the willed and the

118

created – the 'creative will' can say 'I willed it thus!' Nietzsche's emphatic effort to prove that Eternal Recurrence is cosmological has its roots here: he does not want a resigned, passive acceptance of things as they happen to be. Instead, he wants a world in which it is possible to will the Eternal Recurrence of the Same. However, because of the critical premises worked out in his second creative period, he cannot allow himself to formulate the doctrine of Eternal Recurrence as simply the nth account of a supposedly discoverable metaphysical structure of the world, in other words as a new version of the 'real world'.

This explains the link, which we have already outlined, that Nietzsche constructs between the world of Eternal Recurrence and decision, without ever being able to clarify it. This link is supposed to help avoid the situation in which his thought would dissolve in a theoretical design of a real world, which men are supposed to follow unconditionally; an example of this is the 'superficial' version of Eternal Recurrence presented by the dwarf and Zarathustra's animals. Time's circularity and the decision cannot be reconciled, however, at least not in any clearly conceivable way. But does this, as Löwith believes, depend only on a (historical?) *impossibility* of developing a naturalistic metaphysics *à la grecque* when one is already standing on the summit of modernity? Our impression (over and above Löwith's ideas) is more that this impossibility is rooted in Nietzsche's doctrine itself. The difficulty or impossibility of combining the idea of

119

Eternal Recurrence and the decision stems from the fact that, to put it very cursorily, the idea of Eternal Recurrence (and not only the doctrine but also the experience that the men of the age of nihilism have of it) has such a destructuring effect on the subject that it becomes quite literally 'unthinkable'. It becomes inconceivable and can no longer be 'held together' in its various aspects. This leads, however, to a situation in which thought feels giddy.

4. THE WILL TO POWER AND THE FATE OF THE SUBJECT

The concept of the Will to Power acquires some contours when one thinks through the 'selectivity' that Nietzsche bestows upon the idea of Eternal Recurrence in its dual significance as an extreme heightening of nihilism and a new precondition of humanity's happiness.[19] Notes which Nietzsche made in the summer of 1887 under the heading of 'European Nihilism' (N Autumn 1885 – Autumn 1887, VIII.1, 215–22, 5[71]) are particularly informative on this 'selectivity' of Eternal Recurrence. They comprise sixteen short notes, of which the first eight rehearse the developments Nietzsche had gone through in his second creative period: Christian morality enabled man to find his way out of a 'first nihilism' which resulted from his knowledge that chaos was a reality and that 'becoming' had no meaning. However, part of Christian morality entailed an imperative to be truthful; but just as man was following this imperative to the letter, he discovered that morality itself was a lie, a fiction serving life's purposes but lacking any foundation in truth. This discovery was possible because life in the meantime had become less insecure and dangerous, and mankind therefore no longer perceived the need for a discipline as harsh as Christian morality. In the end, God became 'a much too extreme hypothesis' (ibid., para. 3, 216). However, with the downfall of Christian morality, European man plunged into a 'second nihilism' because that Christian moral code had for centuries appeared as the only valid interpretation of the world. No value appeared capable of resisting the mistrust that morality itself had bred in mankind. The world no longer had any aim or purpose: 'life as it is, without meaning or goal, a descent without any finale into nothingness: "Eternal Recurrence"'.

'That is the most extreme form of nihilism: nothingness (the "meaningless") for all eternity!' (ibid., para. 6, 217). But is another attitude possible? An attitude that at every moment affirms this process, precisely because it is no longer 'devalued' by transcendent goals that are supposedly always just around the corner? In addition, the *fundamental characteristic* of each event would have to be capable of examination from the perspective of just this isolated case (ibid., para. 8, 218). One would have to feel the meaning of events as a harmonious conjunction with the meaning of one's own life. That is, however, the 'happiness' which is first announced in the idea of Eternal Recurrence and which is discussed in *The Gay Science* (GS §341, 250). At this point, in the notes of 1887, a *volte-face* occurs (ibid., para. 9, 218). Here, the 'selectivity' of the thought of Eternal Recurrence no longer lies in the statement – 'how well disposed would you have to become to yourself and to life [. . .]' One's own sensation of happiness has now been replaced as the principle of selection by nihilism, by one's recognition that morality is a lie. Morality has invented useful values for life. But while it offered the pretence of implementing values that were supposedly based on 'truth', it has always concealed the locus of these values; it has concealed the fact that they are rooted in the Will to Power of individuals or of whole groups; and by its very nature, morality has always condemned the rulers' Will to Power and its excesses, as well as condemning the renewers and reformers of morality. With the discovery that everything consists of Will to Power, each individual is forced to take up a position. To the weak and those who have turned drawn the short straw in life, morality no longer affords the protection that used to enable them to despise and condemn the strong. These people will go under if they expressly and honestly acknowledge the struggle going on between the fundamentally opposed tendencies of the Will to Power. This will be the case even more, if they do not struggle and remain stubbornly wedded to their moral prejudices; in other words, if they radicalize these prejudices (for example, by encouraging a level-ling-down process at the political level) to the extent

122

that their impact on life becomes still more destructive and hostile. All this does not lead Nietzsche, however, to an unbridled endorsement of struggle or to glorifying the ability to vindicate oneself in that struggle through physical violence. For, in paragraph 15 of the notes we are referring to, he says that those who will prove themselves the strongest will be:

> the most moderate, who do not *need* extreme dogmas, who not only admit to a good chunk of chance and nonsense in themselves but also love the idea, who can think of man as considerably reduced in value without thereby becoming small and weak themselves: those who are richest in health, who can cope with the greatest number of *malheurs* and who therefore do not fear these *malheurs* – those who are *sure of their power* and who represent with conscious pride the *strength* that man has achieved. (ibid., para. 15, 221)

It is above all in the penultimate paragraph of these notes on nihilism that the selectivity of the thought of Eternal Recurrence appears to consist not so much in implementing the struggle of all against all – which has anyway always existed and which the weak have long since won through the bullying force of their moral prejudices –, but rather in the effect produced in man by the knowledge of Eternal Recurrence and by the explicit discovery of the way the Will to Power works in the world. The strong man is characterized less by features that belong to the world of struggle than by a kind of 'hermeneutic' character that is very reminiscent of the 'philosophy of the morning'.

If one may say this, the Will to Power is something hermeneutic, something engaged in interpreting. The struggle between the opposing tendencies of a multiplicity of wills is above all a struggle between competing interpretations, as that fragment concerning European nihilism shows. This corresponds to the real world's becoming a myth: there is nothing but an apparent world and it is brought forth by interpretations which each power centre works out:

> each power centre has its *perspective* on all the *rest*, i.e. its own quite specific *assessment* of them, its own way of acting, its own way of resisting.
> The 'apparent world' reduces itself [. . .] to a specific way of acting on the world, proceeding from a centre. Now there is no other kind of action at all: and the 'world' is only a word for the sum total of these actions. (N 1888, VIII.3, 163, 14[184])

Yet the Will to Power is also hermeneutic in another sense: because it sees the world as a game of competing appearances and perspectives, it is itself one theory among others, an interpretation and nothing else. Nietzsche concedes this point explicitly at the end of an aphorism in *Beyond Good and Evil*: 'Assuming this too is only interpretation [. . .] well, so much the better' (BGE §22,

31). Yet this hermeneutic radicalization in the Will to Power is not the end of the matter:

> Against positivism, which remains stuck on the phenomenon 'there are only facts', I would say: no, there are no facts, only interpretations. We cannot establish any fact 'in itself' ['an sich']: it is perhaps a nonsense to want to do this. 'Everything is subjective', you say: but that is already an *interpretation*; the 'subject' is not a given, but something fabricated, something added on. Is is really necessary to place the interpreter behind the interpretation? That is already fantasy, hypothesis. (N Autumn 1885 – Autumn 1887, VIII.1, 323, 7[60])

Even the interpreting subject is therefore caught in the game of his interpretations, which is itself only a perspectival 'positioning' of a Will to Power. As we can see, we are here running up against the boundaries where Eternal Recurrence and the Will to Power reveal themselves more as disintegrative than as constructive principles. Their selectivity seems inseparably tied to their disintegrative significance. However, even if there is selectivity in both concepts, the selectivity also 'functions' in a certain sense as a decisional principle.

An example is provided by the notion that the world is nothing more than a game of interpretations that proceed from 'power centres'; these are in turn (like the subject) not defining points of relation but instead

Nietzsche: An Introduction

interpretative configurations 'of relative duration' (N Autumn 1887 – March 1888, VIII.2, 278, 11[73]). Must we therefore recognize that all interpreations are equally valid, since there is no truth criterion to which one could appeal, in order to privilege one above another? Even when Nietzsche concedes that the doctrines of Will to Power and Eternal Recurrence are themselves only interpretations, he does not in fact believe that they have the same status as any old interpretation: for instance, he does not believe that the interpretation called Will to Power is on a par with the one called 'Christian morality'. Perspectivism – another term Nietzsche uses to characterize the thought of his final creative period – does not in fact mean that the theory itself, which maintains a plurality of perspectives, should not and must not make a selection from among these perspectives. The theory must at least decide between itself and the many other interpretations available.

The criteria for making such a decision, which Nietzsche cites again and again, are of a 'physiological' nature: strength – weakness, health – sickness, as well as the related ideas of creativity – 'ressentiment' and active – reactive.[20] Strictly speaking, the rejection of metaphysics on account of the errors underlying it cannot be attributed to Nietzsche, since according to him error is vital to life and since in his eyes there is no 'truth' which would be 'more valuable' than error, and to which one could appeal in order to to get beyond error. When morality's metaphysical lie is exposed by the changes in the conditions of life and of morality's logic and when God 'dies', not to acknowledge this is more a sign of physiological degeneration and poor health than is the refusal to acknowledge a truth consisting of facts. Strength and weakness, health and sickness are the only criteria that Nietzsche has left after unmasking metaphysics. His hatred for morality, Christianity and socialism (which as a levelling ideology is simply an extreme form of Christianity) is motivated by a 'physiological' preference for health and strength. Morality is a Will to Power that can be characterized as revenge. It does not suggest new values as alternatives but is instead, according to Nietzsche, the nihilistic denial of every single worldly value and, consequently, the will further to degrade, debase and humiliate man – an example is the way the 'flesh' is despised and humiliated in Christian morality. '*What* is morality actually?

'The instinct of décadence; it is the burned-out and disinherited who in this way *take revenge*' (N Early 1888 – January 1889, VIII.3, 112, 14[135]). Strength and health, in contrast to the spirit of revenge displayed by the weak, which notices the meaninglessness of becoming and rebels against it by despising and degrading the world, are determined precisely by the ability to experience nihilism actively.

I judge the *power* of a *will* according to how much resistance, pain, torture it can endure and; given this yardstick, far be it from me to reproach the evil and

127

painful side of life. (N Autumn 1887 – March 1888, VIII.2, 190, 10[118])

Resistance and the ability to turn suffering to one's own advantage are not, however, mechanisms of a will that wants to *preserve* itself; for, in this case, the evil character of life would have to condemned, even where it is being actively acknowledged and combated. Yet Nietzsche writes in the same passage: ' "I" seize the hope that one day things will be still more evil and painful than they have been until now ...' (ibid.). Resistance and the ability to suffer are not merely forces in the service of the survival instinct because the latter would imply that there are definable units that want to preserve themselves. But:

> there are no durable, definable units, no atoms, no monads: here too 'being' is *imposed* by us (for practical, useful, perspectival reasons) [...] *there is no will:* there are punctations of will, which are constantly increasing or losing their power. (N Autumn 1887 – March 1888, VIII.2, 278f., 11[73])

Strength and weakness, health and sickness cannot therefore be defined with reference to the 'normal' state of any living being, be this man in general or an individual. Yet in the penultimate aphorism of Book Five of *The Gay Science*, Nietzsche defines health as a lust for adventure. Health is personified by: 'Whoever has the soul that thirsts to have experienced the whole panoply of values and desiderata to date, and to have sailed around all the coasts of this ideal "Mediterranean"' (GS §382, 318). And in a note from 1884 we read: 'The highest measure of a wealth of strength is how far one man can live according to *hypotheses* and, as it were, can venture out into limitless seas, instead of into "faith". All lesser spirits perish' (N Spring – Autumn 1884, VII.2, 144, 25[515]). From this point of view, we can see that Nietzsche takes very literally the 'so much the better', with which that aphorism we have already quoted from *Beyond Good and Evil* (§22) closes, and where he discusses the possibility that even the doctrine of the world as Will to Power is 'only' a hypothesis. Only a perspective that presents itself explicitly as an interpretation can be considered 'healthy'; which means that no interpretation disguised as a metaphysical revelation about the eternal structure of things can be considered healthy. All of this can be read without effort outside the scheme of a purely vitalistic rhetoric, but it must be at least be seen in the framework of a more critical and vigilant vitalism. In the process one can appeal to a 'methodological anarchism' *ante litteram*, as this is expressed in *On the Genealogy of Morals*, for example.[21] When combating the myth of objective science which, disregarding an historical view, is attempting to proceed in a one-eyed manner, we must cling fast to the idea that:

There is *only* a perspective seeing, *only* a perspective 'knowing'; the *more* affects we allow to speak about

129

a thing, the *more* eyes, various eyes we are able to use for the same thing, the more complete will be our 'concept' of the thing, our 'objectivity'. (GM III, §12, 383)

It therefore also becomes clear at this point how the selectivity of the idea of Eternal Recurrence or the Will to Power functions. Strength and health can only be defined under the aspects of a lust for adventure and a multiplicity of points of view – hence in terms that we have described as 'disintegrative' – and certainly not as the ability to set in stone any individual perspective or indeed to set it against others. The 'political' applications of the Will to Power, which Nietzsche would like to take into account, have a similarly disintegrative significance. Even though it is risky and perhaps impossible to distil all the notes Nietzsche devoted to this problem into a single formula, a sentence from *The Gay Science* appears to locate its significance beyond its 'socio-biological' rhetoric (the feature emphasized by National Socialist interpreters). It is true, according to this sentence, of all us men of the age of nihilism that: '*All of us are no longer material for a society*' (GS §356, 279). The 'discovery' of the Will to Power by everyone, as described in that fragment on European nihilism, cannot lead to a new start in politics; it can only lead to its disintegration. For how could a politics be established on the idea of the Will to Power? By favouring the victory of the strong over the weak through legislation, perhaps? But if the strong were ever defined as such by legislation (for instance, because they were all supposedly Aryans), they would thereby fall victim to the most evil logic of the spirit of revenge, to a morality of 'ressentiment'; to a straightforward reversal of the levelling spirit of Christianity, which would likewise have a 'moral' foundation. To be fair to Nietzsche, we (like several modern interpreters) must acknowledge that, even in politics, the Will to Power only functions as a selective principle to the extent that it dissolves the political dimension by generalizing it – a phenomenon we can see at work in modern democracy.[22]

The link between selectivity and the disintegrative capacity, which we saw in the example of Eternal Recurrence, also occurs in another central theme of Nietzsche's late thought: the 'Übermensch'. The image of the 'Übermensch' oscillates again and again between that of 'beautiful individuality' with distantly humanistic features ('the strong' in paragraph 15 of the notes on European nihilism) and that of the adventurer who goes beyond all measure and every constructive possibility, driven on by a demand to experiment which also directs itself against him. A 'radiant "Übermensch"' appears above all in Zarathustra's discourses – he is the man of that bestowing virtue, who redeems becoming, who experiences the noontide as the hour when the world is perfectly whole and rounded etc. This image is joined by another which is never clearly opposed to the first. It is that image in which the prefix 'über', which characterizes the new man, refers to the presumptuousness and violence that lie beyond good and evil:

> even using the yardstick of the ancient Greeks, our whole modern existence is nothing but pure *hubris* and godlessness, in so far as it is strength and awareness of strength rather than weakness [...] *Hubris* today characterizes our whole attitude to nature, our rape of nature with the aid of machines and unscrupulous inventiveness of techicians and engineers [...] *hubris* characterizes our attitude to *ourselves* – for we experiment on ourselves in a way we would never allow on animals, and we merrily vivisect our souls out of curiosity: what do we care about the 'salvation' of the soul! (GM III, §9, 375)

Yet experimenting on oneself, the most extreme of experiments, is ultimately also a hypothesis, an idea, the 'discovery' of Eternal Recurrence with all its disintegrative impact. Even the 'I' is 'something fabricated' (N Autumn 1885 – Autumn 1887, VIII.1, 323, 7[60]). The predicates of the self's unity and 'ultimateness', which have been handed down as an extreme bulwark of security by the philosophical tradition – from Descartes' *cogito* to Kant's 'I am thinking' – now appear generally in doubt. Self-consciousness, on which our understanding of the self is based, is in fact not an essential, first or foundational characteristic of man. He could survive very well in a state of 'nature' without a central consciousness. He only developed it under the pressure of the need to communicate when he became a social being. He had to be able to account to himself for himself, in order to be able to account to others. This was true above all in the relationship betwwen 'those who commanded and those who obeyed' (GS §354, 273). It is not only consciousness that is a function of social relations. Even the 'I' is merely a superficial effect. Zarathustra set this out in the discourse 'Of the Despisers of the Body', which is one of the first in Part One of that book: 'You say "I" and are proud of this word. But greater than this – and which you do not want to believe in – is your body and its great intelligence: this does not say "I" but performs "I"' (Z I, iv, 35). Let us re-emphasize that Nietzsche does not want to 'reduce' consciousness to the body, since the phenomenon known as the body serves only as a 'guiding thread' to obtain clarity about the 'multifariousness' of the self, in opposition to that reductionism which morality and metaphysics have always founded upon the hegemony of consciousness (N Autumn 1885 – Autumn 1887, VIII.1, 104, 2[91]). However, an 'I' which recognizes that it is only a superficial effect and which draws its health from this knowledge can in no way be a heightened or intensified 'I', as is so often taken to be case with the 'Übermensch'. It is even debatable whether it can still in any sense be described as a subject.

5. THE WILL TO POWER AS ART

Perhaps only the understanding of art, which Nietzsche develops in his later writings (and above all in the unpublished *Nachlaß* fragments), can aid our understanding of Nietzsche's figure of the 'Übermensch', despite all its inherent difficulties and contradictions – for instance, the antitheses of Eternal Recurrence and decision, of construction and disintegration, and so on. The basis for this can be found as early as *The Gay Science*, Book Five of which admittedly belongs to the final period. In these writings, as was indicated above, Nietzsche takes up many aspects of his early writings, and in particular themes from *The Birth of Tragedy*. This is true, for example, of the idea, presented in the preface to the second edition of *The Gay Science* in 1887, that existence can be justified aesthetically because art protects us from the truth. Now, however, it is no longer a question of a world of beautiful appearances which distract us from looking the chaos and the irrationality of the original Unity in the eye. 'Truth is ugly: *we have art* so that we are not destroyed by truth.' This is only the case, however, because the will to truth is 'already a symptom of decadence' (N Early 1888 – January 1889, VIII.3, 296, 16[40]). Behind its forms, art conceals no objective 'truth' as to how things really are. Instead, as the creative activity and expression of lying it resists the passivity, the reactiveness and the spirit of revenge that characterize the search for truth.

134

No! Do not come to me with science when I am looking for the natural antagonist to the ascetic ideal [. . .] art, in which *lying* sanctifies itself and the *will to deception* has good conscience on its side, is much more fundamentally opposed to the ascetic ideal than science is. (GM III, §25, 420)

All human intellectual activities, not only art, are by their nature lies. In this respect, art is the model of the Will to Power.[23] For a long period Nietzsche planned to call a part of the later abandoned central work 'The Will to Power as Art'. This points to more than a marginal aspect or an incidental application of the doctrine. Nietzsche writes that once one perceives the world from the point of view of Will to Power the consoling opposition between a real and an apparent world disappears:

There is only One world and it is false, cruel, contradictory, seductive, meaningless . . . A world so constituted is the real world . . . *We need lies* in order to conquer this reality, this 'truth', that means in order to *live* [. . .] Metaphysics, morality, religion, science – these are considered merely as various forms of lying: with their aid, life can be *believed* in. 'Life *should* inspire trust': presented in these terms, the task is immense. In order to solve it, man must naturally be a liar; more than anything else, he must be an *artist* [. . .] Metaphysics, morality, religion, science – all simply monstrous products

135

of his will to art. (N Autumn 1887 – March 1888, VIII.2, 435, 11[415])

Nevertheless, there is an essential difference between art as usually understood and the 'creatures' of the will to art, which constitute the world of the remaining intellectual forms. In contradistinction to religion, metaphysics, morality and even science, art does not regress entirely (at least not explicitly and certainly not thematically) into the world of sickness, weakness and vengefulness which manifest themselves in asceticism. The passage from *On the Genealogy of Morals* quoted above already demonstrates this by stating that it is precisely in art where lying sanctifies itself and the will to deception 'has good conscience on its side'. Besides, lying and the will to mask oneself without a bad conscience are named as positive features of art as early as *The Gay Science*. It is hence easy to see how art in the late notes can function, as it were, not only descriptively but also normatively as a model of the Will to Power. If there is a Will to Power which is not the prisoner of an ascetic ideal or of a demand for revenge, in other words a healthy rather than a sick Will to Power, then it can only be realized in the world of art. The other expressions of the mind remain dominated by the moral and metaphysical tradition, utterly enclosed in the circle of reactive nihilism and sickness. Even the 'Übermensch' can only exist as an artist, at least in the current state of our cultural development; the artist is, today, the most visible form of 'Übermensch'. He is a kind of 'stepping stone' in the coming-into-being of the world as Will to Power, 'as a work of art giving birth to itself' (N Autumn 1885 – Autumn 1887, VIII.1, 117, 2[114]). We can see in art a normative model of the Will to Power, and in the artist we can detect the first visible shape of the 'Übermensch', because art can (but need not always) appear in a healthy form. 'Is art a consequence of *dissatisfaction with reality*? Or an expression of *gratitude for happiness enjoyed*? In the first case we have *romanticism*, in the second glorious appearance and dithyramb (in short, *the art of apotheosis*)' (N Autumn 1885 – Autumn 1887, VIII.1, 117, 2[114]). The romantic artist only creates his work from a sense of dissatisfaction or ressentiment (N Autumn 1885 – Autumn 1887, VIII.1, 115, 2[112]). All the negative characteristics that Nietzsche diagnoses and condemns in the art of his time, above all the exaggerated sentimentality he criticizes in Wagner's music, its posturing, its phantasmagoria of stimuli, and not least Wagner's essentially Christian attitude (*Parsifal*!), can be traced to this fundamental distinction he makes between excess and discontent, poverty and ressentiment.

It is a question of the *strength* (of an individual or a nation) *whether* and *where* 'the' judgment 'beautiful' is applied. The feeling of plenitude, of *accumulated strength* (which allows one to accept courageously and cheerfully much that makes the weakling *shudder*) – the feeling of *power* pronounces the judgment 'beautiful' on things that the instinct of impotence can only denigrate as hateful, as ugly. (N Autumn 1887 – March 1888, VIII.2, 221f., 10[168])

These are the bases of the 'physiological aesthetics' conceived by Nietzsche. It is important less a theory of art than as the working out of a picture of life in a world conceived as subordinate to the Will to Power; a world, in other words, free of stable foundations and structures, devoid of ultimate determiners and stripped of any guarantees. It must always be borne in mind that Nietzsche's appeal to strength and health is only a response to the necessity of finding evaluative criteria to decide between interpretations (which alone make up the world), without falling back on essentialist structures or on ultimate and thus necessarily metaphysical arguments. If Nietzsche is thereby following a tendency of modern thought, which is incidentally quite widespread and therefore scarcely coincidental, he nevertheless (for motives of his own) regards art as a privileged locus of a 'positive' (healthy, strong etc.) alternative to the self-definition of human life.

The fact that in his thought this alternative defines itself with reference to art, that the Will to Power and the 'Übermensch' find their models in art (or at least in its 'healthy' variants uncontaminated by nihilism) provides a further pointer to the conception of the figure of the 'Übermensch'. For which art form realizes the non-reactive or nihilistic possibilities of the Will to Power? Here again physiology is the starting point but the argument changes immediately thereafter to an attitude which holds that the fundamental characteristic of strength and health is not any model of 'normality' but simply the capacity to live in a world where there are no normal models either for things or for the subject. The Autumn 1887 note, the beginning of which was quoted above, continues:

> The result, roughly speaking, is that the *preference for questionable and terrible things* is a symptom of *strength*: whereas the taste for the *pretty and delicate* belongs to the weak, the precious. *Pleasure* in tragedy marks out *strong* ages and characters [...] Let us suppose as a counter to this that the *weak* desire enjoyment from an art form that is not designed for them; what will they do to accommodate tragedy to their taste? They will read *their own feelings of value* into it: for example, 'the triumph of the moral world order' or the doctrine of the 'worthlessness of life' or the demand that one be resigned to one's fate [...] The extent to which an individual is prepared to allow things their terrible, their questionable character is a sign of *feeling well and powerful*; and *whether he even needs 'solutions' at the end of the day.* (N Autumn 1887 – March 1888, VIII.2, 222, 10[168] – the last emphasis is the author's)

As we can see, what is being discussed here is tragedy in particular and a theory of art and its significance in general. Besides, in the late Nietzsche's work the concept

139

of tragedy tends to assume a meaning that goes far beyond the specifically theatrical, as well as acquiring an artistic meaning. 'Incipit tragoedia' is the title of the last aphorism of the first edition (1882) of *The Gay Science*, in which Zarathustra is heralded. Here, the concept of tragedy becomes a synonym for every healthy art form, because the enjoyment of tragedy is only open to those who have no need of ultimate solutions, in other words to those who know how to live in the open horizon of a world as Will to Power and an Eternal Recurrence. Even though strength in this analysis is not defined primarily or even exclusively in physiological and biological terms, it is important to bear in mind, not only for Nietzsche's aesthetics but also for his picture of the 'Übermensch' in general, that he does interpret the notion of strength literally. The 'guiding thread' of the body no longer possesses a merely methodological significance and has now become a central element in the overturning of asceticism and of Platonic-Christian morality and metaphysics. The emphasis on the body does not, however, appear to favour any 'materialist' criterion for decision-making (where corporeal values would be 'truer' than those of the mind). Rather, denial of and contempt for the body, at least in our tradition, have always been symptoms of a culture shaped by 'ressentiment' and the demand for ultimate solutions. This emphasis on the body is another reason why Nietzsche believes that art is the only expression of intellect capable of realizing the positive possibilities of the Will to Power. Morality, metaphysics and religion, even science to the

extent that it has reduced the body to a finite, measurable
mass, have all expressed their nihilistic and reactive spirit
by their ascetic distancing of themselves from the body.
When Nietzsche defines art as a 'counter-movement'
against asceticism and nihilism, he is at pains to emphasize its enlivening qualities:

> The feeling of intoxication, corresponding to an
> *increase in strength*:
> most powerfully in the coupling of the sexes:
> new organs, new skills, colours, forms . . .
> 'beautification' is a consequence of *heightened* strength
> beautification as a necessary consequence of strength-
>   heightening
> beautification as the expression of a victorious will, a
>   heightened
> co-ordination, a harmonization of all strong desires
>   [. . .]
> logical and geometrical simplification is a conse-
>   quence of strength-heightening: conversely, the
>   *perception* of such a simplification
> in turn heightens one's feeling of strength . . .
> Peak of development: great style [. . .]
> the state of desire one calls *intoxication* is precisely a
>   high feeling of *power* . . .
> sensations of space and time are transformed:
>   immense distances are surveyed and indeed are
>   only now *perceptible*
> the *extension* of one's gaze over vast subjects and
>   expanses

the *refinement of the organ* used to detect the smallest
  and most fleeting of things
the *power of divining*, the ability to understand with
  only the slightest prompting,
the slightest suggestion, 'intelligent' *sensuality* . . .
strength as a feeling of power in one's muscles, as
  suppleness
and pleasure in movement, as dance, as lightness and
  presto [. . .]
artists, if they can cut the mustard, have strong
  (physically strong) constitutions,
have reserves, are powerhouses, sensual: without a
  certain overheating of the
sexual organs, no Raphael would have been possible.
(N Early 1888 – Early 1889, VIII.3, 85ff., 14[117])

However one interprets Aristotle's teachings, this is the
direct opposite of art as catharsis. Art's task, as defined
here, is neither to soothe the passions by giving them
a momentary outlet nor is it to appease them by declar-
ing that amid the apparent chaos of life there is after
all a governing, guiding rationality. For that would only
be possible, if art were to appear sporting the banner
'ultimate solutions'. Yet outside the horizon of a nihilist
asceticism, all that is left for art are excitations, mani-
festations of strength and the sensation of power. In
addition to the reference to the body and to sensuality in
the passage just quoted, there are two further elements
worthy of note: first, the suggestion that one's sensibility
is sharpened by vital stimuli – and hence a heightened

perceptive capacity, an extension of one's gaze to far horizons, as well as a refinement of one's organs such that they are now capable of grasping the smallest and most fleeting phenomena; and secondly the idea of beauty in its traditional, almost classical sense as the product of this heightened state – beautification as a manifestation of strength, indeed of a victorious will that goes hand in hand with a *simplification* of forms. The first element leads to a 'superabundance of *means of communication*, together with an extreme *receptivity* to stimuli and signs. It is the apogee of communication and transfer between living beings – it is the wellspring of languages' (N Early 1888 – Early 1889, VIII.3, 88, 14[119]). The second element makes clear why Nietzsche could nevertheless be a supporter of 'great style', even though he conceived the Will to Power and the 'Übermensch' in (what appeared to us to be) primarily disintegrative terms.[24] We are dealing here with a late echo of his earlier theory of tragedy, in which beautiful, Apollonian forms had their roots and significance in primal, Dionysian chaos. A phrase from *The Birth of Tragedy* seems to hold good even in the physiological aesthetics of the late Nietzsche: 'Dionysus speaks the language of Apollo, but ultimately Apollo speaks the language of Dionysus' (BT §21, 136). Here, too, the disintegrative, Dionysian, desperately 'experimental' moments appear ultimately to predominate, which renders the concept of 'great style' problematic. However, what are we to make of a fragment like the one dating from the spring of 1888 which, with the title 'Will to Power as art

143

"music" – and great style', appears to doubt that the only form of healthy art as Will to Power obeys the commandment: 'Becoming master of the chaos that one is; doing violence to one's chaos to become form'? Artists who obey this commandment in their work are surrounded by a wilderness, by the fear of their sacrilege:

> All artists know those ambitious for great style: why are they lacking in music? No musician has ever built in the manner of that architect who created the Palazzo Pitti? There is a problem here. Does music perhaps belong to that culture where the sway of men of violence of all kinds has already ended? Would the notion of great style ultimately contradict the soul of music, – the 'woman' in our music? (N Early 1888 – Early 1889, VIII.3, 39, 14[61])

Here the suspicion seems to develop in Nietzsche that the idea of a work of art as a great construction, as a compact form that expresses a 'victory' of the will (over materials, variety etc.), still remains tied to the epoch of violence, to what we would have to call the epoch of 'ressentiment'. Or is music being banished here, improbably so when one considers Nietzsche's texts, to dwell among naturally decadent art forms? Without wishing to exaggerate the significance of this passage, it nevertheless confirms the very real danger inherent in Nietzsche's physiological aesthetics: the problem of reconciling the feeling of overcoming, which carries the Will to Power on its wings, with a will to form. And does not the constructive strength and the purity of form stand opposed to the short-sighted character of judgments on beauty, which is described in another note of the same period? (N Autumn 1887 – March 1888, VIII.3, 220, 10[67]). To say that something is beautiful entails a correspondingly positive evaluation of the demands of our self-preservation and of the increase in our feeling of power. However, we are dealing here with an evaluation which only takes the immediate effects into account and, for that reason, finds itself up against our understanding. And even this shortsightedness seems scarcely reconcilable with the idea of the beautiful as a work possessing great style. At one point in *The Gay Science* Nietzsche raises the question, in an aphorism already cited on the 'Health of the Soul', 'whether the will to health alone, is not a prejudice, cowardice, and perhaps a piece of very subtle barbarism and backwardness' (FW §120, 155). And ultimately this suspicion infiltrates the concepts of form and great style in the physiological aesthetics of Nietzsche's late writings. Admittedly, a strong will is manifest in the beautification, simplification and unity of a form, but beyond this there is something else: the possibility that an art form no longer tied to violence and to the prejudice of an exclusive will to health is better placed to realize Nietzsche's programme of improving the human. We can also perceive in this unreconciled opposition the prophetic character of Nietzsche's aesthetics, with regard to the development of poetics in the twentieth century – in which the

Nietzsche: An Introduction

will to experiment has led on the one hand to ever more dissolutions and destructurings, and to a rigorously constructivist, technical and formalist ideal on the other.

The human is the animal that has invented 'bad conscience' and other devices of self-torture. Contrary to every principle and instinct of self-preservation, this species of animal can move into position against itself. Not only has a new cruelty thereby appeared, but also an utterly unheard-of possibility to reshape life. In *On the Genealogy of Morals*, Nietzsche declares that 'the prospect of an animal soul turning against itself, taking sides against itself, was something so new, profound, unheard-of, puzzling, contradictory *and momentous* on earth that the whole character of the world changed in an essential way' (GM II, §16, 339). Like all the elements that make up the moral and metaphysical vision of the world, asceticism eventually turns into its opposite. In the same way that God dies on account of the religiosity and morality of those who believe in Him, asceticism too (which grew out of the morality of 'ressentiment') ultimately becomes a promise of the future and works towards freeing man from his will to health, survival and security. Only because man achieved, by way of asceticism, the ability to look beyond his own interests of self-preservation, is something like a non-reactive Will to Power, the 'Übermensch' and 'great health' possible; in other words all the things reflected in the ability to live through the experience of the tragic:

The *profundity of the tragic artist* lies in the way that his aesthetic instinct ignores more distant consequences, that he does not become preoccupied with what is nearest, that he affirms the *the economy in great things*, which justifies the *terrible, the evil, the questionable* and not only . . . justifies.

Are we dealing here 'only' with a radicalization of Kant's notion of the disinterestedness of aesthetic judgments in its Schopenhauerian interpretation? This is possibly a feature of Nietzsche's doctrines; but its radicalization consists in the claim that the Will to Power (i.e. 'the world') is art and nothing but art. The human animal's radical disinterestedness is the only thing that appears adequate to Nietzsche to characterize life in a world, in which are no ultimate bases or essences and in which existence can be traced back to the pure event of its interpretation.

IV. Chronology of Nietzsche's Life and Works

1844

15 October: Friedrich Wilhelm Nietzsche born in Röcken, not far from Leipzig, as the first son of the pastor, Karl Ludwig Nietzsche, himself the son of a pastor, and his wife Franziska, née Oehler, whose father had likewise been a pastor. It was the birthday of the Prussian king, much admired by Nietzsche's father, and so the boy was given the king's Christian names. The father had been a tutor at the court of Altenburg. Besides the parents, other members of the Nietzsche household were his paternal grandmother, his father's sister, Rosalie, and his stepsister, Auguste.

1846

10 July: Birth of Nietzsche's sister, Elisabeth.

1848

Birth of a brother, Joseph, who died two years later. The 1848 revolutions greatly disturb Nietzsche's father, an ardent monarchist; at the end of August, he is taken ill with a disease of the nervous system and brain.

1849

30 July: Nietzsche's father dies, following a worsening of the disease contracted the previous year.

1850

Nietzsche's mother moves with both children to Naumburg. The decision to move is taken by Nietzsche's paternal grandmother who has many relatives in the town. Both aunts also move with the family. From Easter Nietzsche attends the municipal boys' school. Becomes friendly with Wilhelm Pinder and Gustav Krug, who are roughly the same age.

1851

Together with Pinder and Krug, Nietzsche enters Dr Weber's Private Institute, where they receive instruction in religion, Latin and Greek. At Krug's home, Nietzsche becomes acquainted with music for the first time. His mother buys him a piano. He takes music lessons.

1856

Nietzsche writes poems and composes pieces of music. His maternal grandmother dies. The family moves to another apartment, this time without Aunt Rosalie.

1858

The family moves for the second time within Naumburg. In October, Nietzsche enters the Landesschule Pforta. Further attempts at composing, in particular sacred music. Nietzsche writes lyric poetry and undertakes various literary projects.

1859

Friendship with Paul Deussen begins. Carl von Gersdorff arrives at Pforta.

1864

Completes his schooling at Pforta. After the summer holidays, Nietzsche registers as a theology student at the University of Bonn. Attends lectures and seminars on art history. Becomes a member of the academic association, Gustav-Adolf. Together with Deussen, Nietzsche joins the student fraternity 'Frankonia'. Attends the lectures of, among others, the classical philologist Friedrich Ritschl.

1865

At the end of January, he resolves not to compose any more music. In May he decides to move to the University of Leipzig in order to study classical philology there. At the same time, Ritschl too decides to move to Leipzig in order to put an end to his quarrel with a colleague, Otto Jahn. The symptoms of ailments that had affected Nietzsche even at school (catarrh and rheumatic pains) become more severe. He begins to suffer acute headaches and nausea. After moving to Leipzig, he is treated by two doctors for syphilis. Continues his study of Theognis and encounters Schopenhauer's works by chance.

1866

Gives papers on Theognis and Suidas and begins to research the sources of Diogenes Laertius. Beginning of friendship with Erwin Rohde.

150

1867

Nietzsche's article on Theognis is published in the journal *Rheinisches Museum für Philologie*, New Series, vol. 22. Gives a paper in January on the tradition of interpreting Aristotle's texts. Studies Homer and Democritus. Reads Kant (though probably only Kuno Fischer's account of Kant's thought). On 9 October, he begins his military service with the mounted section of a field artillery regiment in Naumburg.

1868

Writes various reviews in the field of classical philology. Plans a dissertation on the relationship between Homer and Hesiod. Aims to obtain a doctorate in philosophy with a thesis on Kant. Reads Kant's *Critique of Judgment* and Lange's *History of Materialism*. In March he is involved in a riding accident and sustains a severe chest injury. In mid-October he is permitted to cut short his military service and return to Leipzig. Meets Richard Wagner for the first time on the evening of 8 November at the home of the orientalist Hermann Brockhaus.

1869

Appointed to the Chair of Greek Language and Literature at the University of Basle, thanks to glowing references from Ritschl and Usener. On 28 May, he gives his inaugural lecture on the subject of 'Homer and Classical Philology'. From now on, more frequent visits to Richard and Cosima Wagner in Tribschen, near Lucerne. The University of Leipzig awards him his doctorate on the basis of his publications in the

Rheinisches Museum, including his study of the sources of Diogenes Laertius. Begins a very reverential friendship with Jacob Burckhardt, who is a colleague in Basle. Renounces Prussian citizenship without applying for Swiss nationality.

1870

In January and February, he gives two lectures: one on Greek Music-Drama, the other on Socrates and Tragedy. These two lectures, together with an unpublished text on the Dionysian World-View, form the core of the book on *The Birth of Tragedy*. Nietzsche gets to know Franz Overbeck and becomes his neighbour. Promoted to full professor on 9 April. Rohde visits him in Basle in June. Prompted by the outbreak of the Franco–Prussian War, he requests a sabbatical in August and joins the Prussian army as a volunteer medical auxiliary. However, he contracts dysentery and diptheria in France and is sent home in September on a hospital train. After convalescing in Naumburg, departs for Basle on 21 October. During the second day of the journey, he suffers severe bouts of nausea and vomiting.

1871

Publishes *Certamen quod dicitur Homeri et Hesiodi* and an index to the new series (1842–69) of the journal *Rheinisches Museum für Philologie*. Completes the first version of *The Birth of Tragedy* in January and February. The Leipzig publisher, Engelmann, rejects the manuscript but in October it is accepted by Wagner's publisher, Fritzsch. The book is ready for distribution on 29 December. In January Nietzsche had applied to succeed Gustav Teichmüller in the Chair of Philosophy at Basle but the application was rejected. He had, moreover, suggested that Rohde be his own successor. During July and August he tries to secure his friend a professorship in Zurich, yet even this attempt is unsuccessful. He is a frequent guest at Bachofen's home.

1872
Publication of *The Birth of Tragedy from the Spirit of Music*. Wagner heaps enthusiastic praise on the book in a letter to Nietzsche. From 16 January to 23 March he gives five public lectures *On the Future of our Educational Institutions*. Ulrich von Wilamowitz-Moellendorff, who in a visit the previous year had expressed his admiration for Nietzsche, publishes a polemical attack on *The Birth of Tragedy* in May. Wagner and Rohde defend Nietzsche. Deussen visits him at the end of July. On 31 August he meets Malwida von Meysenbug, an ardent fan of Wagner and the ideas of 1848. Now wishes to withdraw from academic life in order to devote himself entirely to disseminating Wagner's ideas. In May Nietzsche had travelled to Bayreuth, to where Wagner had moved with his wife, in order to supervise the building of the Festspielhaus (Festival Theatre). Unexpectedly, though, he does not journey to Bayreuth in the Christmas vacation. He writes the text *On Truth and Lies in an Extra-Moral Sense* and plans a work on the figure of the philosopher.

1873

Publication, again by Fritzsch in Leipzig, of the first *Untimely Meditation* (on David Strauss). Nietzsche writes a fragmentary text entitled *Philosophy in the Tragic Age of the Greeks*, which was supposed to be the introduction to a more extensive work on the Pre-Socratics. Plans a second *Untimely Meditation* with the title 'Philosophy in Dire Straits'. Borrows numerous books on physics and chemistry from the university library in Basle. From now on, his physical ailments become worse, above all in the shape of severe migraines with vomiting.

1874

Publication of the second edition of *The Birth of Tragedy* as well as the second and third *Untimely Meditations* (*On the Uses and Disadvantages of History for Life* and *Schopenhauer as Educator*). In April Nietzsche composes a piano piece for four hands entitled a *Hymn to Friendship*. Makes plans to marry. Rohde spends two weeks of September in Basle. Becomes closer to Paul Rée, who had attended Nietzsche's lectures on the Pre-Socratics in 1873. Spends the Christmas vacation in Naumburg, where his friends Krug and Pinder introduce him to their wives.

1875

Nietzsche rejects the idea of writing a fourth *Untimely Meditation* with the title *We Philologists* and decides instead to publish *Richard Wagner in Bayreuth* as the fourth in the series, a text which had not originally

154

seemed worthy of publication. Throughout the year his notes are concerned above all with religion. Two of his pupils present him with transcripts of Burckhardt's lectures on the history of Greek culture – one of these pupils was Adolf Baumgartner whose mother, Marie, had been friendly with Nietzsche since the previous year and translated the third *Untimely Meditation* into French. Nietzsche reads with interest Overbeck's *Studies in the History of the Ancient Church* and Rée's *Psychological Observations*. Gersdorff visits him in October. The young musician, Heinrich Köselitz, arrives in Basle at the start of the winter semester and attends lectures given by Nietzsche and Overbeck. He becomes one of Nietzsche's most faithful pupils; Nietzsche advises him to adopt the pseudonym, under which he was to become famous later.

1876

Before the scheduled August opening of the Bayreuth Festival, the fourth *Untimely Meditation* (*Richard Wagner in Bayreuth*) is published by Schmeitzner in Chemnitz. Nietzsche arrives in Bayreuth on 23 July, and leaves again on 27 August, in other words before the end of the Festival. His state of health had deteriorated in the meantime. Even before the summer he reduces his teaching load and, in September, his eye complaint is treated with chemicals. At the beginning of October he is granted a year's leave on medical grounds. He leaves for Italy with Paul Rée. They are joined in Geneva by Albert Brenner, one of Nietzsche's pupils. They arrive

in Genoa on 22 October, where they board a ship
for Naples. From 27 October they are Malwida von
Meysenbug's guests in a villa she had rented, Villa
Rubinacci, in Sorrento. The very evening he arrived,
Nietzsche calls on Richard and Cosima Wagner who
are also staying in Sorrento. Overbeck had married
before Nietzsche's departure and Rohde had announced
his engagement. In June and July Nietzsche had dictated
aphorisms to Peter Gast for another *Untimely Meditation*;
these were, however, later incorporated in *Human, All
Too Human*. Death of Ritschl.

1877

Marie Baumgartner translates the fourth *Untimely Med-
itation* into French, which is published by Schmeitzner.
Reading evenings in Sorrento, at which Thucydides, St
Matthew's Gospel, Voltaire, Diderot, Michelet and
Ranke's *History of the Popes* are read. Around mid-May
Nietzsche arrives in Ragazzo for a thermal cure, where
Overbeck visits him. Nietzsche tells him of his intention
to give up his academic post once and for all. In mid-
June he arrives in Rosenlauibad, having completed the
last part of the journey on foot, from 11 to 17 June.
Once there he reads, among other things, Rée's book on
the origin of moral sensations. Marriage plans again (if
necessary, he will marry the first woman he meets on
the street). Rohde gets married in August. Nietzsche
leaves Rosenlauibad on 1 September, returns to Basle
and resumes his academic duties. On 2 September he
begins dictating the text of *Human, All Too Human* to

Peter Gast. Only three months later, on 3 December, the manuscript is offered to Schmeitzner for publication, who is nevertheless asked to keep it secret until May of the following year. Nietzsche receives his last letter from Cosima Wagner.

1878

The breach with Wagner is now definitive. Nietzsche gives away the scores (with dedications) that Wagner had given him. The first volume of *Human, All Too Human* appears in May. In August a thinly veiled attack by Wagner on Nietzsche is published in the house journal of the Wagner circle (the *Bayreuther Blätter*). The manuscript of the second part of *Human, All Too Human* is ready at the end of December.

1879

Nietzsche's health deteriorates. He is often unable to give his lectures and seminars. On 19 March he abandons his academic activities altogether. Journeys to Geneva for a rest cure. In May his request to be relieved of his academic duties is granted. He spends the weeks that follow in Wiesen and St Moritz. Visits Naumburg in September. In the meantime, the second volume of *Human, All Too Human: A Book for Free Spirits* appears with the title *Assorted Opinions and Maxims*. During the summer in St Moritz, Nietzsche writes *The Wanderer and his Shadow*.

1880

Schmeitzner publishes *The Wanderer and his Shadow*. It

is likely that Nietzsche was writing the notes for *Day-break* as early as January. Intensive reading during this period about problems connected with morality. Also reads Overbeck's *On the Christianity of our Theology Today* (1873). Travels on 10 February from Naumburg to Riva del Garda, where he is joined a few days later by Peter Gast. The pair arrives in Venice on 15 March. Paul Rée is supporting Peter Gast financially with great discretion. July and August are spent in Marienbad. When Nietzsche discovers that Schmeitzner also publishes anti-Semitic writings, he is outraged. Returns to Naumburg at the beginning of September, only to leave again immediately for Heidelberg and Basle (where he meets Overbeck). In October to Locarno and then Stresa. On 8 November withdraws to Genoa with the intention of spending his life in complete isolation.

1881

As with all of Nietzsche's writings, Gast transcribes the manuscript of *Daybreak*, which is then sent to Schmeitzner for printing. The book appears in the first week of July. Nietzsche plans a sojourn in Tunis with Gersdorff. He leaves Genoa in May to meet Peter Gast in Vicenza. Together they travel to Ricoaro. It is during this stay that Nietzsche invents the pseudonym Peter Gast for Köselitz. At the beginning of July he goes for the first time to Sils-Maria which from now on he will visit every summer. During a walk, the idea of Eternal Recurrence comes to him. Returns to Genoa on

1 October. His health is still poor – even his vision is worsening. On 27 November he attends a performance of Bizet's *Carmen* for the first time and is filled with enthusiasm.

1882

At the beginning of the year he works on a continuation of *Daybreak*. Peter Gast receives the first three parts at the beginning of January; these, together with a fourth part, are published at the end of August by Schmeitzner under the title *The Gay Science*. In February Paul Rée visits Nietzsche in Genoa and presents him with a typewriter. At the end of March Nietzsche sails in a cargo ship to Messina, where he stays until 20 April. However, the draft of his *Idylls of Messina* predates this journey by several days. The 'Idylls', the only poems Nietzsche published outside his aphoristic work, appear in the May number of the *Internationale Monatsschrift* (pp. 269–75). Responding to an invitation from Malwida von Meysenbug and Paul Rée, Nietzsche arrives in Rome on his way back from Messina. In the Meysenbug home he is introduced to Lou von Salomé, whom he would like to marry. He entrusts Rée with the task of asking for Lou's hand in marriage on his behalf. Lou leaves with her mother for Lago d'Orta where Nietzsche and Rée also arrive a few days later. Lou and Nietzsche take a long walk up the Monte Sacro. Rée is extremely annoyed by their lengthy absence. The three had previously planned to stay in Vienna or Paris. Nietzsche visits Overbeck in Basle from 8 to 13 May. He then meets Lou and Rée in Lucerne. On 16 May Nietzsche returns to Naumburg, while Lou and Rée travel to Stibbe in East Prussia to visit Rée's mother. Nietzsche, who has revealed his intentions to his sister, rents three rooms in Tautenburg, in order to live there for a while with Lou and his sister. Lou stays in Tautenburg from 7 to 26 August. The following day Nietzsche travels to Naumburg and thence to Leipzig where, in October, he meets Lou and Rée for the last time. He leaves for Genoa once again on 18 November. Thence he travels to Portofino, Santa Margherita and then, on 3 December, to Rapallo. The first part of *Thus Spake Zarathustra* can be traced back to this time.

1883

Nietzsche stays in Rapallo until the end of February, where the news of Richard Wagner's death reaches him. He then travels to Genoa again. While the first part of *Zarathustra* is being published, he works on the second part (which also appeared in that year) and starts preparing the third. Frequent rows and reconciliation with his sister, whom he sees again in June while staying with Malwida von Meysenbug in Rome. Nietzsche spends the summer in Sils-Maria. He returns to Naumburg in September and decides to spend the winter in Nice.

1884

Completes work on the third part of *Zarathustra*, which appears in April. Further quarrels with his sister on account of her engagement to Bernhard Förster, an anti-Semite and Wagnerian. In February Nietzsche writes to Gast from Nice: 'Music is by far the best; I would like now more than ever to be a musician' (Letters III, 1, 480). Conversations with Dr Joseph Paneth from Vienna, a philosophically inclined zoologist and friend of Sigmund Freud. Nietzsche leaves Nice on 20 April and travels to Venice, where Peter Gast awaits him. Breaks off relations with his mother. Stays in Sils-Maria from mid-June until the end of September. Heinrich von Stein visits him there at the end of August and makes a very good impression on Nietzsche. As he had done before, he considers living monastically and founding a philosophical order with Lou and Rée. His mother and sister offer him an olive branch by suggesting a meeting in Naumburg. Initially, Nietzsche declines but then agrees to a meeting halfway, in Zurich. From the end of September to the end of October he stays in Zurich where he and his sister made it up. He writes a conciliatory letter to his mother on 4 October. He meets Gottfried Keller. He spends November in Menton before returning to Nice. Drafts the fourth part of *Zarathustra* in mid-November.

1885

As Nietzsche can find no publisher for the fourth part of *Zarathustra*, he asks Gersdorff for financial help so that he can have the book printed privately. He leaves Nice on 9 April and arrives at Peter Gast's in Venice. The first copies of the fourth part of *Zarathustra* are sent to Overbeck at the beginning of May. The publisher of the private printing is Naumann in Leipzig. His sister marries Dr Förster on 22 May, whose intention is to set up a German colony in South America based on racist principles. Nietzsche does not attend the wedding. On 7 June he arrives in Sils-Maria, where he remains until mid-September. He is then in Naumburg until 1 November, travels to Munich and thence to Florence. He is in Nice again on 11 November.

1886

Even *Beyond Good and Evil* has to be published privately by Naumann. The first copies are ready at the beginning of August. After Schmeitzner's bankruptcy, the works of Nietzsche that he had published are reissued by Fritzsch. He publishes a new edition of the two volumes of *Human, All Too Human* with new prefaces. Similarly, Fritzsch publishes a new edition of *The Birth of Tragedy* (with a new subtitle: *Or: Greekness and Pessimism*), for which Nietzsche provides a new preface entitled 'Attempt at a Self-Criticism'. Burckhardt writes to him about *Beyond Good and Evil*: 'The book goes way above my old head and it makes me feel quite stupid'. During the summer in Sils-Maria, Nietzsche draws up plans for a four-volume work with the title *The Will to Power*, as well as for a book on Eternal Recurrence. Meanwhile, in February, his sister had left for Paraguay with her husband. Between May and June Nietzsche leaves Nice to stay in Naumburg and Leipzig, where he attends Rohde's lectures – Rohde had been appointed to a chair there in April. After a summer in Sils-Maria, Nietzsche spends part of October in Ruta Ligure before returning to Nice. He works on the forewords to the new editions of *Daybreak* and *The Gay Science*.

1887

In June, Fritzsch publishes the new editions of *Daybreak* and *The Gay Science* (the latter now containing a fifth book and an appendix entitled 'Songs of Prince Vogelfrei'). The same publisher also reissues *Zarathustra*, which contains only the first three parts. On 3 April Nietzsche leaves Nice for Cannobio on Lago Maggiore. He then spends a week in Zurich until 6 May before going to Chur until 8 June. Here he receives the news of Lou's engagement to Dr Andreas, which causes him to lapse into a deep depression. Nietzsche announces to Rohde the end of their friendship, because the latter had made disparaging remarks about Hippolyte Taine, with whom Nietzsche had had an intensive correspondence the previous autumn. From 12 June he is again in Sils-Maria, where he writes *On the Genealogy of Morals*, which is published by Naumann in November. Once again, Nietzsche has to meet the printing costs. After spending a few weeks in Venice, he returns to Nice on 12 October, where he receives a letter from Georg Brandes, a university professor in Copenhagen, who will give a lecture on Nietzsche the following year. Among the 1887 publications there is also a musical composition, the 'Hymn to Life', for mixed choir and orchestra. The music dates back to 1873–74, while the text is a strophe from Lou von Salomé's poem 'Life's Prayer'. This work, too, is also published by Fritzsch.

1888

Nietzsche remains in Nice until 2 April and then journeys to Turin, a city that makes a very good impression on him. In Nice he works on the text concerning the 'Transvaluation of All Values', from which *The Antichrist* will later emerge. In Turin he works on *The Case of Wagner*; he sends the manuscript to Naumann for printing on 17 July. He leaves Turin on 5 June for Sils-Maria, where he remains until 20 September. He spends the last part of the year in Turin again. In he works on the Will to Power and writes *Twilight of the Idols*. In Turin he writes *Ecce Homo*, which he completes on 4 November and sends to Naumann, as well as *Nietzsche contra Wagner*, which he sends to Naumann on 4 November. Meanwhile, *The Case of Wagner* has appeared. All remaining works that Nietzsche wrote in 1888, including *Dionysos-Dithyramben*, have also been sent for printing.

1889

On 3 January, Nietzsche displays signs of a serious mental disorder. In the days that follow he writes effusive letters to friends and well-known figures in public life. Burckhardt receives one of these letters and, alarmed, he informs Overbeck who arrives in Turin on 8 January. He returns to Basle with Nietzsche, where he is admitted to a psychiatric hospital; the diagnosis is 'progressive paralysis'. Nietzsche's mother, who had hurried to Basle, travels on 17 January with her son and two escorts to Jena, where Nietzsche is admitted to the university's psychiatric clinic. Naumann publishes *Twilight of the Idols*, *Nietzsche contra Wagner*, and *Ecce Homo*. Overbeck had advised Peter Gast temporarily to postpone publication of *Ecce Homo*. At the beginning of June, Nietzsche's brother-in-law takes his own life as a result of the financial failure of his Paraguayan colony. In November Julius Langbehn, an art historian, offers to collaborate with Nietzsche; he accompanies Nietzsche on walks outside the clinic and converses with him. After three weeks, Nietzsche reacts negatively to Langbehn. The latter disappears at the end of February 1890, after managing to secure the guardianship of Nietzsche.

1890

On 24 March, Nietzsche is able to leave the clinic and live with his mother in Jena. Mother and son return to Naumburg on 13 May. Their departure is almost akin to an escape. His sister returns from Paraguay on 16 December.

1891–97

Nietzsche's health continues to deteriorate. By 1892 he can no longer recognize the friends who come to visit him. He often flies into rages which are so violent that Peter Gast fears for the life of Nietzsche's mother. In 1893 he suffers a stiffening of the back, which prevents him from leaving the house for walks (something he had hitherto done at his mother's insistence). In the house he has to rely on a wheelchair. From 1894 Nietzsche, who can no longer speak otherwise, roars out from time to time while his face has an expression of great serenity. His mother dies on 20 April 1897 at the age of 71. Elisabeth takes her sick brother into her house in Weimar. For all practical purposes, however, he is cared for by Alwine Freytag who had assisted his mother for years.

In 1892 the publisher Fritzsch transfers the rights to Nietzsche's works to Naumann, and Peter Gast begins working on a complete edition. In the autumn of that year, *Zarathustra* is published for the first time in its entirety. The *Untimely Meditations* then appear together with the chapters from *Ecce Homo*, inwhich they are 'reviewed'. 1893 sees the publication of *Human, All Too Human*, *Beyond Good and Evil* and *On the Genealogy of Morals*. At the beginning of 1894, Nietzsche's sister arranges the immediate interruption of Gast's edition and establishes the Nietzsche Archive, which will henceforth dedicate itself to publishing a complete edition.

1900
Nietzsche dies on Saturday 25 August 1900, at around midday.

V. History of Nietzsche Reception

Even in the summer of 1888 in Sils-Maria, Nietzsche was fully aware of his fame. Admittedly, none of his books had found particular favour with academic philosophers. Clearly they were unable to detect that link to philosophical tradition in his thought, which would have enabled them to enter into a dialogue with him. For many years, Nietzsche's influence was felt above all by artists. Yet it appears from the documents and citations collected by Krummel that Nietzsche was also very quickly accorded a place in the history of philosophy.[1] For example, in the 1880 edition of Ueberweg's *Grundriß der Geschichte der Philosophie* [*Outline of the History of Philosophy*] Nietzsche is described as a successor to Schleiermacher, Schopenhauer and Beneke, while he is mentioned in Falkenberg's *Geschichte der neueren Philosophie* [*History of Modern Philosophy*], in the chapter on the opponents of conservative Idealism, as a pupil of Schopenhauer and Wagner. In this account, Nietzsche appears as a German Rousseau who metamorphosed into a disciple of Voltaire before returning, in *Zarathustra*, to a mystical-religious position.[2] Even in *Philosophie der Gegenwart* [*Contemporary Philosophy*] by Brasch, which

167

was published in 1888, Nietzsche is discussed as undoubtedly one of the most interesting and fascinating of all Schopenhauer's followers. Yet such recognition served only to increase Nietzsche's fame among artists, above all writers.[3] This fame was founded less on his works dealing with aesthetic theory (in other words, the writings of the early 1870s), and more on the later works, in which he himself appears as an artist. The impulses generated by Nietzsche became a fateful model for his friends and pupils (as well as for a wider audience) in the sense that, in these impulses, the artist with all his whims, moods and premonitions had gained access to philosophy. It was precisely this attitude (which Nietzsche had consciously taken over from the earliest Greek philosophers and had rediscovered in the French moralists, as well as in Tolstoy and Dostoevsky) which influenced the great writers of the twentieth century, from Kafka to Musil, Rilke to Thomas Mann, and Strindberg to Gide. For this reason, the experiment Nietzsche conducted as educator was in no sense a failure, even though it had no substantial impact on his immediate audience. Even Nietzsche's mental 'collapse' was ultimately perceived as an 'artistic' event. The starting-point for an engagement with his work was the debate concerning the nature and cause of this collapse. At one extreme, Nietzsche's sister tried to explain away her brother's illness as either a chance occurrence or the result of his overworking in the final months of 1888, in order to prevent the stigma of mental illness attaching itself to the family or to her brother's work; and at the other extreme, the physician Möbius believed he could detect signs of mental illness in all of Nietzsche's published works.[4] In reality, the cause of Nietzsche's illness, whether it was syphilitic or not, could not be reliably established. This hampered philosophical discussion of Nietzsche's work until at least the First World War, because the suspicion that his brain may have been infected by syphilis even before 1870 constituted a decisive objection to his entire thought. Independent of this, it was thought that the style of his aphorisms was more typical of a moralist than a philosopher.

Theologians, at least those of them who had known Nietzsche personally, attributed his psychological breakdown to his unsuccessful attempt to overcome Christianity and his enduring, irrepressible desire to find his way back to God.[5] This argument was supported by his mother's reports of conversations with her son during the long years of his illness.[6] In their engagement with Nietzsche, the theologians often pointed to the possibility that Nietzsche's Antichrist(ian) was in fact a new Christ(ian).[7]

Until 1900, interest in Nietzsche focused either on his biography (the main concern of both his sister in the inner circle of friends and of Lou Salomé)[8] or on the significance his thought had assumed for literature and the plastic arts. It is no coincidence that Georg Brandes, who is often regarded as the discoverer of Nietzsche, was a literary scholar,[9] and that Julius Langbehn, an art historian and friend of Nietzsche towards the end, should have entitled his most important book *Rembrandt as Educator*.[10]

At this time, the possible influence that Nietzsche's possible reading of Stirner may had on his development was also heavily discussed. At the beginning of the 1890s, Schellwien saw a parallel between the two thinkers without, however, pursuing the question of whether Nietzsche had ever read Stirner's work.[11] However hard Nietzsche's sister struggled to refute the assumption, the idea gradually took hold that Nietzsche had been influenced by Stirner. Frau Overbeck, for one, claimed that Nietzsche had read Stirner. Peter Gast, on the other hand, was undecided on the question since he was sure that Nietzsche had never spoken to him about Stirner and was equally sure that Nietzsche was in the habit of speaking to his nearest and dearest about books that were important to him.[12]

Numerous accounts attempting a comprehensive survey of Nietzsche's thought were published in the first decade of the twentieth century. In the main, their intention was to establish a connection between Nietzsche's various doctrines, identify the contradictions underlying them, and ask what possible meaning could be ascribed to them. In the process, Nietzsche's philosophy was generally read with moral spectacles. Drews[13] describes Nietzsche's transition to his third creative period in the following terms:

> Nietzsche is not striving to to go beyond morality as such, but merely beyond *heteronomous* morality,

which imposes its commandments from without and results in the diminishment and subjugation of the individual self. He would like to confront this old, life-denying morality with a new, *autonomous* morality, which stems directly from the individual will and is therefore in tune with the individual being. (Drews, 1904, 311f.)

According to Drews, Nietzsche had sought, like all the great German moralists from Kant to Eduard von Hartmann, to keep man on the straight road of autonomy. He therefore no longer conceived of the will, as Schopenhauer had, as a will to life, as something that must be preserved that would otherwise die, but instead as a Will to Power which sought to stretch the feeling of power to the point that it coincided with the necessity of transforming every agony into a motive force for life. Hence the immoralism, the exaggerated egoism, individualism, and relativism that were often ascribed to Nietzsche in those early years; hence also his poetic inspiration and his idea that he was dynamite (Drews, 1904, 313–22). According to Drews, Nietzsche's ethical aims had a further dimension: to him, the Will to Power is seen as the sublation ('Aufhebung') of the objective laws of nature. In this sense, Drews aligns Nietzsche with Kant:

Kant also denied real nature (the world of things in themselves) any objective status and argued that all so-called natural laws are merely the laws of our own

171

mind, which we unconsciously project onto, and read into nature. (Drews, 1904, 402f.)

Unlike Kant, however, Nietzsche makes no distinction between immanent nature (the world of appearances) and transcendental nature (the world of things in themselves), because he is concerned both to demonstrate the absurdity of assuming that there is a 'real' world and to expose the motives that have led to such an assumption. Given that the real world is false, only an apparent world would remain at this point. In his argument, Drews stresses Nietzsche's propensity for paradox, without asking why this should be. For behind these paradoxes Nietzsche is concealing the impossibility of clarifying his realism concerning the will without resorting to metaphysics. Yet, in Drews's opinion, this impossibility can be traced to Nietzsche's positivist past (cf. Drews, 1904, 407).

Riehl,[14] Ernst Horneffer,[15] and Ewald[16] had already attempted to suggest an affinity between Nietzsche's thought and Kantian philosophy by focusing in particular on the idea of an imperative which these interpreters regarded as an obligation to eternalize human life in an ethical sense. Taking their cue from Drews, other scholars, including Georg Simmel, continued to pursue this approach.[17]

Vaihinger interpreted Nietzsche's thought epistemologically and stressed Kant's importance to Nietzsche.[18] In Vaihinger's view, this importance is best expressed in his famous phrase that the understanding prescribes to nature its laws rather than taking them away from her. At the centre of Vaihinger's analysis is the role of those regulative fictions posited by Nietzsche, which, according to Nietzsche, constitute the world, without being reducible to anything true or false. What is at stake here are aspects of the world, which can only be understood as fictions and their loss, as might be the case with myth and religion, and can only entail an impoverishment of the world. Clearly, Vaihinger's approach here is coloured by his philosophy of 'Als ob' ['As if'].

An examination of Nietzsche's intellectual contacts with (German) Romanticism, opens up perspectives that go far beyond a narrowly defined concern with the area. According to Karl Joël, the appeal to Dionysus and his Dionysian overcoming of nihilism display a fundamentally romantic tendency in Nietzsche.[19] On this interpretation, Nietzsche's interest in early Greece is the most important aspect of this tendency, in so far as as it reveals a preference for Asiatic characteristics alien to the tradition of Western rationality. The latter appears as an impoverishment of a richer life that drew on the originality of the infinite. The battle that Nietzsche nevertheless fought against romanticism was, according to Joël, a battle against an inauthentic and debased romanticism. By comparing passages from Nietzsche with quotations from Novalis, Tieck and Friedrich Schlegel, Joël succeeds in demonstrating Nietzsche's spiritual proximity to early German Romanticism. This connection is often discussed in later studies of Nietzsche, even when it is not the main object of the inquiry.[20] This is true of Ernst Bertram's study, for example, a figure closely associated with Stefan George's circle.[21] For Bertram, Nietzsche had to become a 'legend' because the picture history gives us is never made up of an objective composition of facts. In Bertram's view, Nietzsche's thought therefore also had to be mythologically reconstructed. The 'work' itself, which is admittedly something concrete, only remains preserved in this process to the extent that it finds its way in to the legend of its author. What remains of a person beyond his or her temporal boundaries is always, as Bertram says (with an appeal to Burckhardt), magic, religious gesture, something that eludes any mechanical or rational correspondence. 'Legend is in truth what a word expresses in its baldest sense: it is not something written but rather something to be *read* anew time and again, which only comes into being through being read differently over and over again' (Bertram, 1918, p. 6). But this is necessarily the case because there is no objective or definitive reading. Nietzsche's impact therefore rests on the 'symbol' that he represents: the passion for insight as well as for the Eleusian mysteries, for Christianity, paganism, the Dionysian spirit and late Lutheranism (and this despite Nietzsche's dislike of Lutheranism which, in Bertram's opinion, corresponds to his reservations about Wagner). On this reading, then, there is a Nordic element in Nietzsche alongside the Greek component, Christian asceticism next to the Greek love of appearance, the horror of unveiled truth and the passion for myth. Ultimately, though, the will to knowledge triumphs in Nietzsche, even if this will should turn out to be a will to death. For Nietzsche knew, like Hebbel, that man resembles a basilisk who dies as soon as he catches sight of himself (Bertram, 1918, p. 390).

Ludwig Klages was concerned to establish a more precise relationship with Nietzsche's thought, although he too gave his interpretation a certain 'inner' slant.[22] According to Klages, Nietzsche's full significance had not yet been understood because no-one had grasped what he had inaugurated. In Klages' view, Nietzsche provided the decisive impulse for examining the characters of humans by directing attention to the soul and the spirit. Recognising the soul is extremely difficult because it cannot rely on anything external for its unfolding. Zarathustra's claim that You are older than I is decisive, according to Klages, because it overturns an axiom which gained metaphysical expression in Descartes. If I have to turn to an external reality when encountering an Other, I will have to refrain from this when encountering myself and become alien to myself. 'The Other confronts me in the form of an appearance, in other words as a primary reality, whereas one's own Self ("das Eigenich") must first become alien to itself in order to become graspable' (Klages, 1926, p. 18). According to Klages, Nietzsche was the first to see that the 'psychology' which investigates the facts of the soul (i.e. psychology as it has existed for more than two thousand years) will never grasp the soul precisely because it has never made the effort to become alien to itself. Yet the demand 'Know thyself' is also a demand to know 'Being'. The Being that has been 'brought in' in this way opposes itself to the flow of time in the soul. The formula with which Nietzsche expressed this is the 'Will to Power'. In order to be able to live, he must relate to values. He thereby decides in favour of values which he possesses and denies those which he does not. In Klages' opinion, Nietzsche decided in favour of self-deception as a means of combating despair. For this reason, he (Nietzsche) was able to undertake an extremely precise analysis of those means which individuals, whole nations, and indeed humanity as a whole have selected in order to deceive themselves. This was nothing negative, however, for whoever has taken all these means into account, according to Klages, is on the way to knowing himself. Concealed trust in the external world and the conviction that one has a personal identity can be traced back to this will to deceive oneself.

A new phase in the history of Nietzsche reception begins with Alfred Baeumler's book, not only because it represents the National Socialist interpretation of Nietzsche's thought but also because it employs and develops one of the great terms of Nietzsche's philosophy, the Will to Power, against the metaphysical tradition of the West.[23] Baeumler regards the Will to Power as the central thought of Nietzsche's 'metaphysics', and the work he had conceived to spell out this thought (namely, *The Will to Power*) is, to Baeumler,

Nietzsche's central work. According to Baeumler, the Will to Power is not a willing of power but rather a formula which expresses Becoming itself. A will which ceaselessly desires struggle has no goal, because it is itself an event or, in Baeumler's version, will *as* power. At this point, however, Baeumler has to banish the doctrine of Eternal Recurrence from Nietzsche's thought in the name of the system he has adopted to interpret that thought, because it would reintroduce something alien to struggle into the world. In fact, Baeumler does distinguish between a Heraclitean world of ceaseless flux and a Dionysian world of recurrence. The thought of Eternal Recurrence, in Baeumler's view, is only the expression of a highly personal experience of Nietzsche's and is of no consequence to the system of the Will to Power. If there is thus only an Innocence of Becoming ('Unschuld des Werdens') in the Heraclitean world, then Nietzsche's attempt (in aphorism 617 of *The Will to Power*) 'to stamp the character of Being onto Becoming' is necessarily an attempt that must remain irreconcilable with a system dominated by the Will to Power. In fact, in such a system, Becoming has to remain free of any determination by Being. Baeumler spells out how the doctrine of Eternal Recurrence came about in Nietzsche's thought before arriving at the system of the Will to Power, which is therefore intended as an overcoming of doctrine of Eternal Recurrence. The Will to Power is simply another name for what Baeumler calls 'the highest justice', in other words for the kind of justice which raises itself above

177

the petty definitions of good and evil and is, ultimately, a will of the whole. Baeumler writes:

> Justice is but another word for the presence of this whole, for the self-preservation of this whole which, in order to be power for all eternity, preserves its balance for all eternity, and which only preserves its balance in order to affirm itself for all eternity in the struggle of all its qualities against one another. *The Will to Power is therefore only another expression for the highest justice.* (Baeumler, 1937, p. 78)

Mastery therefore belongs to the strongest and slavery to the weakest. In the context of this metaphysical perspective, the second part of the book interprets Nietzsche's political thought. Nietzsche's politics, according to this interpretation, consist of an attack upon contemporary Western values. Its wars should lead to a state governed by the Nordic race. Nietzsche's sympathetic attitude to France does not contradict this perspective, for this sympathy was a deliberate and provocative move on Nietzsche's part, designed to arouse interest in his ideas.

As already suggested, Baeumler's book led to the great Nietzsche interpretations of the thirties, those by Jaspers, Löwith and Heidegger, which were in part an answer to Baeumler's attempt to cast Nietzsche as a precursor of National Socialism and racial violence.

Karl Jaspers, who set himself the task of understanding Nietzsche's 'philosophizing' (and not just the philosophical results of his thought), looked above all in the unpublished fragments of the 1880s for those transcendent moments where Nietzsche's thought attempts to go beyond the boundaries set by existing values and truths.[24] At the heart of Jaspers' interest is a will to truth inherent in Nietzsche's thought, which corresponds to a will to death. Nietzsche's whole thought, which is light and labyrinth, spirit and Being, circles around this ambiguity of truth. Truth's ultimate secret, at which Nietzsche arrives via myth, is that truth is death and that concealed in the passion for truth there is again only death (cf. Jaspers, 1936, p. 230). In the labyrinth, in which Nietzsche finds himself as Theseus searching for truth, it is in fact Ariadne who is death's last disguise. Of this perceived ambiguity, an ambiguity that brings Jaspers close to Hölderlin's conception of the tragic (where the god himself appears in death), modern man has only experienced nothingness and, on the chessboard of his earthly existence, only registered the silence of an absent God. However, in the light of this existential approach the doctrines of the 'Übermensch', the Will to Power, and Eternal Recurrence are ciphers of a transcendence whose goal is neither God nor the world but instead the ceaseless opening-up of possibilities. According to Jaspers, Nietzsche's thought therefore oscillates in almost Kierkegaardian fashion between godlessness and a scarcely tangible religiosity.

Karl Löwith connects the expressions 'Thou shalt', 'I will' and 'I am' with the figures of the wanderer, Zarathustra and Dionysus respectively. For their part these figures have correspondences in the philosophy of the morning (which, in its search for truth, pushes through to the boundary of nothingness) in the discovery of the noontide hour (i.e. the death of God and the 'Übermensch') and also ultimately in the doctrine of Eternal Recurrence (as the most extreme affirmation of life).[25] The birth of nihilism corresponds to the negative event of God's death. Nihilism is understood here as a denigration of the highest values, which leads not to despair but life affirming itself. According to Löwith, then, Nietzsche is re-presenting (at the height of modernity's crisis) an antique understanding of the world, in which everything recurs eternally and, temporally, the circle takes the place of the line. Yet he fails, because he fails to solve the connection between man and the world. Nietzsche, who with the idea of Eternal Recurrence had wanted to be a Greek, basically remained profoundly Christian. At the moment of expressing an irrepressible will to the future, this will was doomed to failure after the loss of that Christian God whose appearance ought to have given that will a direction: 'His philosophy breaks in two because the will to eternalize the existence of the modern ego does not square with the show of an eternal circularity of the natural world.' According to Löwith, therefore, the doctrine of Eternal Recurrence is a theodicy which seeks a balance between the way of the world and human existence.

Martin Heidegger, whose work is probably the most convincing riposte to Baeumler's arguments, wants to place

Nietzsche alongside Plato and Aristotle in the history of metaphysics.[26] For, according to Heidegger, his problem was the problem of metaphysics, the question of Being. And this problem was most apparent in Nietzsche's last (posthumously published) work, *The Will to Power*. This will is precisely the characteristic that Nietzsche ascribes to that which is being that defines itself in its own Being. This metaphysics of the will stands firmly in the tradition of German philosophy since Leibniz. From Platonism and the Judaeo-Christian tradition it has inherited forgetfulness of Being ('Seinsvergessenheit'). The systematic organization of Being attempted by the Western tradition therefore finds its most complete expression in Nietzsche. In his thought, nothing remains of Being, whereas the world is made subordinate to the control of technology, that planetary happening, in which metaphysics completes itself. If the Will to Power is therefore the fundamental characteristic of a being thing in its organized totality, then this necessarily requires that the *essence* of a thing so being, because a being thing as Will to Power can only will itself. Eternal Recurrence is therefore the 'how' of existence ('Dasein') or its *existentia*. According to Heidegger, even Nietzsche's conception of truth must be understood as proceeding from the Will to Power. The Will to Power is the truth criterion in knowledge and, simultaneously, the measure of life's re-formation in art. We have the Will to Power to thank for the fact that art and truth manifest themselves as that seizure of possession of the self ('Selbstbesitzergreifung') which is peculiar to

181

them. In this sense, truth remains bound up with another fundamental concept that Heidegger discerns in Nietzsche: justice. Since Descartes, the modern epoch has tended to transform truth into self-certainty and conceived of things as objects of the self's representation. Nietzsche put an end to this tendency by realizing that it was nihilism.

> Nihilism is the historical process through which the 'supersensible' becomes irrelevant and nugatory with the result that Being itself loses its value and meaning. Nihilism is the history of Being itself, through which the death of the Christian God slowly but relentlessly emerges. (Heidegger, 1961, p. 33)

Nietzsche's predicted transvaluation of all values would lead, according to Heidegger, to the end of all hitherto credible values and ultimately, in Nietzsche's case, to the end of any *need* for values. But precisely for this reason, Nietzsche still thought in terms of valuational yardsticks and conceived of Being as a value in his thought (cf. Heidegger, 1961, p. 35).

In the years immediately after the Second World War, Nietzsche scholarship concerned itself above all with freeing him of association with the crimes of the Nazis, who had labelled him their 'spiritual' and 'German' legitimizer.[27] Thomas Mann's *Doctor Faustus*, written during the war years, captured with great sensitivity the painful feeling that the German catastrophe was in some sense bound up with Nietzsche's spiritual experience.

Friedrich Georg Jünger[28] also noticed this and attempted to show how Nietzsche's prophecy should not be read in a directly historical sense because one would then be putting the cart before the horse and making Nietzsche responsible for a catastrophe of which he was in fact the result and consequence (cf. Jünger, 1949, pp. 169–72).

In these immediate postwar years, Nietzsche was often read from an existentialist perspective (in the wake of Jaspers) as the theoretician of the European consciousness. At this time, Nietzsche was often viewed as Kierkegaard's cousin (again following Jaspers), as Löwith had already endeavoured to show as early as 1933.[29] Studies by Struve,[30] Giesz,[31] Rehm[32] and Lavrin[33] all pursued this tendency. This philosophical reappropriation of Nietzsche's works was moreover determined by a certain preference for the writings of his middle period, from *Human, All Too Human* to *The Gay Science*. Schoeck's book ushered in these efforts, which enjoyed considerable prominence in the 1950s.[34] In the meantime, Nietzsche's relation to Christianity was also reawakening interest. Flake perceived in Nietzsche the climax of a religious and moral subjectivism that began with Luther and could only end in nihilism;[35] and in the emptiness of this nihilism only the idols of race, the state and violence could triumph. Weymann-Weye put forward another point of view, namely, that

Nietzsche's thought has a positive meaning in the history of Christian consciousness because it is one of the possible forms of expression of that consciousness.[36] In this sense Nietzsche was on a par with Kierkegaard, though only the latter was able to give human history a foundation by confronting man with God rather than releasing him into a suprahuman loneliness. In fact, as we have already indicated, the idea that Nietzsche could be read as a Christian thinker went back to the earliest years of his reception. Benz reinforced this idea when he spoke of Nietzsche as the initiator of a particular *imitatio Christi*.[37] Karl-Heinz Volkmann-Schluck, on the hand, commented that contemporary theology was still not prepared to deal with the problems raised by Nietzsche's attacks on Christianity.[38]

In 1946 Jaspers returned to the theme of Christianity in Nietzsche.[39] He emphasized above all the need to distinguish between the reality of Christianity and the demands that gave expression to it. In order better to understand Nietzsche, therefore, there is a need to separate the Pauline doctrine of faith in a Beyond, to which only the 'good' can have access, and the doctrine, practised by Christ himself, of an experience of the heart. Taking this as his starting-point, Jaspers argues that Nietzsche merely watered the seeds of self-realization which Christianity had carried within itself from the outset. According to Jaspers, the origin of Nietzsche's nihilism must be sought in his Christian attitude (cf. Jaspers, 1946, p. 43). The suffering Nietzsche experienced at the hands of man can be traced back to the biblical account of original sin. In this context Jaspers quotes the sentence: 'There is something fundamentally flawed in man'. Christianity's tendency towards self-disintegration is, however, not the only thing that connects Nietzsche with this religion. Jaspers is at pains to demonstrate how Nietzsche sets up a dialectic between the figures of Dionysus and Jesus, which mirrors a debate (between transcendence and immanence) that has run through the history of Western thought. Nietzsche's juxtaposing of Jesus and Dionysus contains for Jaspers the oppositions of two interpretative models of suffering, the Christian and the tragic. In the first, suffering becomes a symbol of the world's fragility and irredeemability and is thus an objection to life; while, in the tragic model, suffering becomes absorbed into a totality of Being which, in its sacredness, is able to justify infinite pain (cf. aphorism 1052 of *The Will to Power*).

The argument that Nietzsche's attack on Christianity was an expression of his religiosity was also endorsed by Nigg, who regarded Nietzsche as a religious revolutionary.[40] He saw in him the embodiment of modern man's metaphysical fate (cf. Nigg, 1948, p. 226). Admittedly, in order to prove Nietzsche's religiosity, Nigg had to make a distinction between Christianity and religiosity. In this way he succeeded in interpreting Nietzsche's atheism religiously, even at those points where Nietzsche states that belief in God is a lie. In this context, Paul Tillich also speaks of a search for God beyond God with the title 'Der Gott

185

über Gott und der Mut zum Sein' ['The God Above God and the Courage To Be'].[41]

Werte also evaluated Nietzsche's atheism positively.[42] He spoke of a 'dual dialectic' of the human will, culminating in a 'tragic ambivalence'. For, on the one hand, human passions are pushing the will to realize itself even in conditions of temporal limitation, and dialectically together with the will to the unlimited, which then in turn metamorphoses into a negative will as a result of demonic withdrawal ('Entzugsdämonie'). On the other hand, the unconditionality of the will metamorphoses into a will to the unconditional. Belief in God appears here as a way of withdrawing from the proximity of the finite. Welte writes:

> In this way, man is constantly and simultaneously attracted and repelled by the poles of his two great possibilities. In the believing willing of the unconditional he will always have a will not to believe, and in the unconditional willing of that which he has he will always sense the pain and the impotence of contradictory finitude. He will everywhere and in all his possibilities of realization (that lie in the these extreme poles or somewhere between them) find himself caught up in a yes *and* a no, and one way or another this dilemma will not let him come to rest. (Welte, 1958, p. 49)

The idea that Nietzsche belongs in the history of Christian consciousness was subsequently taken up many times and elaborated upon. Let it suffice here to mention some of the important contributors to this debate: Grau,[43] Wein,[44] Ulrich,[45] Valadier,[46] and Biser.[47] In Biser's view, Nietzsche's statement 'God is dead' belongs to that theological tradition which has freed the concept of Being from that of God, in order to push forward to a realm of Being Beyond; this is the tradition of Pseudo-Dionysios Areopagites, John Scotus Eriugena, Nikolaus von Kues and also, in Biser's opinion, Augustine and Thomas Aquinas.

Blumenberg, too, places Nietzsche in the historical movement of a religious and cultural change.[48] According to him, every teleology is a theology to Nietzsche and is criticized as such. On this reading, Nietzsche is a late but nevertheless decisive expression of the second overcoming of gnosis. Nietzsche is not content with the idea that man could not have created the world from the outset; rather he wants autonomy with regard to reality as it actually is; in other words, he wants man to create a space for his works, for 'our salvation lies not in knowing but in creating'.[49] In this sense, after the end of natural teleology, technology has become its replacement, and Nietzsche would appear to be the philosopher of the technological age, despite his contempt for modernity's preoccupation with the practical.

The debate concerning Nietzsche's relationship with Christianity has in no way exhausted the interest he has aroused in the last few decades. Blumenberg's reference to technology demonstrates that, even after Heidegger, further possibilities of interpreting Nietzsche's work have opened up.

In the 1950s, Nietzsche research was dominated by Karl Schlechta's new edition of his works.[50] In this edition, Nietzsche's notes on the Will to Power are organized chronologically (rather than systematically), with the title 'From the Unpublished Material of the 1880s'. Schlechta noted, moreover, in the afterword to his edition that there was nothing important in these notes that could not be found in the published writings. According to Schlechta, Nietzsche's thought found its true expression in the latter. As we have already pointed out, Nietzsche was read in the immediate postwar years with reference above all to the published texts of his middle period. Leaving aside the various attempts at complete accounts of his thought, we must nevertheless highlight the studies by Kaufmann,[51] Schlechta himself,[52] and Wolff.[53]

Kaufmann wanted to see the Apollonian reevaluated because, in his opinion, it had become forgotten and subsumed by Dionysian intoxication. Kaufmann argued that Nietzsche had placed particular importance on sketching a morality of the 'Übermensch', which remained intact even beyond its destructive aspects in confronting traditional morality. The Apollonian, the model of which was Socrates, was expressed as sublimation and spiritualization.

In Nietzsche's image of 'noontide' ('Mittag'), Schlechta found both pagan and Christian resonances. The unrest expressed by Nietzsche at noon was the unrest of the man who has turned away from Christianity without then regaining the antique serenity of the circle. Eternal Recurrence thus becomes a secularized inferno, according to Schlechta.

Wolff gives a chronological account of Nietzsche's thought, paying particular attention to the philosopher's intellectual personality. He, too, regards the published texts as more important than the unpublished; and, according to Wolff, the problems Nietzsche raises with regard to the mind, life and consciousness are of more interest than those concerning art, culture and politics.

An account of Nietzsche scholarship in the 1950s would be incomplete without a mention of Lukács's interpretation.[54] The reason for this is not so much because of any particular value it had for an understanding of Nietzsche, but rather for the negative effects it had, above all within Marxism. It has often been remarked that this interpretation essentially agrees with that of the Nazis, differing from it only in its choice of ideological label. Lukács presents Nietzsche as *the* thinker of bourgeois irrationalism in the imperialist era. According to Lukács, the content of Nietzsche's resulted from 'a fear that his own class was doomed, expressed in a flight to myth' (Lukács, 1962, p. 350); and the perversity of bourgeois society found its most brilliant and simultaneously most irrational expression in Nietzsche's aphorisms. Despite Lukács's authority, this interpretation was not uncontroversial, even within Marxist circles. It was contradicted by, among others, the Frankfurt School, which felt indebted to Nietzsche in view of its concept of a dialectic of Enlightenment and acknowledged explicitly that they had inherited from him the Heraclitean idea that historicity and nihilism are interlinked.[55]

It is clear, however, that there was greater interest in Nietzsche after the Second World War outside Germany. There was a renaissance in Nietzsche scholarship, particularly in France, Italy and the United States.[56] In the 1960s this tendency increased, if anything, when the Italians Colli and Montinari began work on a new edition of Nietzsche's work. As well as appearing in Italian, this edition appeared almost simultaneously in German, French and Japanese.

However, before we turn to the interpretations outside the German-speaking world, we must mention Eugen Fink's book which appeared in 1960.[57] Although it essentially rehearses Heidegger's interpretation, it also introduces an important correction. According to Fink, Nietzsche's thought is not only the culmination of the history of metaphysics but also the first attempt to abandon it. Fink interpreted the 'Übermensch' on the basis of an ontology of play, which he developed simultaneously, and independent of his Nietzsche interpretation, as the foundation of his own philosophy. On this reading, Nietzsche's 'Übermensch' recognizes in play his free participation in a world of appearance. This does not mean that 'this' world is the only world but only that 'this' world is an apparent world.

Even before the 1960s, interest in Nietzsche was very strong in France, as is clear from the works of Andler,[58]

Bataille,[59] Gide[60] and Camus.[61] It was Deleuze, however, who created a new vision of Nietzsche in France.[62] According to Deleuze, too, Nietzsche's philosophy is an attempt to abandon metaphysics. This attempt was made concrete in Nietzsche's resistance to dialectics, which contains all the ingredients of metaphysical thinking: from Socrates' invention of the concept to the Christian notion of suffering, from theology to merely reactive thinking. Deleuze introduced the concept of 'difference' in order to show how, in Nietzsche's thought, the conception of living Becoming as a force presents itself primarily in a 'flowing' that crosses 'different' planes. Klossowski's reading reveals a certain proximity to this interpretation.[63] According to him, however, the force expressed in Nietzsche's thought is directed towards a 'plot' whose premiss is the idea of Eternal Recurrence. Yet the idea of the eternity of recurrence plunges personal identity into crisis, in Klossowski's view, and thus reveals itself as ill-suited to a plot. In practical terms, this plot would not therefore require any political organization of, say, a Marxian kind, but would have to impose itself as the gradual autonomization of the pathological; in other words, it would have to proceed from marginal groups and schizophrenics. Klossowski therefore believes that Nietzsche cannot be aligned with either Marx or Freud, because his efforts are moving in another direction, towards a 'délir' and emotional enthusiasm.

In contrast to the two authors just mentioned, Granier set out his examination of Nietzsche's concept of truth more conventionally.[64] Nietzsche's thought appeared to him as a 'meta-philosophy'. Nietzsche's conception of truth was two-fold: first, as something 'original' and, secondly, as wisdom. As wisdom it has the function of accepting appearance, in other words of preventing life becoming paralysed by the realization that all action is merely apparent. This is where art has its main function.

The relation of art and philosophy is also the starting-point of Pautrat's book.[65] In his view, Nietzsche's orientation towards Dionysus meant the disappearance of the traditional distinction between art and philosophy as well as the appearance of the problems of style and the textuality of the text. Nietzsche's philologically orientated early writings had to be aligned with *Zarathustra*. The confronting of the Apollonian with the Dionysian in *The Birth of Tragedy* as the opposition of *melos* and *logos*, of music understood in a Schopenhauerian sense and a language reduced by abstractions and generalizations to words and concepts, leads to what Pautrat terms the 'law of impurity'. This law owes its existence to the fact that the Apollonian and the Dionysian are not absolute opposites; it is more the case that the Apollonian derives from the Dionysian. A derivation of this kind clearly has no historical sense, either in Nietzsche's thought or in the general development of culture; it is to be understood more as a 'structure'. On the basis of this structure, Nietzsche conceived of difference instead of Being, according to Pautrat, understood as impurity (in other words, as the Dionysian) that places itself outside metaphysics. In this way the problem of meta-physics became a problem of language. Metaphysics is the subjection of language by certain social conditions. Taking account of the textuality of a text is not only a method of reading Nietzsche but is to be found in the texts themselves, because Nietzsche understood his work as the deconstruction of a metaphysical edifice. As Lacoue-Labarthe has shown, with reference to Derrida, it is a question of reconstructing how Nietzsche him-self conceived of the problem of how textuality arises.[66] The initial impurity, the opposition and interdepend-ence of Apollo and Dionysus, has no beginning there-fore but is instead constantly renewed, whether it be in tragedy, in the thought of Eternal Recurrence or in the Will the Power. According to this interpretative model, a 'text' is no longer, as it is in metaphysics, a sign implying a signified (in other words, something outside the text) but is instead a totality of *signifiants* (signifiers) which refer to one another and do not allow access to a clearly defined state of affairs underlying them. By renouncing the signified, Nietzsche has there-fore come down in favour of poetry and parody in the metaphysical text.

Another approach to Nietzsche in the 1960s was undertaken by a member of the group associated with the journal *Praxis*, Grlic, who attempted an anti-aesthetic interpretation.[67] According to Grlic, we should not understand aesthetics in Nietzsche as a particular disci-pline but as an ontology dealing with the truth of human existence. If Nietzsche used aesthetic categories,

193

then this was only to refute the idea that aesthetics was a discipline designed to examine a particular area of human activity. Djuric, who follows broadly the same line, buttresses his argument primarily with reference to Heidegger and Fink.[68] He emphasizes that Nietzsche knew full well that nihilism was a pathological and transitory condition, the result of an 'enormous generalization', according to which everything is meaningless. To Nietzsche, the outbreak of nihilism was therefore not an attack on metaphysics but a recognition of a radical break with its history. Yet only a 'completed' nihilism was in a position to endure this situation with all its implications, while an 'incomplete' nihilism was only a sign of the weakness of that Western culture which believed it could save itself by seeking another meaning for the world. Djuric leads nihilism back to the radical overcoming of any conception of the Beyond and then aligns it with the demands of the young Marx, which point in the same direction.[69] Marx had written: 'It is therefore the *task of history*, after the disappearance of the *Beyond of truth*, to establish the *truth of the here and now*' (Karl Marx, 'Zur Kritik der Hegelschen Rechtsphilosophie' ['Critique of Hegel's Philosophy of Right'], in Marx/Engels, *Werke* [Berlin, 1957], vol. i, 379). According to Djuric, Nietzsche's 'Übermensch' is thus the human being who has understood that everything is Will to Power, while hitherto men had covered up this truth. In relation to Marx's revolutionary demand, even completed nihilism does not correspond to the overcoming of the current situation, and leads

back, as Heidegger correctly saw, to traditional metaphysics. However, the nihilism of the late Nietzsche,
according to Djuric, is a preparatory moment of revolution, in the sense that it favours the dissolution of
rigid ways of thinking.

Jähnig tried to demonstrate that, to Nietzsche, art
was not able to constitute any privileged position.[70] In
Jähnig's opinion, Nietzsche's concern was primarily to
draw up a new image of the Greeks. For, as was the
case with the Greeks, so too, according to Jähnig, art
was the completion of the totality of the world, in other
words the production of that which is not present in
reality. In the same way that the Dionysian orgies of the
Greeks interrupted concrete life from time to time, in
order to open man's access to the totality of Being, art
is also primarily fulfilment and completion. Tragedy,
which unifies Apollonian and Dionysian tendencies,
expresses this nature of art. Its birth coincides with the
end of mythical sensibility.

In Italy meanwhile, efforts were concentrated on
defending or freeing Nietzsche from Lukács's interpretation. Even here, though, there existed a tradition of
Nietzsche scholarship, whose most important represen-
tatives were Giusso,[71] Banfi,[72] Della Volpe,[73] and Paci.[74]
In this scholarship, Nietzsche was interpreted critically,
anti-dogmatically and anti-metaphysically. In 1965 De
Feo's book on Nietzsche appeared, which paid particular attention to the problem of finitude in Nietzsche's
work.[75] In De Feo's view, Nietzsche had developed this
problem out of a dialectic of contradictions which

consisted of a ceaseless reversal of existing perspectives. On this reading, even the Transvaluation of All Values was not aimed so much at their negation but rather at an investigation of their inversion. De Feo claimed Jaspers was right to regard Nietzsche as the first existential philosopher.

Masini's starting point was also a perceived dialectic in Nietzsche's thought, which Masini used to demonstrate that the absolute negativity of nihilism, which had proclaimed the death of God, was turned on its head in Nietzsche's positive Dionysian affirmation of life.[76] According to Masini, this movement does not lead to irrationalism and unfolds not only in capitalism but is also a continually self-renewing discussion of the preconditions of our existence in the direction of a new rationality.

In Vattimo's opinion, Nietzsche's thought places metaphysical subjectivity in crisis and thereby opens up a new perspective, in which the relations between Being, truth and interpretation combine to produce a creative conception of man: liberated, the Dionysian consciously opts for a multiplicity of masks.[77]

Cacciari argues that Nietzsche anticipated the crisis of our perception and knowledge that shook the first two decades of the twentieth century.[78] With Nietzsche, the relation of subject and object became definitively critical. His 'negative thinking' renounces any rationalization of the real, preferring instead to tackle a rationalization of perception. Foregoing any metaphysical project did not make Nietzsche an irrationalist; on the contrary, it made him the most conclusive rationalist.

There has also been a revival of Nietzsche scholarship in Germany in the last few years, not least in the circles of 'hermeneutic' philosophy inaugurated by Heidegger and perpetuated by Gadamer.

According to Müller-Lauter, Nietzsche conceived of the will as an opposition of various competing Wills to Power from the outset, unlike Schopenhauer who had conceived of the will as something originally undifferentiated that only acquires various individuations in the course of its development.[79] For in Nietzsche's thought there is no negation of the will. Even the will to nothingness is a will, though it is admittedly no longer possible in this case to establish what is being willed. The Wills to Power are quanta of power which can only express themselves by resisting other quanta. It is not a question here of either Being or Becoming but of a pathos, as Nietzsche himself formulates it. It represents the quality of will encountered by another will. According to Müller-Lauter, the Will to Power is opposed by the will to truth, which is an expression by the weak of their *ressentiment* and desire for revenge. Life does not need truth, in fact, but rather those perspectives in which the world appears as Will to Power. From this perspectivism, according to Müller-Lauter, there emerges the need for the 'Übermensch' as the man capable of bringing contradictory perspectives under a single yoke and harnessing the various Wills to Power.

This happens either in destructive rage or through a preparedness to die. But precisely here Nietzsche's philosophy of contradictions fails because these two conceptions of the 'Übermensch' cannot be reconciled. In Müller-Lauter's view, this failure is confirmed by the doctrine of Eternal Recurrence which leads to divergent consequences, depending upon which of the two conceptions of the 'Übermensch' is invoked.

According to Kaulbach, Nietzsche's philosophy had not yet been considered from the point of view of the unity of content and method.[80] The idea of an experimental philosophy allows us to approach this problem. In this philosophy, the Cartesian methodical doubt that underlies the entire experimental work of the Will to Power expresses itself at its most radical. The doctrine of Eternal Recurrence also finds a way into this work as one of the temporarily accepted variants. The radicality of the doubt expressed in this experimental philosophy consists, according to Kaulbach, in the effort of freeing oneself from the foundations of knowledge, because as such it suppresses the methodical doubt. In the face of Being there can be no truth criteria, only gradations of significance. The tension towards truth only conceals the will to significance. However, this inevitably produces conflicts within the perspectives, which require a recourse to rationality. Nietzsche calls this rationality *justice*. This justice does not, however, apportion the individual perspectives their places distributively, because it is nothing more than the acknowledgment of the significance that each perspective has achieved in its conflict with the others. Nietzsche's *meditatio vitae* here radically contradicts the message of the philosophy of modernity. According to Kaulbach, Nietzsche makes it his task to go beyond the antithesis of a Baconian dominance over nature and an Idealism of human freedom, by means of an 'aesthetic reason' embedded in a pluralistic universe of perspectives. In this context, Kaulbach refers to what Nietzsche calls the 'psychology of art' which resembles a continuation of Kant's third Critique. He speaks of a free play of our powers of perception and of freedom under the law.

According to Paul Ricoeur, every philosophy is interpretation. To him, Nietzsche represents a decisive turn by virtue of his radical understanding of philology. Figl has pursued this idea. He sees the key to reading Nietzsche's notes on the Will to Power in the formula 'to be is to interpret', which is discernible in Nietzsche's language.[81] The intuition that existence is terrible and groundless prompted Nietzsche to regard all interpretations hitherto as masks that were designed to conceal this groundlessness. Underlying this attitude, according to Figl, is a nihilist ontology which approaches a tendency to unmask as well as an ontology, in which man is the animal who interprets his world with the aid of signs. The reference to the Will to Power necessitates the introduction of a subject of the 'interpretative event'. According to Figl, this subject is pluralistically constituted, i.e. made up of various wills that only become a subject within the interpretative event itself.

In the last few years, Nietzsche monographs have

concentrated above all on locating Nietzsche's place within modernity. On a new historical basis, they have attempted primarily to set out Nietzsche's relations to other authors and to the thought of his contemporaries. On the other hand few comprehensive studies have been published, presenting Nietzsche's thought on the basis of personal and extraordinary, indeed historic experiences. Exceptions to this are the posthumously published lectures of Picht and Volkmann-Schluck.[82] Both studies refer to Heidegger. While Nietzsche represents to Picht not only the end of Western metaphysics but also its radical overcoming in the sense of a transcendental philosophy (where reflexion is no longer supported by a subject but exclusively by history, in which every thinking subject is enmeshed), Nietzsche's renunciation of a truth becomes, to Volkmann-Schluck, an event of this truth. A claim is thereby readopted, which had remained hidden since the time of the Greeks.

Readopting Adorno's dialectical approach and rejecting Lukács's theory of an irrationalist Nietzsche, the most recent criticism has been at pains to reconstruct Nietzsche's thought on the basis of that work of understanding that is characteristic of modernity. In the process, this criticism attempts to establish connections between the claims to validity of the various cultural, political, social and religious parts of society as well as presenting a critique of these claims. In this way, the attempt to see the understanding of these claims to validity as either a critique of their own authority, or as the removal of these claims, has become a guiding thread in the understanding of Nietzsche's social philosophy.[83] A further object of investigation has been Nietzsche's vision of a 'madness of reason'.[84] It has been explained in this study that Nietzsche was the first to recognize the dangers of a rationalist critique. Precisely because of his passion for reason, he decided in favour of a ban on totalitarianism, and it is here that the causes of his turn against Christianity and nihilism should be looked for. It has been considered whether his thought might not permit an ethical refoundation of the concept of value in the light of Protestant theology.[85] Lastly, the new order has been discussed which can bring his thought into the matrix of subjectivity and politics[86] as well as of history and modernity, on the basis of a renewed concept of life.[87] There have, moreover, been studies of the relation between man's historicity and his utopian destiny[88] as well as between suffering and that health ('great health') which is produced by self-overcoming in the face of suffering. According to this view, Nietzsche had developed through his understanding of health (which also encompassed sickness as the sublimation of individual suffering) a 'pathosophy' as a radical critique of modernity, which permitted the transition from Christian to tragic suffering. Although they work towards health, sickness and pain become, to him, moments of health.[89]

The secondary literature has, moreover, established a connection between Nietzsche's thought and the maturation process of modernity. In this way, the literature was hoping to arrive at a better understanding of modernity. These attempts were supported by the comparison of Nietzsche with those thinkers who, together with him, have contributed to shaping modernity. In this context, the evaluation of religion (and the phrase 'God is dead') plays as important a role as the opening of a new, post-metaphysical epoch. In the process, Nietzsche is not supposed to have reinforced either atheism against existing religions or nihilism against traditional metaphysics in the face of a completely developed rationality which was, moreover, carried by scientific progress. Instead, according to some critics, Nietzsche was concerned to clear up those hermeneutic processes by which religion and metaphysics define their objects. This unmasking aligned Nietzsche with Marx and Freud in particular, but also the Frankfurt School and postwar French philosophy.[90] There have also been studies comparing Nietzsche with apparently unconnected thinkers. For example, Nietzsche's view of love has been compared to Hölderlin's,[91] and Nietzsche's understanding of the 'Übermensch' has been compared to the thought of Sri Aurobindo.[92] There have also been attempts to demonstrate the presence of the Apollo-Dionysus conflict (as well as a more general Nietzschean influence) in some of Ernst Bloch's works (*Spirit of Utopia*, for example, *Legacy of Our Time* and *The Principle of Hope*).[93]

More precise details have also been gleaned of how Nietzsche established connections in his thought to the past and to the events of his own time. On the one hand, scholars have conducted new investigations into

Nietzsche's relations with ancient Greece and attempted to discover the importance to him of Greek decadence (of which Socrates is most important symptom) and hence what importance to attribute to the emergence of a rationality without beauty.[94] And, on the other hand, critics have been concerned with the problem of whether decadence can be restricted to the phenomenon of art and what role Greek *mousiké* plays in the context of a rebirth of art (in music). There have also been investigations of Nietzsche's attitude to the interpretations of Viennese classicism (and Beethoven's in particular) through Hanslinck, Wagner and Schopenhauer.[95]

Studies of Nietzsche's view of language have proved particularly fruitful in recent years. In the process the early Nietzsche's complex relations to the linguistic theories of Kant, Schopenhauer, Lange and, above all, Gustav Gerber (*Language as Art*, 2 vols (Bromberg, 1871–74)). In the context of these investigations, Nietzsche's writings 'On Theology' (1867–68), 'On the Origin of Language' (1869–70), as well as the lectures on rhetoric and the text 'On Truth and Lies in an Extra-Moral Sense' have all been interpreted more precisely.[96]

Ultimately, perhaps, no conclusions can be drawn. The interpretation of Nietzsche's thought has oscillated between the claim that it is absolutely not topical, indeed is 'only an artistic phenomenon', and the assertion that it is utterly topical, as the National Socialists argued, for instance. An oscillation of this kind is, however, part of his thought, whose topicality derives from its very non-topicality, in other words the way it denies access to any given 'period'. So the central aim of his thought is thus always elsewhere, in the 'suspicion' towards Being and its truth, which pursues and unmasks the genealogies of truth from which the world is made. A history of Nietzsche interpretations must therefore do justice to the interpretations of a given period, on the one hand, and track down the residual non-topicality in Nietzsche's thought, on the other, until this non-topicality ultimately reveals the problem of interpretation in his 'text'.

Notes

I. FROM PHILOLOGY TO PHILOSOPHY

1. Heidegger, *Nietzsche*, 2 Vols (Pfullingen, 1961).
2. Heidegger, op. cit., i, 76ff.
3. Dilthey, *Das Wesen der Philosophie*, ed. O. Pöggeler (Hamburg, 1984), p. 39.
4. For a divergent hermeneutic reading of Nietzsche, see J. Figl, 'Nietzsche und die philosophische Hermeneutik des 20. Jahrhunderts', *Nietzsche-Studien*, 10/11 (1981/82), 408–30. See also my lecture, 'Nietzsche and Contemporary Hermeneutics', *V. Philosophical Colloquium (Nietzsche as Affirmative Thinker)*, Jerusalem, April 1983.
5. C. P. Janz, *Nietzsche. Biographie*, 3 vols (Munich and Vienna, 1978–79), i, 254.
6. Janz, op. cit., i, 142–63.
7. The notes from the period when he was preparing the fourth *Untimely Meditation* and, in particular, the preliminary work on the fifth, *Wir Philologen*, are illuminating on this point.
8. See my *Ipotesi su Nietzsche* (Turin, 1967), Ch. 3.
9. For a detailed account of Nietzsche's attitude to German Romantic philosophy, see Charles Andler, *Nietzsche, sa vie et sa pensée* (Paris, 1958), Vol. i, Ch. 4 (first edn 1920–31).
10. See Andler, op. cit., Vol. i, Ch. 4.
11. See H. Jeanmaire, *Dionysos. Histoire du culte de Bacchus* (Paris, 1951).
12. Here and henceforth, italics in the text, unless otherwise

Notes

indicated, reflect the emphases (in expanded spacing) in Nietzsche's texts.

13. See Ulrich von Wilamowitz-Moellendorff, *Zukunftsphilologie! I und II* (Berlin, 1872–73).

14. For further discussion, see my *Il soggetto e la maschera. Nietzsche e il problema della liberazione*, second edn (Milan, 1983).

15. See Colli and Montinari's discussion of this issue in the commentary ('Nachbericht') to volume III.1 of *Nietzsche. Werke. Kritische Gesamtausgabe* (Berlin and New York, 1967ff).

16. *Science*: throughout BT, Nietzsche uses the term *Wissenschaft* to describe the rational pursuit of knowledge and truth in any field, not just the natural sciences – translator's note.

17. Cf. Janz, op. cit., Vol. i, and M. Montinari, 'Nietzsche contra Wagner: estate 1878', in E. Fubini (ed.), 'R. Wagner e F. Nietzsche. Atti del seminario tenuto al Goethe Institut mdi Torino il 10–11 marzo 1983', in *Quaderni di 'Musica e realtà'*, no. 4, Unicopli (Milan, 1984), pp. 73–85.

18. Cf. Thomas Mann, *Reflections of an Unpolitical Man* (1918).

19. Cf. M. Heidegger, *Sein und Zeit* [*Being and Time*], eleventh edition (Tübingen, 1967), §76, pp. 392–7. Benjamin quotes the second *Untimely Meditation* explicitly in his 'Über den Begriff der Geschichte' ['On the Concept of History'], in *Gesammelte Schriften* [*Collected Writings*], Vol. i, 2 (Frankfurt/M, 1980), p. 700.

20. cf. W. Benjamin, op. cit., These VIII, p. 696f.

21. Burckhardt's *Weltgeschichtliche Betrachtungen* [*World-Historical Reflections*] (Berlin and Stuttgart, 1905) was published posthumously by his pupil and nephew Jakob Oeri. They contain material from lectures Burckhardt delivered in Basle from 1868. Therefore Nietzsche may well have known Burckhardt's reflections in this lecture form. (cf. Janz, op. cit., Vol. i, 387).

Notes

II. THE DECONSTRUCTION OF METAPHYSICS

1. Heidegger, op. cit., ii, 259f.
2. Cf. Nietzsche's 'Attempt at a Self-Criticism' (the foreword to the new edition of *The Birth of Tragedy* of 1886) and Colli and Montinari's remarks at the end of Volume III.2, 387f. of the Italian edition of Nietzsche's works on *Su verita è menzogna* (*On Truth and Lies* ...). This commentary has yet to appear in the German (or indeed English) editions.
3. Cf. the remarks in the fourth *Untimely Meditation*; see also Janz's comments on the significance to Nietzsche of the first Bayreuth Festival, op. cit., i, 717ff.
4. On Nietzsche's purpose in acquiring knowledge of the natural sciences while in Basle, see Janz, op. cit., i, 555f., and K. Schlechta/A. Anders, *Nietzsche* (Stuttgart, 1962).
5. Cf. Andler, op. cit., i, 105–75, and W. D. Williams, *Nietzsche and the French* (Oxford, 1952).
6. The term 'deconstruction' has acquired a particular meaning in contemporary philosophy and literary criticism, above all with reference to the work of Jacques Derrida (cf. M. Ferraris, *La svolta testuale* (Pavia, 1984)). However, it may be used legitimately with reference to Nietzsche, because not only does a large part of contemporary deconstructionism invoke Nietzsche, but also and above all because his work (in its 'genealogical' more than in its 'critical' approach) leads to an analysis of the moral and metaphysical traditions of the West, which it dissolves into its elements without destroying them. And it is precisely there that the sense of deconstruction can be seen.
7. Nietzsche knew the work of Ludwig Feuerbach, whose book *Das Wesen des Christentums* [*The Essence of Christianity*] (Leipzig, 1841) he had read while still a schoolboy at Pforta.
8. 'Unconditional and honest atheism is simply the *presupposition* of the way he [Schopenhauer] poses his problem, this being a triumph achieved finally and with great difficulty by the European mind, the most fateful act of two thousand years of

Notes

discipline for truth, which in the end forbids itself the *lie* which is faith in God. One can see *what* really triumphed over the Christian god: Christian morality itself' (GS §357, 282).

9. It should be remembered that the first edition of *The Gay Science* in 1882 contained only four books (up to and including §342). Book Five, the preface and the 'Appendix: Songs of Prince Vogelfrei' were added to the 1887 edition.

10. See F. Massini, *Lo scriba del caos: Interpretazione di Nietzsche* (Bologna, 1978)

III. THE PHILOSOPHY OF ZARATHUSTRA

1. The distinction between a 'philosophy of Zarathustra' and Nietzsche's late thought can be found in Mazzino Montinari, *Che cosa ha veramente detto Nietzsche* (Rome, 1975), for example, a study which does not, however, tackle questions of periodization explicitly. The first edition of the work known as *The Will to Power*, edited by Ernst and August Horneffer, was published in 1901 by Naumann in Leipzig; it incorporated 483 fragments. The second edition, edited by Peter Gast and Nietzsche's sister (Elisabeth Förster-Nietzsche), appeared in 1906 and contained 1067 fragments. It was reissued, with minor alterations, by Kröner in 1911 and this became the 'definitive' edition. The work had been cobbled together by the editors on the basis of one of many draft proposals (and titles) that Nietzsche had envisaged in his last notebooks. But as Colli and Montinari were able conclusively to demonstrate (see the relevant notes to vols VI.3, VIII.1, and VIII.2 of the Italian edition – there is as yet no critical apparatus to vol VIII in German), Nietzsche had abandoned once and for all any intention of publishing a work with the title *The Will to Power* in August 1888. He published large parts of the material that he had already worked through in texts that appeared in the last years of his life, such as *The Antichrist* (1895) and *Twilight of the Idols* (1888).

208

Notes

2. C. P. Janz, *Friedrich Nietzsche: Biographie* (Munich and Vienna, 1978–79).

3. Nietzsche had invented this pseudonym for Köselitz, who wanted to make a name for himself as a composer, because he (Nietzsche) thought the pseudonym would appeal more to the public and help to spread his friend's fame.

4. Quoted in Janz, op. cit., ii, 75f. The same chapter in Janz documents a climate of transformation and 'prophetic' excitement characteristic of Nietzsche's life during these months.

5. Cf. Janz, op. cit., ii, 375 and 381f.

6. See the letters to Paul Deussen and Georg Brandes, quoted in Montinari, 1975, p. 127.

7. For further discussion of this issue, see Colli and Montinari's notes in the Italian edition (VIII.2, 426; VIII.1, 328) – these commentary volumes have yet to appear in German. See also Janz, op. cit., ii, 595.

8. Cf. Karl Löwith, *Nietzsches Philosophie der ewigen Wiederkunft des Gleichen* (Berlin, 1935), repr. as *Nietzsches Philosophie der ewigen Wiederkehr des Gleichen*, in K.L., *Sämtliche Schriften*, vol. vi (Stuttgart, 1987).

9. For further discussion of the significance of noontide in Nietzsche's work, see Karl Schlechta, *Nietzsches großer Mittag* (Frankfurt/M, 1954).

10. Cf. Löwith, 1987.

11. Cf. Löwith, 1987, Ch. 4.

12. For further discussion of the significance of Heidegger's concept of metaphysics, and for a fuller survey of his interpretation of Nietzsche, see my *Essere, storia e linguaggio in Heidegger* (Turin, 1963) and *Introduzione a Heidegger*, third edition (Rome and Bari, 1982).

13. That summer he had Overbeck send him the volume on Spinoza from Kuno Fischer's *Geschichte der neuern Philosophie* that he had borrowed from the Basle library; see Janz, op. cit., ii, 78.

14. See the letter to Overbeck quoted in Janz, op. cit., ii, 78.

15. See my *Il soggetto e la maschera*, op. cit., p. 249, where I refer

Notes

to a very beautiful passage concerning time in Nietzsche's *Philosophy in the Tragic Age of the Greeks*.

16. For a comprehensive survey of the problem of (dis)proving the doctrine of Eternal Recurrence, see Bernd Magnus, *Nietzsche's Existential Imperative* (Bloomington/Ind., 1978), in particular Ch. 4.

17. Montinari takes his cue from Henri Lichtenberger (*La philosophie de Nietzsche* (Paris, 1898)) and names, among other important 'precursors' of Nietzsche's theory of Eternal Recurrence, A. Blanqui's work of 1872, *L'éternité par les astres* (Montinari, 1975, pp. 91–3). It transpires from Nietzsche's notes, however, that he did not read it until 1883, by which time he had already formulated his theory of Eternal Recurrence.

18. I have attempted to provide a commentary on this discourse in *Il soggetto e la maschera*, op. cit., p. 195ff.

19. Nietzsche ascribes a dual significance to nihilism: on the one hand, it is passive or reactive in so far as it sees through the meaninglessness of the world and is thus prepared to take revenge upon and hate a life seen as lost. On the other hand, it is active in the sense that it is a feature of the Übermensch who deliberately establishes himself in the meaninglessness of the world for the purpose of creating new values in that world. On this point, see my *Il soggetto e la maschera*, op. cit., and a note of autumn 1887 (N Autumn 1887 – March 1888, VIII.2, 14–16, 9[35]).

20. Gilles Deleuze's Nietzsche interpretation is based above all on the antithesis 'active – reactive': see his *Nietzsche et la philosophie* (Paris, 1962), trans. as *Nietzsche und die Philosophie* (Munich, 1976). The problem of the 'criteria' was formulated in the terms we are following here in a paper entitled 'Nietzsche als affirmativer Denker' ['Nietzsche as Affirmative Thinker'] given by D. C. Hoy at the S. H. Bergman Center for Philosophical Studies in Jerusalem in April 1983. Hoy's paper 'Is Nietzsche's Genealogy a Feasible Philosophical Method Today?' has been published in the proceedings of the colloquium.

210

21. This is the position that D. C. Hoy appears to adopt in the paper we have already cited.
22. See the informative work by M. Cacciari ('L'impolitico nietzscheano'), in M. Beer and M. Ciampa (eds), *F. Nietzsche: Il libro del filosofo* (Rome, 1978), which contains contributions by M. Cacciari, F. Masini, S. Moravia and G. Vattimo.
23. Elsewhere I have set out the importance of art to an understanding of the Will to Power and attempted to avoid the the aporias of a 'technicistic' or 'neo-rationalist' reading of this concept, which drives Heidegger's interpretation of Nietzsche to extremes: cf. G. Vattimo, *Le avventure della differenza* (Milan, 1980), ch. 4.
24. For further discussion of the problem of 'great style' in Nietzsche's works and its reverberations in twentieth-century culture and literature, see the sensational remarks in C. Magris, *L'anello di Clarisse* (Turin, 1984), ch. 1.

V. HISTORY OF NIETZSCHE RECEPTION

1. R. F. Krummel, *Nietzsche und der deutsche Geist* [*Nietzsche and the German Mind*], 2 Vols (Berlin and New York, 1974; 1983).
2. R. Falkenberg, *Geschichte der neueren Philosophie von Nikolaus von Kues bis zur Gegenwart* [*History of Modern Philosophy from Nikolaus von Kues to the Present*] (Leipzig, 1886).
3. Cf. Bruno Hillebrand (ed.), *Nietzsche und die deutsche Literatur* [*Nietzsche and German Literature*] (Tübingen and Munich, 1978).
4. J. Möbius, *Nietzsche* (Leipzig, 1902).
5. Cf., above all, Franz Overbeck, 'Erinnerungen an F. Nietzsche' ['Memories of F. Nietzsche'], *Die neue Rundschau*, 17 (1906), 206–31, 320–30; J. Kaftan, 'Aus der Werkstatt des Übermenschen' ['Out of the Workshop of the "Übermensch"'], *Deutsche Rundschau*, 31 (1905), 90–110, 237–60; and the same author's *Das Christentum und Nietzsches Herrenmoral* [*Christianity*

Notes

and Nietzsche's Master Morality] (Berlin, 1897). For further discussion of Nietzsche and Kaftan, see C. P. Janz, *Nietzsche: Biographie*, 3 vols (Munich and Vienna, 1978–79), ii, 617–22.

6. Cf. Janz, op. cit., iii, 122.

7. For a discussion of Nietzsche's positive influence on theology, see P. Köster, 'Nietzsche-Kritik und Nietzsche-Rezeption in der Theologie des 20. Jahrhunderts' ['Nietzsche Criticism and Nietzsche Reception in the Theology of the Twentieth Century'], *Nietzsche-Studien*, 10/11 (1981–82), 615–85.

8. In the appendix to his book on Eternal Recurrence, Löwith describes Lou Salomé's text as the first significant attempt to come to terms with Nietzsche; see Karl Löwith, *Nietzsches Philosophie der ewigen Wiederkunft des Gleichen* (Berlin, 1935), repr. as *Nietzsches Philosophie der ewigen Wiederkehr des Gleichen*, in *Sämtliche Schriften* (Stuttgart, 1987), vol. 6.

9. Georg Brandes, 'Aristokratischer Radikalismus: Eine Abhandlung über F. Nietzsche' ['Aristocratic Radicalism: A Treatise on F. Nietzsche'], *Deutsche Rundschau*, 63 (1890), 52–99. The article had appeared in Danish the previous year.

10. Julius Langbehn, *Rembrandt als Erzieher. Von einem Deutschen* [*Rembrandt as Educator: By a German*] (Leipzig, 1890). For discussion of Langbehn's role after Nietzsche's breakdown, see Janz, op. cit., iii, 91–113. For a more general survey of Nietzsche's influence on the plastic arts, see D. Schubert, 'Nietzsche-Konkretionsformen in der bildenden Kunst 1890–1933: Ein Überblick' ['Nietzschean Instantiations in the Plastic Arts, 1890–1933: An Overview'], *Nietzsche-Studien*, 10/11 (1981–82), 278–317.

11. R. Schellwien, *Max Stirner und Nietzsche: Erscheinungen des modernen Geistes und das Wesen des Menschen* [*Max Stirner and Nietzsche: Phenomena of the Modern Spirit and the Essence of Man*] (Leipzig, 1892).

12. Cf. Janz, op. cit., iii, 212ff.

13. A. Drews, *Nietzsches Philosophie* (Heidelberg, 1904).

14. Alois Riehl, *Friedrich Nietzsche: Der Künstler und der Denker* [*Friedrich Nietzsche: The Artist and the Thinker*] (Stuttgart, 1897).

Notes

15. Ernst Horneffer, *Nietzsches Lehre von der ewigen Wiederkunft und deren bisherige Veröffentlichungen* [*Nietzsche's Doctrine of Eternal Recurrence and Publications of It To Date*] (Leipzig, 1900).

16. O. Ewald, *Nietzsches Lehre in ihren Grundbegriffen: Die ewige Wiederkunft des Gleichen und der Sinn des Übermenschen* [*Nietzsche's Teaching in its Essential Concepts: The Eternal Recurrence of the Same and the Meaning of the 'Übermensch'*] (Berlin, 1903).

17. Georg Simmel, *Schopenhauer und Nietzsche* (Leipzig, 1907).

18. Hans Vaihinger, *Nietzsche als Philosoph* [*Nietzsche as Philosopher*] (Berlin, 1902).

19. Karl Joël, *Nietzsche und die Romantik* [*Nietzsche and Romanticism*] (Jena, 1905).

20. The connection is discussed very thoroughly in three studies by Ernst Behler: 'Die Kunst der Reflexion: Das frühromantische Denken im Hinblick auf Nietzsche' ['The Art of Reflexion: Early Romantic Thought and Nietzsche'] in Benno von Wiese (ed.), *Untersuchungen zur Literatur als Geschichte* [*Examinations of Literature as History*], (Berlin, 1973), pp. 219–48; 'Nietzsches Auffassung der Ironie' ['Nietzsche's Conception of Irony'], *Nietzsche-Studien*, 4 (1975), 1–35; 'Friedrich Schlegels "Rede über die Mythologie" im Hinblick auf Nietzsche' ['Friedrich Schlegel's "Speech on Mythology" with Regard to Nietzsche'], *Nietzsche-Studien*, 8 (1979), 182–209.

21. Ernst Bertram, *Nietzsche: Versuch einer Mythologie* [*Nietzsche: Attempt at a Mythology*] (Berlin, 1918). Bertram's interpretation took on particular importance for Thomas Mann's understanding of Nietzsche; cf. B. Boeschenstein, 'Ernst Bertrams *Nietzsche* – eine Quelle für Thomas Manns *Doktor Faustus*' ['Ernst Bertram's *Nietzsche* – A Source for Thomas Mann's *Doktor Faustus*'], *Euphorion*, 72 (1978) H.1, 68–83; for a discussion of Nietzsche's role in the George Circle, see H. Raschel, *Das Nietzsche-Bild im George-Kreis: Ein Beitrag zur Geschichte der deutschen Mythologeme* [*The Image of Nietzsche in the George Circle: A Contribution to the History of German Mythologemes*] (Berlin and New York, 1983).

Notes

22. Ludwig Klages, *Die psychologischen Errungenschaften Friedrich Nietzsches* [*The Psychological Achievements of Friedrich Nietzsche*] (Leipzig, 1926).

23. Alfred Baeumler, *Nietzsche, der Philosoph und Politiker* [*Nietzsche, the Philosopher und Politician*], third edition (Leipzig, 1937); first edition, Leipzig, 1931.

24. Karl Jaspers, *Nietzsche: Einführung in das Verständnis seines Philosophierens* [*Nietzsche: An Introduction to Understanding his Philosophizing*] (Berlin, 1936); third edition, Berlin, 1950.

25. Karl Löwith, op. cit.

26. Martin Heidegger, *Nietzsche* 2 vols (Pfullingen, 1961); the work consists of (revised) lectures that Heidegger gave in Freiburg between 1935 and 1940 as well as essays written between 1940 and 1946.

27. For an excellent survey of Nietzsche's alleged responsibility for the rise and development of National Socialism, see E. Sandvoss, *Hitler und Nietzsche* (Göttingen, 1969).

28. F. G. Jünger, *Nietzsche* (Frankfurt/M, 1949).

29. Karl Löwith, 'Kierkegaard und Nietzsche oder philosophische und theologische Überwindung des Nihilismus' ['Kierkegaard and Nietzsche or the Philosophical and Theological Overcoming of Nihilism'], *Deutsche Vierteljahresschrift für Literaturwissenschaft und Geistesgeschichte*, 11 (1933), 43–66; and K. L., *Kierkegaard und Nietzsche oder philosophische und theologische Überwindung des Nihilismus* ['Kierkegaard and Nietzsche or the Philosophical and Theological Overcoming of Nihilism'] (Frankfurt/M, 1933); both repr. in *Sämtliche Schriften*, vol. 6 (Stuttgart, 1987). For a comprehensive survey of Nietzsche research since the Thirties, and in particular of the connections between Nietzsche's and Kierkegaard's thought, see W. Ries, *Grundzüge des Nietzsche-Verständnisses in der Deutung seiner Philosophie: Zur Geschichte der Nietzsche-Literatur in Deutschland (1932–1963)* [*The Main Tendencies of Nietzsche Interpretation: A Study of Nietzsche Literature in Germany (1932–1963)*], dissertation, University of Heidelberg, 1967.

30. W. Struve, *Die neuzeitliche Philosophie als Metaphysik der*

214

Notes

Subjektivität: Kierkegaard und Nietzsche [*Modern Philosophy as the Metaphysics of Subjectivity: Kierkegaard and Nietzsche*] (Freiburg I. B., 1949).

31. L. Giesz, *Nietzsches Existentialismus und Wille zur Macht* [*Nietzsche's Existentialism and Will to Power*] (Stuttgart, 1950).

32. W. Rehm, *Kierkegaard und der Verführer* [*Kierkegaard and the Seducer*] (Munich, 1949); Ch. 22 (pp. 513–22) is devoted to the opposition of Nietzsche and Kierkegaard.

33. Janko Lavrin, *Nietzsche: An Approach* (London, 1948)

34. H. Schoeck, *Nietzsches Philosophie des 'Menschlich-Allzumenschlichen': Kritische Darstellung der Aphorismen-Welt der mittleren Schaffenszeit als Versuch einer Neuorientierung des Gesamtbildes* [*Nietzsche's Philosophy of the 'Human-All Too Human': A Critical Account of the World of Aphorisms in the Middle Period as an Attempt to Reorientate the Whole Picture*] (Tübingen, 1948).

35. O. Flake, *Nietzsche: Rückblick auf eine Philosophie* [*Nietzsche: A Retrospective on a Philosophy*] (Baden-Baden, 1946).

36. W. Weymann-Weye, *Die Entscheidung des Menschen: Nietzsche als geschichtliche Wirklichkeit* [The Decision of Man: Nietzsche as Historical Reality] (Freiburg i. B., 1948).

37. E. Benz, 'Nietzsches Ideen zur Geschichte des Christentums und der Kirche' ['Nietzsche's Ideas on the History of Christianity and the Church'], *Zeitschrift für Kirchengeschichte*, 56 (1937), 169–312; second, revised edition, Leiden, 1956.

38. Karl-Heinz Volkmann-Schluck, 'Zur Gottesfrage bei Nietzsche' ['On the Question of God in Nietzsche's Work'], in *Leben und Denken: Interpretationen zur Philosophie Nietzsches* [*Life and Thought: Interpretations of Nietzsche's Philosophy*] (Frankfurt/M, 1968), pp. 25–47 (p. 40). This essay first appeared in *Anteile* (Frankfurt/M, 1950).

39. Karl Jaspers, *Nietzsche und das Christentum* [*Nietzsche and Christianity*] (Hameln, 1946); second edition, Munich, 1952.

40. W. Nigg, *Religiöse Denker* [*Religious Thinkers*] (Zurich, 1948), pp. 217–312; and *Prophetische Denker* [*Prophetic Thinkers*] (Zurich and Stuttgart, 1957), pp. 437–538.

Notes

41. Paul Tillich, *Sein und Sinn* [*Being and Meaning*], in *Gesammelte Werke* (Stuttgart, 1969), vol. xi, 132–9.

42. B. Welte, *Nietzsches Atheismus und das Christentum* [*Nietzsche's Atheism and Christianity*] (Darmstadt, 1958).

43. G-G. Grau, *Christlicher Glaube und intellektuelle Redlichkeit: Eine religions-philosophische Studie über Nietzsche* [*Christian Faith and Intellectual Honesty: A Study of Nietzsche in the Philosophy of Religion*] (Frankfurt/M, 1958).

44. H. Wein, *Positives Antichristentum: Nietzsches Christusbild im Brennpunkt nachchristlicher Anthropologie* [*Positive Antichristianity: Nietzsche's Image of Christ as the Focal Point of Postchristian Anthropology*] (Den Haag, 1962).

45. F. Ulrich, *Die Macht des Menschen bei Friedrich Nietzsche* [*The Power of Man in Friedrich Nietzsche*], in AA.VV: *Potere e responsabilità* (Brescia, 1963), pp. 154–98.

46. P. Valadier, *Nietzsche et la critique du christianisme* [*Nietzsche and the Critique of Christianity*] (Paris, 1974).

47. E. Biser, '*Gott ist tot': Nietzsches Destruktion des christlichen Bewußtseins* [*'God is dead': Nietzsche's Destruction of the Christian Consciousness*] (Munich, 1962).

48. H. Blumenberg, *Die Legitimität der Neuzeit* [*The Legitimacy of Modernity*] (Frankfurt/M, 1966).

49. Quoted in Blumenberg, op. cit., p. 95; this note dates back to 1872 and is part of Nietzsche's preparatory work on a text about the philosopher.

50. Friedrich Nietzsche, *Werke in drei Bänden* [*Works in Three Volumes*] (Munich, 1954–56); Schlechta's afterword can be found in Vol. iii, 1433–52.

51. Walter Kaufmann, *Nietzsche: Philosopher, Psychologist, Antichrist* (Princeton, 1950); new edition, New York, 1968.

52. Karl Schlechta, *Nietzsches großer Mittag* [*Nietzsche's Great Noontide*] (Frankfurt/M, 1954).

53. H. M. Wolff, *Friedrich Nietzsche: Der Weg zum Nichts* [*Friedrich Nietzsche: The Way to Nothingness*] (Berne, 1956).

54. Georg Lukács, *Die Zerstörung der Vernunft* [*The Destruction of*

Reason] (Berlin, 1954); repr. in *Werke* (Neuwied and Berlin, 1962), Vol. ix, 270–350.

55. For discussions of Nietzsche and the Frankfurt School, see: Heinz Röttges, *Nietzsche und die Dialektik der Aufklärung* [*Nietzsche and the Dialectic of Enlightenment*] (Berlin and New York, 1972); Peter Pütz, 'Nietzsche im Lichte der kritischen Theorie' ['Nietzsche in the Light of Critical Theory'], *Nietzsche-Studien*, 3 (1974), 175–91; R. Maurer, 'Nietzsche und die kritische Theorie' ['Nietzsche and Critical Theory'], *Nietzsche-Studien*, 10/11 (1981–82), 34–58.

56. See, for example, Peter Pütz, *Nietzsche*, Second Edition (Stuttgart, 1978), p. 106.

57. Eugen Fink, *Nietzsches Philosophie* [*Nietzsche's Philosophy*] (Stuttgart, 1960).

58. Charles Andler, *Nietzsche: sa vie et sa pensée* [*Nietzsche: His Life and his Thought*], 6 vols (Paris, 1920–31); new edition in three vols, Paris, 1958.

59. Georges Bataille, *Somme athéologique. III: Sur Nietzsche* [*Atheological Sum. III: On Nietzsche*] (Paris, 1945).

60. André Gide devoted one of the 'Lettres à Angèle' to Nietzsche's thought in the volume *Prétextes* (Paris, 1923), pp. 166–82; first edition, 1903.

61. Albert Camus, 'Nietzsche et le nihilisme' ['Nietzsche and Nihilism'], in *L'homme révolté* [*Man in Revolt*] (Paris, 1951).

62. Gilles Deleuze, *Nietzsche et la philosophie* [*Nietzsche and Philosophy*] (Paris, 1962).

63. Pierre Klossowski, *Nietzsche et le cercle vicieux* (Paris, 1969); translated as *Nietzsche and the Vicious Circle* (London, 1997).

64. J. Granier, *Le problème de la vérité dans la philosophie de Nietzsche* [*The Problem of Truth in Nietzsche's Philosophy*] (Paris, 1966).

65. B. Pautrat, *Versions du soleil* [*Versions of the Sun*] (Paris, 1971). For a discussion of 'French' interpretations of Nietzsche, see Gianni Vattimo, 'Nietzsche e il testo della metafisica', in *Riscoprire Nietzsche* (Palermo, 1980), pp. 99–128.

Notes

66. Philippe Lacoue-Labarthe, in *Nietzsche aujourd'hui?* [*Nietzsche Today?*] (Paris, 1973), vol. ii, p. 21. Recent Nietzsche interpretations, Pautrat's, for instance, or the late Sarah Kofman's, are heavily influenced by Derrida, who has often drawn upon Nietzsche in his writings, particularly in *Éperons: Les styles de Nietzsche* [*Spurs: Nietzsche's Styles*] (Venice, 1976).
67. D. Grlic, 'L'antiésthetisme de Friedrich Nietzsche' ['Friedrich Nietzsche's Anti-Aestheticism'], *Praxis*, 2 (1966), 338–42.
68. M. Djuric, 'Die geschichtliche Erfahrung des Nihilismus' ['The Historical Experience of Nihilism'], *Wiener Jahrbuch für Philosophie*, 8 (1975), 212–49. Two further articles by Djuric have appeared in *Nietzsche-Studien*. They deal with the ancient sources of the thought of Eternal Recurrence (1979) and with other aspects of Nietzsche's nihilism (1980).
69. Cf. Djuric, op. cit., p. 234.
70. See D. Jähnig, 'Nietzsches Kunstbegriff (erläutert an der "Geburt der Tragödie")' ['Nietzsche's Concept of Art (with reference to the "The Birth of Tragedy")'], *Beiträge zur Theorie der Künste im 19. Jahrhundert* (Frankfurt/M, 1972), Vol. ii, 29–68; and the same author's *Welt-Geschichte: Kunst-Geschichte: Zum Verhältnis von Vergangenheitserkenntnis und Veränderung* [*World-History: Art-History: On the Relationship between Recognition of the Past and Change*] (Cologne, 1975). Jähnig collected his thoughts on Nietzsche in this volume (pp. 68–196). His essays deal with Nietzsche's conception of history and the 'classical', as well as with Nietzsche's troubled relationship with Wagner.
71. See L. Giusso, *Leopardi, Stendhal e Nietzsche* (Naples, 1933); and the same author's *Nietzsche* (Naples, 1936), second edition, Milan, 1942.
72. A. Banfi, *Nietzsche* (Milan, 1974). D. Formaggio has published Banfi's 1933–34 lectures on Nietzsche as *Introduzione a Nietzsche* [*Introduction to Nietzsche*] (Milan, 1974).
73. G. Della Volpe, *Nietzsche e i problemi di un'estetica antiromantica* [*Nietzsche and the Problems of an Antiromantic Aesthetic*] (Messina, 1941).
74. E. Paci, *Friedrich Nietzsche* (Milan, 1940).

Notes

75. N. M. De Feo, *Analitica e dialettica in Nietzsche* [*Analytics and Dialectics in Nietzsche*] (Bari, 1965). For a survey of more recent Nietzsche interpretations in Italy, see A. Maggiore, 'Alcune recenti riletture di Nietzsche in Italia' ['Recent Rereadings of Nietzsche in Italy], *Rivista di storia della filosofia*, 39 (1984) n. 2, 303–22.

76. F. Masini, *Lo scriba del caos: Interpretazione di Nietzsche* (Bologna, 1978); this volume contains Masini's essays on Nietzsche since 1967.

77. G. Vattimo, *Il soggetto e la maschera: Nietzsche e il problema della liberazione* (Milan, 1974); *Ipotesi su Nietzsche* (Turin, 1967); and various essays in *Le avventure della differenza* (Milan, 1979) and *Al di là del soggetto: Nietzsche, Heidegger e l'ermeneutica* (Milan, 1981).

78. M. Cacciari, *Krisis: Saggio sulla crisi del pensiero negativo da Nietzsche a Wittgenstein* (Milan, 1976); *Pensiero negativo e razionalizzazione* (Venice, 1977); in addition, Cacciari, Masini, Moravia and Vattimo published four essays on Nietzsche in *Friedrich Nietzsche: Il libro del filosofo* (Rome, 1978).

79. Walter Müller-Lauter, *Nietzsche: Seine Philosophie der Gegensätze und die Gegensätze seiner Philosophie* [*Nietzsche: His Philosophy of Antitheses and the Antitheses of his Philosophy*] (Berlin and New York, 1971).

80. F. Kaulbach, *Nietzsches Idee einer Experimentalphilosophie* [*Nietzsche's Idea of an Experimental Philosophy*] (Cologne and Vienna, 1980).

81. J. Figl, *Interpretation als philosophisches Prinzip: Friedrich Nietzsches universale Theorie der Auslegung im späten Nachlaß* [*Interpretation as Philosophical Principle: Friedrich Nietzsche's Universal Theory of Interpretation in the Late Nachlass*] (Berlin and New York, 1982).

82. G. Picht, *Nietzsche*, ed. C. Eisenbart and E. Rudolph (Stuttgart, 1988); K. H. Volkmann-Schluck, *Die Philosophie Nietzsches: Der Untergang der abendländischen Metaphysik* [*Nietzsche's Philosophy: The Decline of Western Metaphysics*], ed. B. Heimbüchel (Würzburg, 1991).

83. L. Alfieri, *Apollo tra gli schiavi: La filosofia sociale e politica di Nietzsche (1869–1876)* (Milan, 1984); B. H. F. Taurek, *Nietzsche und der Faschismus: Eine Studie über Nietzsches politische Philosophie und ihre Folgen* [*Nietzsche and Fascism: A Study of Nietzsche's Political Philosophy and Its Consequences*] (Hamburg, 1989); K. Brose, *Sklavenmoral: Nietzsches Sozialphilosophie* [*Slave Morality: Nietzsche's Social Philosophy*] (Bonn, 1990).

84. C. Türcke, *Der tolle Mensch: Nietzsche und der Wahnsinn der Vernunft* [*The Madman: Nietzsche and the Madness of Reason*] (Frankfurt/M, 1989).

85. H. Kreß, *Ethische Werte und der Gottesgedanke: Probleme und Perspecktiven des neuzeitlichen Wertbegriffs* [*Ethical Values and the Thought of God: Problems and Perspectives of the Modern Concept of Value*] (Cologne, 1990).

86. Mark Warren, *Nietzsche and Political Thought* (Cambridge/ Mass. and London, 1988).

87. E. Mazzarella, *Nietzsche e la storia: Storicità e ontologia della vita* (Naples, 1983).

88. V. Vitiello, *Utopia del nichilismo: Tra Nietzsche e Heidegger* (Naples, 1983).

89. Th. Velt, *Die Bedeutung des Leidens für den Menschen: Nietzsches Leidenskonzept einer tragischen Moderne* [*The Meaning of Suffering for Man: Nietzsche's Conception of Suffering of a Tragic Modernity*] (Berne, Frankfurt/M and New York, 1988).

90. W. Steinde, *Friedrich Nietzsche und der moderne Atheismus* [*Friedrich Nietzsche and Modern Atheism*] (Stuttgart, 1981); W. L. Newell, *The Secular Magi: Marx, Freud and Nietzsche on Religion* (New York, 1986); G. Stauth and B. Turner, *Nietzsche's Dance: Resentment, Reciprocity and Resistance in Social Life* (Oxford and New York, 1988).

91. C. Littek, *Versöhnungs-Ontologie: Zum Liebesbegriff Hölderlins und Nietzsches* [*Ontology of Reconciliation: On Hölderlin's and Nietzsche's Concept of Love*] (Düsseldorf, 1985).

92. W. Huchzermeyer, *Der Übermensch bei Friedrich Nietzsche und Sri Aurobindo* [*The Übermensch in the Thought of Friedrich Nietzsche and Sri Aurobindo*] (Gladbach, 1986).

Notes

93. H. Gekle, *Die Tränen des Apoll: Zur Bedeutung des Dionysos in der Philosophie Ernst Blochs* [*The Tears of Apollo: On the Importance of Dionysos in Ernst Bloch's Philosophy*] (Tübingen, 1990).
94. V. Tejera, *Nietzsche and Greek Thought* (Dordrecht, Boston and Lancaster, 1987); H. Schmid, *Nietzsches Gedanke der tragischen Erkenntnis* [*Nietzsche's Thought of Tragic Insight*] (Würzburg, 1984) and *Nietzsche und die philosophische Tradition* [*Nietzsche and the Philosophical Tradition*], 2 vols (Würzburg, 1985).
95. B. Schmidt, *Der ethische Aspekt der Musik: Nietzsches 'Geburt der Tragödie' und die Wiener klassische Musik* [*The Ethical Aspect of Music: Nietzsche's 'Birth of Tragedy' and Viennese Classical Music*] (Würzburg, 1981).
96. Thomas Böning, *Metaphysik, Kunst und Sprache beim frühen Nietzsche* [*Metaphysics, Art and Language in the Early Nietzsche*] (Berlin and New York, 1988); A. Meijers and H. Stingelin, 'Konkordanz zu den wörtlichen Abschriften und Übernahmen von Beispielen und Zitaten aus Gustav Gerber: "Die Sprache als Kunst"' ['Concordance to the Literal Copies and Borrowings of Examples and Quotations from Gustav Gerber's "Die Sprache als Kunst"'], *Nietzsche-Studien*, 17 (1988), 350ff.; A. Meijers, 'Gustav Gerber und Friedrich Nietzsche: Zum historischen Hintergrund der sprachphilosophischen Auffassungen des frühen Nietzsche' ['Gustav Gerber and Friedrich Nietzsche: On the Historical Background to the Early Nietzsche's Views on Linguistic Philosophy'], *Nietzsche-Studien*, 17 (1988), 369ff.; C. Crawford, *The Beginnings of Nietzsche's Theory of Language* (Berlin and New York, 1988).

Bibliography

1. BIBLIOGRAPHICAL WORKS

A bibliographical compilation of Nietzsche's works can be found in 'Verzeichnis der bis 1939 erschienenen Ausgaben der Werke, Kompositionen und Briefe Nietzsches' ['Index of the pre-1939 Editions of Nietzsche's Works, Compositions and Letters'], which appeared in Weimar in the 1939 Yearbook of the Nietzsche Archive Foundation[*Jahresheft für 1939 der Stiftung Nietzsche-Archiv*]. Fundamental to the secondary literature is the *International Nietzsche Bibliography*, edited by H. W. Reichert and Karl Schlechta (Chapel Hill, 1960). An expanded second edition appeared in 1968. For the period 1968–72, Reichert prepared a new edition which was published in the second volume of *Nietzsche-Studien* (1973). This journal has appeared annually, published by de Gruyter in Berlin and edited by Mazzino Montinari, Walter Müller-Lauter and Heinz Wenzel. It includes articles and reviews covering the latest developments in Nietzsche studies.

Detailed coverage of secondary material on Nietzsche can also be found in: Karl Löwith, *Nietzsches Philosophie der ewigen Wiederkunft des Gleichen* (Berlin, 1935), which has been reprinted as *Nietzsches Philosophie der ewigen Wiederkehr des Gleichen*; Löwith's *Sämtliche Schriften*, vol. vi (Stuttgart, 1987) – for the period 1894–1954; Walter Kaufmann, *Nietzsche: Philosopher, Psychologist, Antichrist*, third edition (New York, 1968); and Gianni Vattimo, *Ipotesi su Nietzsche* (Turin, 1967) – for the period 1945–66.

Apart from the reviews in *Nietzsche-Studien*, references to the

Bibliography

most recent secondary literature can be found in the 'Bulletin
Nietzschéen' which has appeared at irregular intervals since 1971,
is edited by P. Valadier and published in the *Archives de Philosophie*.
In 1981 and 1982, B. Lypp produced a two-part survey of the most
recent publications on Nietzsche in the *Philosophische Rundschau*.

2. EDITIONS OF WORKS AND CORRESPONDENCE

The first comprehensive edition of Nietzsche's works was published by the Nietzsche Archive in Weimar, whose first director
was Nietzsche's sister, Frau Elisabeth Förster-Nietzsche. This
edition is generally known as the 'Großoktavausgabe' (royal octavo
edition) and appeared from 1895 to 1926, published by Naumann
in Leipzig. It also exists in small octavo format with the same
pagination, though volumes 17 to 19 of the larger edition are not
reproduced here. It is divided into three sections: volumes 1–8
contain the published writings as well as those which Nietzsche
himself had prepared for publication; volumes 9–16 contain the
posthumously published texts, though the 'definitive' edition of *The
Will to Power* appeared separately (in small octavo format) in 1906
with 1,067 aphorisms; and volumes 17–19 contain the philological
writings. The edition was completed in 1926 with the appearance
of an index volume. Another edition frequently referred to is the
23-volume Musarion edition (1920–29), edited by Richard and Max
Oehler. Its last two volumes contain an index.

In 1933 the Nietzsche Archive began a *Historisch-Kritische
Gesamtausgabe* [*Historical-Critical Complete Edition*] of Nietzsche's
works and correspondence, published by C. H. Beck in Munich.
Five volumes of works and four of letters were published. One of
the editors was Karl Schlechta who, after the Second World War,
presented a new, 3-volume edition of all Nietzsche's works and a
selection of his letters (Friedrich Nietzsche, *Werke in drei Bänden*
[Munich: Hanser, 1956], with an index in a fourth volume [1965]).
The significance of Schlechta's edition lay in its chronological

Bibliography

presentation of not only the works published by Nietzsche himself but also of all the material that Elisabeth Förster-Nietzsche and Peter Gast, who followed only one of Nietzsche's many sketches, had arbitrarily assembled in 1906 as *The Will to Power*. When conceiving this controversial edition (see the November 1957 and August 1958 numbers of *Merkur*), Schlechta (rightly) assumed that in the last months of his conscious life Nietzsche had abandoned the idea of putting together a systematic *magnum opus* from his many notes and that the 'systematic work' produced by his sister and Peter Gast in 1906 was thus a forgery. Furthermore, Schlechta put forward the argument (which attracted the most controversy) that Nietzsche's late unpublished notes of 1887–89 contained nothing substantially new, when compared to his published works (cf. Schlechta [1956], vol iii, 1402).

In the Colli-Montinari edition all of Nietzsche's writings and notes are reproduced in chronological order. This 40-volume edition, the publication of which was begun by de Gruyter in Berlin in 1967 and almost simultaneously by Adelphi in Milan, is divided chronologically into eight large sections, with a commentary volume to accompany each section. By the end of 1999, 32 of the projected 40 volumes had appeared, including all of Nietzsche's published writings and the unpublished material from 1869 to 1889.*

Plan of the Colli-Montinari Edition
Sect. I   Early and Philological Writings before Spring 1868
Sect. II   Philological Writings and Lecture Notes 1867–79
Sect. III   *The Birth of Tragedy, Untimely Meditations I–III,* Unpublished Writings and Notes 1869–73
Sect. IV   *Untimely Meditations IV, Human All Too Human,* Unpublished Fragments 1875–79
Sect. V   *Daybreak, Idylls from Messina, The Gay Science,* Unpublished Fragments 1880 – July 1882

---

* The translator has updated this information to take account of publication progress since Vattimo's work appeared in 1985.

Bibliography

A special 15-volume paperback edition of Nietzsche's works, based on the Colli-Montinari edition, was published in 1980. It does not include Nietzsche's unpublished writings before 1869, his philological writings or his Basle lectures. In other words, it does not contain the first two sections of the hardback edition. The publication of Nietzsche's correspondence began in 1975, once again edited by Colli and Montinari and published by de Gruyter and Adelphi. It contains three sections, covering the periods 1844–69, 1869–79 and 1880–89 respectively. All three sections have now been published. The only volume yet to appear by the end of 1999 was the commentary volume to the third section, which will include an index to the whole edition. (An eight volume paperback edition of Nietzsche's letters [*Kritische Studienausgabe der Sämtlichen Briefe*] was published by de Gruyter and dtv in 1986.) A fourth section of the larger edition, containing five volumes, is proposed. The plan is to publish letters between third parties in which Nietzsche is mentioned, as well as other documents relating to his life (1844–1900). In the Italian editions of Nietzsche's works and correspondence there are no separate commentary volumes. Instead each volume contains an appendix with notes.

The only comprehensive edition of Nietzsche's correspondence before Colli and Montinari's and the four volumes of the *Historical-Critical Complete Edition* mentioned above, which only go as far as 1877, was the Nietzsche Archive's edition of collected letters [*F. Nietzsche's Gesammelte Briefe*]. It comprises five volumes, the last of which is divided into two parts, and the correspondence is organised by recipient. Volumes I–III were published by Schuster and Loeffler in Berlin and Leipzig (1900–4) and the remaining two by Insel in Leipzig (1907–9). This collection did not include the

225

Bibliography

correspondence with Franz Overbeck, which was published separately by Richard Oehler and C. A. Bernouilli with the title Friedrich Nietzsche, *Briefwechsel mit Franz Overbeck* (Leipzig: Insel, 1916). A thorough study of the editorial problems surrounding Nietzsche's letters has been undertaken by C. P. Janz (*Die Briefe Friedrich Nietzsches: Textprobleme und ihre Bedeutung für Biographie und Doxographie* [Zurich, 1972]). Janz has also published all of Nietzsche's musical compositions in *Friedrich Nietzsche: Der musikalische Nachlaß* (Basle, 1976).

3. SECONDARY LITERATURE

a) Biographical Studies

In addition to the extensive and detailed notes on the individual volumes of the Colli-Montinari edition, the following (in order of their appearance) are the most important studies of Nietzsche's life:

Andreas-Salomé, Lou, *Friedrich Nietzsche in seinen Werken* (Vienna, 1894; second edn, Dresden 1924; new edn Frankfurt/M, 1983).

Förster-Nietzsche, Elisabeth, *Das Leben Friedrich Nietzsches* (3 vols, Leipzig, 1895; second edn, Leipzig, 1904).

Deussen, Paul, *Erinnerungen an Friedrich Nietzsche* (Leipzig, 1901).

Bernoulli, C. A., *Nietzsche und Overbeck* (2 vols, Jena, 1908).

Halévy, Daniel, *La vie de Nietzsche* (Paris, 1909, enlarged new edn 1944).

Stroux, J., *Nietzsches Professur in Basel* (Jena, 1925).

Schever, F., *Nietzsche als Student* (Bonn, 1933).

Andler, Charles, *Nietzsche: Sa vie et sa pensée* (6 vols, Paris, 1920–31; new edn in 3 vols, Paris, 1958). [A standard work].

Podach, Ernst, *Nietzsches Zusammenbruch: Beiträge zu einer Biographie auf Grund unveröffentlichter Dokumente* (Heidelberg, 1930).

—— *Gestalten um Nietzsche: Mit unveroffentlichten Dokumenten zur Geschichte seines Lebens und seines Werkes* (Weimar, 1932).

226

Bibliography

Förster-Nietzsche, Elisabeth, *Nietzsche und die Frauen seiner Zeit*, with notes by Karl Schlechta (Munich, 1935).

Podach, Ernst, *Der kranke Nietzsche: Briefe seiner Mutter an Franz Overbeck* (Vienna, 1937). [Nietzsche's mother's letters to Overbeck, 1889–97.]

Würzbach, Friedrich, *Nietzsche: Sein Leben in Selbstzeugnissen, Briefen und Berichten* (Berlin, 1942).

Zahn, L., *Friedrich Nietzsche: Eine Lebenschronik* (Darmstadt, 1950).

Blunck, R., *Friedrich Nietzsche: Kindheit und Jugend* (Munich and Basle, 1953).

Frenzel, Ivo, *Friedrich Nietzsche in Selbstzeugnissen und Bilddokumenten* (Hamburg, 1966).

Schlechta, Karl, *Nietzsche-Chronik: Daten zu Leben und Werk* (Munich and Vienna, 1975).

Peters, H. F., *Zarathustra's Sister: The Case of Elisabeth and Friedrich Nietzsche* (New York, 1977).

Janz, Curt Paul, *Nietzsche: Biographie*, 3 vols (Munich and Vienna, 1978–79). [The first part of the first volume consists of Blunck, op. cit.]

Verrecchia, A., *La catastrofe di Nietzsche a Torino* (Turin, 1978).

Ross, Werner, *Der ängstliche Adler: Friedrich Nietzsches Leben* (Stuttgart, 1980).

Specific Biographical Aspects

Nietzsche's Illness

Steiner, Rudolf, 'Die Philosophie Nietzsches als psychopathologisches Problem', *Wiener klinische Rundschau* (1900), repr. in *Friedrich Nietzsche: Ein Kämpfer gegen seine Zeit* (Dornach, 1926).

Ireland, W., 'Friedrich Nietzsche: A study in mental pathology', *Journal of Mental Science*, 47 (1901), 1–28.

Moebius, P. J., *Über das Pathologische bei Nietzsche* (Wiesbaden, 1902).

Bibliography

Gould, G., 'The origins of the ill health of Nietzsche', in *Biographic Clinicis* (Philadelphia, 1903), ii, 285–322.

Hildebrandt, Kurt, 'Der Beginn von Nietzsches Geisteskrankheit', *Zeitschrift für die gesamte Neurologie und Psychiatrie*, 89 (1924), 283–309.

Benda, E., 'Nietzsches Krankheit', *Monatsschrift für Psychiatrie und Neurologie*, 60 (1925), 65–80.

Hildebrandt, Kurt, *Gesundheit und Krankheit in Nietzsches Leben und Werk* (Berlin, 1926).

Lange-Eichbaum, W., *Nietzsche: Krankheit und Wirkung* (Hamburg, 1946).

Podach, E. F., *Friedrich Nietzsches Werke des Zusammenbruchs* (Heidelberg, 1961) [A new edition of Nietzsche's last four works: *Nietzsche contra Wagner*, *Der Antichrist*, *Dionysos-Dithyramben* and *Ecce Homo*, and the text of *Ecce Homo* was completely rearranged for this edition. Podach wanted to demonstrate that Nietzsche's late works were connected to his mental illness. Cf. also the next entry.]

—— *Ein Blick in Notizbücher Nietzsches* (Heidelberg, 1963) [Podach's claims are critically discussed in the following two works].

Heftrich, Eckhard, 'Die Grenzen der psychologischen Nietzsche-Erklärung', *Revue internationale de philosophie*, 1, Nr. 67 (1964), 74–90.

Champromis, P., 'Nietzsches Werke des Zusammenbruchs oder Zusammenbruch der editorischen Werke Podachs', *Philosophische Rundschau* (1964–65), 246–63.

Nietzsche's Relations with Wagner

Kulke, E., *Richard Wagner und Friedrich Nietzsche* (Leipzig, 1890).

Bellaigue, C., 'L'évolution musicale de Nietzsche', *Revue des deux mondes* (1905), 898–923.

Glasenapp, C. F., *Das Leben Richard Wagners*, vols iv–vi (Leipzig, 1905–11).

Bélart, H., *Nietzsches Freundschaftstragödie mit Richard Wagner und Cosima Wagner-Liszt* (Dresden, 1912).

Bibliography

Förster-Nietzsche, Elisabeth, *Wagner und Nietzsche zur Zeit ihrer Freundschaft* (Munich, 1915).

Stefan, P., *Die Feindschaft gegen Wagner: Eine geschichtliche und psychologische Untersuchung* (Regensburg, 1919). [For discussion of Nietzsche, see pp. 24–60.]

Griesser, L., *Nietzsche und Wagner: Neue Beiträge zur Geschichte und Psychologie ihrer Freundschaft*, Vienna, 1923.

Verweyen, J. M., *Wagner und Nietzsche*, Stuttgart, 1926.

Abraham, G., 'Friedrich Nietzsche's Attitude toward Richard Wagner', *Music and Letters* [London], 13 (1932), 64–74.

Dippel, P., *Nietzsche und Wagner: Eine Untersuchung über die Grundlagen und Motive ihrer Trennung* (Berne, 1934).

Fehr, M., *Richard Wagners Schweizer Zeit*, Vol. ii [1855–72] (Frankfurt/M., 1953).

Love, Frederick R., *Young Nietzsche and the Wagnerian Experience* (Chapel Hill/NC, 1963).

Hollinrake, Roger, 'Nietzsche and Wagner's Parsifal', *Oxford German Studies*, 4 (1969), 118–41.

Fubini, E. (ed.), *Richard Wagner e Friedrich Nietzsche* (Milan, 1984) (Quaderni di 'Musica e realta', 4).

Further Aspects of Nietzsche's Biography and Educational Development

Fouillée, A., 'Les jugements de Nietzsche sur Guyau d'après des documents inédits', *Revue de philosophie de la France et de l'étranger*, 52 (1901), 569–99.

Crusius, O., *Erwin Rohde: Ein biographischer Versuch* (Tübingen, 1902).

Joël, Carl, *Nietzsche und die Romantik* (Jena. 1905).

Faguet, E.: 'Nietzsche et les femmes', *Revue des deux mondes* (1912), 81–95.

Binder, E., *Malwida von Meysenbug und Friedrich Nietzsche*, Berlin, 1917.

Hirsch, E., 'Nietzsche und Luther', *Jahrbuch der Gesellschaft* (1921), 61–106.

229

Bibliography

Strecker, K., *Nietzsche und Strindberg: Mit ihrem Briefwechsel*, Munich, 1921.

Clisson, E., 'Nietzsche et Bizet', *Revue musicale*, 1922 (May), 147–54.

Klein, J., 'Nietzsche and Bizet', *Musical Quarterly*, 1925 (October), 482–505.

Bouillier, V., 'Baltasar Graciàn et Nietzsche', *Revue de la littérature comparée*, 6 (1926), 381–401.

Wahnes, G. H., *H. von Stein und sein Verhältnis zu Richard Wagner und Friedrich Nietzsche* (Leipzig, 1926).

Adam, Margarete, 'Nietzsches Stellung zur Frau', *Die Frau* [Berlin] (1929), 329–35.

Baeumler, Alfred, *Bachofen und Nietzsche* (Zurich, 1929), repr. in A. B., *Studien zur deutschen Geistesgeschichte* (Berlin, 1937).

Brann, H. W, *Nietzsche und die Frauen* (Leipzig, 1931); second edn, Bonn 1978.

Gaby, V., *Malwida de Meysenbug, sa vie et ses amis* (Paris, 1932).

Giusso, L., *Leopardi, Stendhal e Nietzsche* (Naples, 1932).

Kolpaktschy, G. and De La Herverie, B., 'Le mot d'une énigme: la source maçonnique de "Ainsi parlait Zarathustra"', *Mercure de France* (1934), 498–510.

Podach, Ernst, *Friedrich Nietzsche und Lou Salomé: Ihre Begegnung 1882* (Zurich, 1938).

Salin, Edgar, *Jacob Burckhardt und Nietzsche* (Basle, 1938).

Martin, Alfred von, *Nietzsche und Burckhardt* (Munich, 1941).

Oehler, Max, *Nietzsches Bibliothek* (Weimar, 1942).

Bluhm, H., 'Das Lutherbild des jungen Nietzsche', *Publications of the Modern Language Association of America*, 58 (1943), 264–88.

Williams, W. D., *Nietzsche and the French* (Oxford, 1952) [the importance of French writers and thinkers to Nietzsche's development].

Gerber, H. E., *Nietzsche und Goethe* (Berne, 1954).

Baumgartner, E., *Das Vorbild Emersons in Werk und Leben Nietzsches* (Heidelberg, 1957).

Champromis, P., 'Nietzsche devant la culture française', *Romanische Forschungen*, 68 (1957), 74–115.

230

Bibliography

Binion, R., *Frau Lou: Nietzsche's Wayward Disciple* (Princeton, 1968).

Dickopp, K. H., 'Zum Wandel von Nietzsches Selbstverständnis', *Zeitschrift für philosophische Forschung*, 24 (1970), 50–71.

Bludau, B., *Frankreich im Werk Nietzsches: Geschichte und Kritik der Einflußthese* (Bonn, 1979).

Böning, Thomas, *Metaphysik, Kunst und Sprache beim frühen Nietzsche* (Berlin and New York, 1988).

Meijers, A., and H. Stingelin, 'Konkordanz zu den wörtlichen Abschriften und Übernahmen von Beispielen und Zitaten aus Gustav Berber: Die Sprache als Kunst', *Nietzsche-Studien*, 17 (1988), 350 ff.

Diethe, Carol, *Nietzsche's Women: Beyond the Whip* (Berlin and New York, 1996).

b) Studies of Nietzsche's Philosophy

This part of the bibliography is divided into three sections: the first (A) contains a list of the most important works on Nietzsche's philosophy. It also includes works with a marked theoretical bias, such as those by Jaspers and Heidegger; the second (B) contains studies representative of *philosophical engagement* with Nietzsche's writings, in other words studies that are more 'theoretically' than 'historically' orientated; the final section (C) lists works whose animus is less philosophical but which are nevertheless indispensable to an understanding of Nietzsche's impact in the twentieth century.

A

In addition to the works already listed above by Charles Andler, Lou Salomé and Curt Paul Janz, the following studies must be mentioned:

Eisler, R., *Nietzsches Erkenntnistheorie und Metaphysik* (Leipzig, 1902).

Bibliography

Ewald, O., *Nietzsches Lehre in ihren Grundbegriffen: Die ewige Wiederkehr des Gleichen und der Sinn des Übermenschen* (Berlin, 1903).

Drews, A., *Nietzsches Philosophie* (Heidelberg, 1904).

Hofmiller, Josef, *Versuche* (Munich, 1909); new edn entitled *Letzte Versuche*, Munich, 1952.

Scheler, M., *Abhandlungen und Aufsätze*, 2 vols (Leipzig, 1915).

Bertram, Ernst, *Nietzsche: Versuch einer Mythologie* (Berlin, 1918); eighth edn including unpublished manuscripts, ed. H. Buchner, Bonn, 1965.

Römer, H., *Nietzsche*, 2 vols (Leipzig, 1921).

Heckel, K., *Nietzsche: Sein Leben und seine Lehre* (Leipzig, 1922).

Banfi, A., *Nietzsche* (Milan, 1924).

Klages, Ludwig, *Die psychologischen Errungenschaften Friedrich Nietzsches* (Leipzig, 1926).

Baeumler, Alfred, *Nietzsche, der Philosoph und der Politiker* (Leipzig, 1931).

Hofmiller, Josef, *Friedrich Nietzsche* (Lübeck, 1933), repr. Hamburg, 1947.

Löwith, Karl, *Nietzsches Philosophie der ewigen Wiederkunft des Gleichen* (Berlin, 1935); reissued as *Nietzsches Philosophie der ewigen Wiederkehr des Gleichen*, in K.L., *Sämtliche Schriften* (Stuttgart, 1987), vol. vi.

Giusso, L., *Nietzsche* (Naples, 1936).

Jaspers, Karl, *Nietzsche: Einführung in das Verständnis seines Philosophierens* (Berlin, 1936).

Heintel, E., *Nietzsches 'System' in seinen Grundbegriffen* (Leipzig, 1939).

Paci, E., *Friedrich Nietzsche* (Milan, 1940) [an anthology with a substantial introduction].

Brinton, Crane, *Nietzsche* (Cambridge, Mass., 1941); new edn, New York 1965.

Morgan, G. A., *What Nietzsche Means* (New York, 1941); new edn, New York 1965.

Copleston, Frederick, *Friedrich Nietzsche: Philosopher of Culture* (London, 1942).

232

Bibliography

Kaufmann, Walter A., *Nietzsche: Philosopher, Psychologist, Antichrist* (Princeton, 1950); new edn, New York and Princeton, 1968.

Heimsoeth, Heinz, *Metaphysische Voraussetzungen und Antriebe in Nietzsches Immoralismus* (Wiesbaden, 1955).

Schlechta, Karl, *Der Fall Nietzsche* (Munich, 1958).

Wolff, H. M., *Friedrich Nietzsche: Der Weg zum Nichts* (Berne, 1956).

Fink, Eugen, *Nietzsches Philosophie* (Stuttgart, 1960).

Heidegger, Martin, *Nietzsche*, 2 vols (Pfullingen, 1961).

Heftrich, Eckhard, *Nietzsches Philosophie: Identität von Welt und Nichts* (Frankfurt/M, 1962).

Ulmer, K., *Nietzsche: Einheit und Sinn seines Werks* (Berne, 1962).

Schlechta, Karl, and Anders, Anni, *Nietzsche* (Stuttgart, 1962).

Deleuze, Gilles, *Nietzsche et la philosophie* (Paris, 1962).

Danto, A. C., *Nietzsche as Philosopher* (New York, 1965).

Morel, G., *Nietzsche: Introduction à une première lecture*, 3 vols (Paris, 1971).

Hollingdale, R. J., *Nietzsche* (London, 1973).

Baroni, C., *Ce que Nietzsche a vraiment dit* (Paris, 1975).

Montinari, Mazzino, *Che cosa ha veramente detto Nietzsche* (Roma, 1975).

Chaix-Ruy, J., *Pour connaître la pensée de Nietzsche* (Paris, 1977).

Picht, Georg, *Nietzsche*, ed. C. Eisenbart and E. Rudolph (Stuttgart, 1988).

Volkmann-Schluck, Karl-Heinz, *Die Philosophie Nietzsches: Der Untergang der abendländischen Metaphysik*, ed. B. Heimbüchel (Würzburg, 1991).

The following journal numbers and collections of essays also contain important contributions to an understanding of Nietzsche's work:

Revue internationale de Philosophie, 67/1 (1964).

Nietzsche: Actes du VII colloque international de philosophie, Juillet 1964 (Paris, 1967).

Bibliography

Revue philosophique de la France et de l'Étranger, 96/3 (1971).
Nietzsche aujourd'hui?: Actes du colloque international de Cérisy-La-Salle, Juillet 1972 (Paris, 1973).
Il caso Nietzsche (Cremona, 1973).
Nuova Corrente, 68–9 (1979).
Salaquarda, Jörg (ed.), *Nietzsche* (Darmstadt, 1980).
Marini, A. (ed.), *Amicizie stellari* (Milan, 1982).
Nietzsche: verità-interpretazione: Atti del convegno di Rapallo, dicembre 1982 (Genoa, 1983).

B

Riehl, Alois, *Friedrich Nietzsche: Der Künstler und der Denker* (Stuttgart, 1897).
Ziegler, Th., *Friedrich Nietzsche* (Berlin, 1900).
Lasserre, Pierre, *La morale de Nietzsche* (Paris, 1902).
Vaihinger, Hans, *Nietzsche als Philosoph* (Berlin, 1902).
Rensi, G., *Studi e note* (Milan, 1903).
—— 'L'immoralismo di Friedrich Nietzsche', *Rivista ligure* (1906), no. 5, 287–322.
Sestov, L., *Tolstoi und Nietzsche* (Cologne, 1923) (Russian edn, St Petersburg, 1907).
—— *La filosofia della tragedia: Dostoevskij e Nietzsche* (Naples, 1950) (Russian edn, St Petersburg 1909).
Grützmacher, R. H., *Nietzsche* (Leipzig, 1910); new edn, 1939.
De Pallarès, V ., *Le crépuscule d'un idole: Nietzsche, nietzschéisme, nietzschéens* (Paris, 1910).
Croce, Benedetto, *Saggio sullo Hegel, seguito da altri scritti di storia della filosofia* (Bari, 1913).
Rickert, H., *Die Philosophie des Lebens: Darstellung und Kritik der philosophischen Modeströmungen unserer Zeit* (Tübingen, 1920).
Del Negro, W., *Die Rolle der Fiktionen in der Erkenntnistheorie Nietzsches* (Munich, 1923).
Hirsch, M., *Friedrich Nietzsche, der Philosoph der abendländischen Kultur* (Stuttgart, 1924).

234

Bibliography

Balthasar, H. U. von, *Apokalypse der deutschen Seele*, 3 vols (Leipzig, 1936–39) [vol. 2 bears the title 'Im Zeichen Nietzsches'].

Della Volpe, G., *Crisi critica dell'estetica romantica e altri saggi* (Messina, 1941); second edn, Rome, 1963.

Bataille, Georges, *Somme athéologique. III: Sur Nietzsche* (Paris, 1945).

Weber, A., *Abschied von der bisherigen Geschichte: Überwindung des Nihilismus* (Berne, 1946) [for discussion of Nietzsche, see pp. 144–208].

Giesz, L., *Nietzsches Existentialismus und Wille zur Macht* (Stuttgart, 1950).

Landmann, M., *Geist und Leben: Varia nietzscheana* (Bonn, 1951).

Lukács, Georg, *Die Zerstörung der Vernunft* (Berlin, 1954).

Mirri, E., *La metafisica nel Nietzsche* (Bologna, 1961).

Bartuschat, W., *Nietzsche: Selbstsein und Negativität*, dissertation (Heidelberg, 1964).

De Feo, N. M., *Analitica e dialettica in Nietzsche* (Bari, 1965).

Granier, J., *Le problème de la vérité dans la philosophie de Nietzsche* (Paris, 1966).

Pütz, Peter, *Nietzsche* (Stuttgart, 1967).

Purkhart, W., *Metaphysische Perspektiven im Denken Friedrich Nietzsches* (Vienna, 1967).

Vattimo, Gianni, *Ipotesi su Nietzsche* (Turin, 1967).

Habermas, Jürgen, 'Nachwort' ['Postscript'] to Nietzsche, *Erkenntnistheoretische Schriften* (Frankfurt/M, 1968).

Volkmann-Schluck, Karl-Heinz, *Leben und Denken: Interpretationen zur Philosophie Nietzsches* (Frankfurt/M, 1968).

Klossowski, Pierre, *Nietzsche et le cercle vicieux* (Paris, 1969).

Rey, J. M., *L'enjeu des signes: Lecture de Nietzsche* (Paris, 1971).

Foucault, Michel, 'Nietzsche, la généalogie, l'histoire', in *Hommage à Jean Hyppolite* (Paris, 1971).

Rohrmoser, Günter, *Nietzsche und das Ende der Emanzipation* (Freiburg i. B., 1971).

Müller-Lauter, Wolfgang, *Nietzsche: Seine Philosophie der Gegensätze und die Gegensätze seiner Philosophie* (Berlin and New York, 1971).

Bibliography

Pautrat, B., *Versions du soleil* (Paris, 1971).

Kofman, Sarah, *Nietzsche et la métaphore* (Paris, 1972).

Greiner, B., *Friedrich Nietzsche: Versuch und Versuchung in seinen Aphorismen* (Munich, 1972).

Kremer-Marietti, A., *L'homme et ses labyrinthes: Essai sur Friedrich Nietzsche* (Paris, 1972).

Vattimo, Gianni, *Il soggetto e la maschera: Nietzsche e il problema della liberazione* (Milan, 1974).

Colli, Giorgio, *Dopo Nietzsche* (Milan, 1974).

Guerin, M., *Nietzsche, Socrate héroique* (Paris, 1975).

Djúric, Mihailo, 'Die geschichtliche Erfahrung des Nihilismus', *Wiener Jahrbuch für Philosophie*, 8 (1975), 212–49.

Jähnig, Dieter, *Welt-Geschichte: Kunst-Geschichte. Zum Verhältnis von Vergangenheits-erkenntnis und Veränderung* (Cologne, 1975) [essays on Nietzsche, pp. 68–196].

Derrida, Jacques, *Éperons: Les styles de Nietzsche* (Venice, 1976).

Rupp, G., *Rhetorische Strukturen und kommunikative Determinanz. Studien zur Textkonstitution des philosophischen Diskurses im Werk Friedrich Nietzsches* (Berne and Frankfurt/M, 1976).

Magnus, Bernd, *Nietzsche's Existential Imperative* (Bloomington/ Ind., 1978).

Masini, F., *Lo scriba del caos: Interpretazione di Nietzsche* (Bologna, 1978).

Margreiter, R., *Ontologie und Gottesfrage bei Nietzsche* (Meisenheim/ Glan, 1978).

Bouda, R., *Kulturkritik und Utopie beim frühen Nietzsche* (Frankfurt/M and Berne, 1980).

Kaulbach, Friedrich, *Nietzsches Idee einer Experimentalphilosophie* (Cologne and Vienna, 1980).

Vattimo, Gianni, *Al di là del soggetto: Nietzsche, Heidegger e l'ermeneutica* (Milan, 1981).

Figl, Johann, *Interpretation als philosophisches Prinzip: Friedrich Nietzsches universale Theorie der Auslegung im späten Nachlass* (Berlin and New York, 1982).

Mazzarella, E., *Nietzsche e la storia: Storicità e ontologia della vita* (Naples, 1983).

236

Bibliography

Vitiello, V., *Utopia del nichilismo: Tra Nietzsche e Heidegger* (Naples, 1983).

Türcke, C., *Der tolle Mensch: Nietzsche und der Wahnsinn der Vernunft* (Frankfurt/M, 1989).

C

The history of Nietzsche reception in various countries:

Bianquis, G., *Nietzsche en France* (Paris, 1929).

Petzold, G. von, 'Nietzsche in englisch-amerikanischer Beurteilung bis zum Ausgang des Weltkrieges', *Anglia* [Halle], 53 (1929), 134–218.

Deesz, G., *Die Entwicklung des Nietzsche-Bildes in Deutschland*, dissertation (Bonn, 1933).

Lengyel, B., 'Nietzsches ungarische Nachwelt', *Jahrbuch des deutschen Instituts der Universität Budapest*, 5 (1939), 457–541.

Marcuse, L., 'Nietzsche in America', *South Atlantic Quarterly*, 50 (1951), 330–9.

Rusker, U., *Nietzsche in der Hispania* (Munich and Berne, 1962).

Sobejano, G., *Nietzsche en España* (Madrid, 1967).

Ries, W., *Grundzüge des Nietzsche-Verständnisses in der Deutung seiner Philosophie: Zur Geschichte der Nietzsche-Literatur in Deutschland (1932–1963)*, dissertation (Heidelberg, 1967).

Boudot, P ., *Nietzsche et l'au-delà de la crise: Nietzsche et les écrivains français de 1930 à 1960* (Paris, 1970).

Thatcher, David S., *Nietzsche in England 1890–1914: The Growth of a Reputation* (Toronto, 1970).

Strong, B., 'Images of Nietzsche in America 1900–1970', *South Atlantic Quarterly*, Autumn 1971, 575–94.

Krummel, Richard Frank, *Nietzsche und der deutsche Geist: Ausbreitung und Wirkung des Nietzscheschen Werkes im deutschen Sprachraum bis zum Todesjahr des Philosophen. Ein Schrifttumsverzeichnis der Jahre 1867–1900* (Berlin and New York, 1974); [a second volume, covering the period 1901 to 1918, appeared in

Bibliography

1983, and a third volume, covering the period 1918 to 1945, appeared in 1998].

Stefani, M. A., *Nietzsche in Italia: Rassegna bibliografica 1893–1970* (Assisi and Rome, 1975).

Brandl, H., *Persönlichkeitsidealismus und Willenskult: Aspekte der Nietzsche-Rezeption in Schweden* (Heidelberg, 1977).

Michelini, G., *Nietzsche nell'Italia di D'Annunzio* (Palermo, 1978).

Davis, R. D., 'Nietzsche in Russia: A preliminary bibliography', *Germano-Slavica* (Waterloo, Canada), 2 (1977) no. 3, 201–20.

Kiss, E., 'Über die ungarische Wirkung Friedrich Nietzsches bis 1918–19', *Annales Universitatis Scientiarum Budapestinensis de Rolando Eötvös nominatae*, 2 (1978), 137–51.

Gabel, Gernot E., *Friedrich Nietzsche: Leben und Werk im Spiegel westeuropäischer Hochschulschriften. Eine Bibliographie* (Hamburg, 1978).

The following studies also need to be mentioned:

Lichtenberger, Henri, *La philosophie de Nietzsche* (Paris, 1898).

Zoccoli, E., *Friedrich Nietzsche, la filosofia religiosa – la morale, l'estetica* (Modena, 1898).

Brandes, Georg, *En Afhandling om aristokratisk radikalisme* (Copenhagen, 1899).

De Gaultier, J., *De Kant à Nietzsche* (Paris, 1900).

Richter, R., *Friedrich Nietzsche: Sein Leben und sein Werk. 15 Vorlesungen gehalten an der Universität Leipzig* (Leipzig, 1903).

Orestano, F., *Le idee fondamentali di Friedrich Nietzsche nelloro progessivo svolgimento: Esposizione e critica* (Palermo, 1903).

Willy, R., *Nietzsche: Eine Gesamtschilderung* (Zurich, 1904).

Seillière, E., *La philosophie de l'impérialisme*, vol. 2: *Apollon ou Dionysos: Étude critique sur Friedrich Nietzsche et l'utilitarisme impérialiste* (Paris, 1905).

Papini, G., *Il crepusculo dei filosofi* (Milan, 1906).

Mencken, H. L., *The Philosophy of Nietzsche* (Boston, 1908) [new edn, Port Washington/NY, 1967].

Bibliography

Mussolini, Benito, 'La filosofia della forza', *Pensiero romagnolo* (Autumn 1908).

Borgese, G. A., *Gabriele d'Annunzio* (Naples, 1909).

Meyer, R. M., *Nietzsche: Sein Leben und seine Werke* (Munich, 1910).

Chatterton-Hill, G., *The Philosophy of Nietzsche* (London, 1913).

Hammer, W., *Nietzsches Metaphysik* (Leipzig, 1914).

Salter, W., *Nietzsche: The Thinker* (New York, 1917).

Muckle, F., *Friedrich Nietzsche und der Zusammenbruch der Kultur* (Munich, 1921).

Gundolf, E., and Hildebrandt, K., *Nietzsche als Richter unserer Zeit* (Breslau, 1923).

Buhnoff, N., *Nietzsches Kulturphilosophie und Umwertungslehre* (Leipzig, 1924).

Castiglioni, M., *Il poema eroico di Friedrich Nietzsche* (Turin, 1924).

Hildebrandt, Kurt, *Wagner und Nietzsche: Ihr Kampf gegen das 19. Jahrhundert* (Breslau, 1924).

Zweig, Stefan, *Die Baumeister der Welt* (Leipzig, 1925) [vol. 2 is entitled *Der Kampf mit dem Dämon: Holderlin, Kleist, Nietzsche*].

Lessing, Th., *Nietzsche* (Berlin, 1925).

De Gaultier, J., *Les maîtres de la pensée antichrétienne: Nietzsche* (Paris, 1926).

Vetter, A., *Nietzsche* (Munich, 1926).

Landry, H., *Friedrich Nietzsche* (Berlin, 1931).

Maulnier, T., *Nietzsche* (Paris, 1933).

Hildebrandt, Kurt, 'Über Deutung und Einordnung von Nietzsches "System"', *Kant-Studien*, 41 (1936), 221–93.

Lefebvre, H., *Nietzsche* (Paris, 1939) [an anthology with a substantial introduction].

Cresson, A., *Nietzsche, sa vie, son œuvre, avec un exposé de sa philosophie* (Paris, 1942).

Engelke, K., *Die metaphysischen Grundlagen in Nietzsches Werk* (Würzburg, 1942).

Barth, H., *Wahrheit und Ideologie* (Zurich, 1945) [cf. the essay 'Nietzsches Philosophie als Kunst des Mißtrauens', pp. 207–83].

Bibliography

Flake, Otto, *Nietzsche: Ruckblick auf eine Philosophie* (Baden-Baden, 1946).

Weymann-Weye, W., *Die Entscheidung des Menschen: Nietzsche als geschichtliche Wirklichkeit* (Freiburg i. B., 1948).

Mann, Thomas, *Nietzsches Philosophie im Lichte unserer Erfahrung* (Berlin, 1948).

Lavrin, Janko, *Nietzsche: An Approach* (London, 1948).

Jünger, Friedrich Georg, *Nietzsche* (Frankfurt/M, 1949).

Camus, Albert, *L'homme revolté* (Paris, 1951).

Heller, Erich, *The Disinherited Mind: Essays in Modern German Literature and Thought* (Cambridge, 1952).

Holz, H. H., *Die abenteuerliche Rebellion: Burgerliche Protestbewegungen in der Philosophie. Stirner, Nietzsche, Sartre, Marcuse* (Darmstadt and Neuwied, 1976).

Heller, P., *Probleme der Zivilisation: Versuche über Goethe, Th. Mann, Nietzsche und Freud* (Bonn, 1978).

Sini, C., *Semiotica e filosofia: Segno e linguaggio in Peirce, Nietzsche, Heidegger, Foucault* (Milan, 1978).

Stelzer, S., *Der Zug der Zeit: Nietzsches Versuch der Philosophie* (Meisenheim/Glan, 1979).

Marcel, G., 'Nietzsche, l'homme devant la mort de Dieu', in *G. Marcel et la pensée allemande* (Paris, 1979), pp. 9–24.

Thiel, M., *Nietzsche: ein analytischer Aufbau seiner Denkstruktur* (Heidelberg, 1908).

Colli, Giorgio, *Scritti su Nietzsche* (Milan, 1980).

Cacciari, M. (ed.), *Crucialità del tempo: Saggi sulla concezione nietzscheana del tempo* (Naples, 1980).

Montinari, Mazzino, *Su Nietzsche* (Rome, 1982).

Velt, Th., *Die Bedeutung des Leidens fur den Menschen: Nietzsches Leidenskonzept einer tragischen Moderne* (Berne, Frankfurt/M and New York, 1988).

c) Relations, Influences, Comparisons

Schellwien, R.: *Max Stirner und Nietzsche: Erscheinungen des modernen Geistes und das Wesen des Menschen* (Leipzig, 1892).

Bibliography

Kreibig (Laurentius), J. C., *Kropotkins Morallehre und deren Beziehung zu Nietzsche* (Dresden, 1896).

Falkenfeld, M., *Marx und Nietzsche* (Leipzig, 1899).

Oudinot, G., 'Carlyle et Friedrich Nietzsche', *Mercure de France* (1899) n. 31, 622–46.

Selle, C. F., *Die Philosophie der Weltmacht* (Leipzig, 1902) [examines Spencer and Nietzsche].

Fouillée, A., *Nietzsche et l'immoralisme* (Paris, 1902).

Demoschek, G. A., *Das Problem des egoistischen Perfektionismus in der Ethik Spinozas und Nietzsches* (Leipzig, 1905).

Caussy, F.: 'La théorie des sacrifices d'après Nietzsche et Joseph de Maistre', *Mercure de France* (1906), 344–66.

Simmel, Georg, *Schopenhauer und Nietzsche* (Leipzig, 1907).

Berthelot, R., *Évolutionisme et platonisme* (Paris, 1908) [see pp. 88–138 for discussion of the idea of life in the works of Guyau, Nietzsche and Bergson].

Schiedt, R. C., 'Ernst Haeckel und Friedrich Nietzsche', *Reformed Church Review*, 12 (1908), 29–47 and 213–33.

Ewald, Oskar, 'Darwin und Nietzsche', *Zeitschrift für Philosophie und philosophische Kritik* (1909) Supplement 1, 159–79.

Jackh, E., 'Friedrich Nietzsche und David Friedrich Strauss', *Patria* [Berlin] (1909), 210–47.

Allen, G., 'Self-Assertion in Nietzsche and Self-Surrender in Boehme: a Contrast and an Identity', *Hibbert Journal*, (1909–10), 411–27.

Baumgartner, O., 'Hölderlin und Nietzsches Zarathustra', *Wissen und Leben* [Zurich] (1911), 853–63.

Berthelot, R., *Un romantisme utilitaire: Étude sur le mouvement pragmatiste* (Paris, 1911) [contains discussions of Nietzsche and Peirce as well as of Nietzsche and Poincaré].

Fischer, O., 'Nietzsche und Kleist', *Neue Jahrbücher für das klassische Altertum, Geschichte und deutsche Literatur* (1911), 506–19.

Miiller-Freienfels, R., 'Nietzsche und der Pragmatismus', *Archiv für Geschichte der Philosophie* (1913), 339–58.

Bauer, H., 'Pascal et Nietzsche', *La revue germanique*, 10 (1914), 1–51.

Bibliography

Sodeur, G., *Kierkegaard und Nietzsche* (Tübingen, 1914).

Ziegler, Th., *Menschen und Probleme* (Berlin, 1914) [contains essays on Nietzsche and Hölderlin and on Nietzsche and Socrates].

Bauch, Bruno, 'Nietzsche und der deutsche Idealismus', *Der Panther*, 5 (1917), 496–519.

Bertram, Ernst, 'Nietzsches Goethebild', in *Festschrift B. Litzmann* (Bonn, 1920), pp. 318–61.

Ludwig, A., 'Nietzsche und Shakespeare', *Jahrbuch der deutschen Shakespeare-Gesellschaft* (1920), 24–57.

Caffi, E., *Nietzsches Stellung zu Macchiavellis Lehre* (Vienna, 1921).

Dietrich, A., 'Marx' und Nietzsches Bedeutung für die deutsche Philosophie der Gegenwart', *Die Dioskuren* (1920), 338–80.

Gabetti, G., 'Nietzsche e Leopardi', *Il convegno*,(1923), 441–61 and 513–31 (concluded in the 1924 volume, pp. 5–30).

Liebmann, W., *Nietzsche für und gegen Vaihinger: Die Rolle der Fiktionen in der Erkenntnistheorie Nietzsches* (Munich, 1923).

Jacob, G., *Thomas Mann und Nietzsche: Zum Problem der Decadence* (Munich, 1926).

Löwith, Karl, 'Nietzsche im Lichte der Philosophie von Ludwig Klages', in *Reichls philosophischer Almanach* (Darmstadt, 1927), pp. 285–348; repr. in K.L., *Sämtliche Schriften*, Stuttgart, 1987, Vol. vi.

Hasse, H., 'Vorstufen der Lehre Nietzsches von der ewigen Wiederkunft bei Schopenhauer', *Jahrbuch der Schopenhauer-Gesellschaft*, 16 (1929), 45–56.

Langer, N., *Das Problem der Romantik bei Nietzsche* (Münster, 1929).

Depenheuer, K., *Nietzsche–Maeterlinck: Ein Beitrag zum Problem des Individualismus* (Krefeld, 1930).

Rehm, W., *Jakob Burckhardt* (Leipzig, 1930) [cf. pp. 172–200 for discussion of Nietzsche's relationship with Burckhardt].

Jankelevitch, S., 'L'unique et le surhomme, le problème de la personnalité chez Stirner et chez Nietzsche', *Revue d'Allemagne* (1931), 27–40 and 216–43.

Litt, Th., 'Nietzsche und die Philosophie des Lebens', in *Handbuch der Philosophie* (Munich, 1931).

Bibliography

Spencer, M., 'Spinoza and Nietzsche: a Comparison', *Monist* (1931), 67–90.

Berning, A. H., 'Ringen um die Idee: Nietzsche, Hölderlin und Karoline von Günderrode', *Das Wort in der Zeit*,1 (1933), 1–12.

Drain, H., *Nietzsche et Gide* (Paris, 1933).

Löwith, Karl, *Kierkegaard und Nietzsche oder philosophische und theologische Überwindung des Nihilismus* (Frankfurt/M, 1933); repr. in K.L., *Sämtliche Schriften* (Stuttgart, 1987), Vol. vi.

Brodersen, A., and Jablonski, W., ' Herder und Nietzsche oder die philosophische Einheit des Goethejahrhunderts', *Skrifter: Norske videnskabers selskab* [Trondheim] (1934) no. 10, 1–45.

Fairley, Barker, 'Nietzsche and Goethe', *Bulletin of the John Rylands Library*, 18 (1934), 298–314.

Gurlitt, W., 'Von Nietzsche zu Rudolf Steiner', *Anthroposophie* [Stuttgart], 16 (1934), 237–48.

Rosengarten, W., *Nietzsche und George, ihre Sendung und ihr Menschtum* (Leipzig, 1934).

Bernhart, J., *Meister Eckhart und Nietzsche: Ein Vergleich für die Gegenwart* (Berlin, 1935).

Kein, O., *Das Apollinische und das Dionysische bei Nietzsche und Schelling* (Berlin, 1935).

Dehn, F., 'Rilke und Nietzsche', *Dichtung und Volkstum*, 37 (1936), 1–22.

Löwith, Karl, *Jakob Burckhardt*, Lucerne 1936 (Nietzsche's relations with Burckhardt are discussed on pp. 11–61); repr. in K.L., *Sämtliche Schriften* (Stuttgart, 1987), Vol. vi.

Przywara, E, 'Th. von Aquin, Ignaz von Loyola und Friedrich Nietzsche', *Zeitschrift für Askese und Mystik* [Innsbruck], 11 (1936), 257–95.

Platz, H., 'Nietzsche und Bourget', *Neuphilologische Monatsschrift*, 8 (1937), 177–86.

Ackermann, O., *Kant im Urteil Nietzsches* (Tübingen, 1939).

Jolivet, H., 'Strindberg et Nietzsche', *Revue de la littérature comparée*, 19 (1939), 390–406.

Schubart, W., *Dostojewski und Nietzsche: Symbolik ihres Lebens* (Lucerne, 1939).

243

Bibliography

Hultsch, G., *Nietzsche und Luther* (Gütersloh, 1940).

Kuehnemund, R., 'Faust and Zarathustra in our Time', *Germanic Review*, 15 (1940), 116–36.

Weber-Colonius, E., *Nietzsche und Plotin: Versuch eines Vergleichs* (Kassel, 1941).

Heyse, H., 'Kant und Nietzsche', *Kant-Studien*, 42 (1942–43), 3–27.

Bentley, E. R., *A Century of Hero-Worship: A Study of the Idea of Heroism in Carlyle and Nietzsche with Notes on other Hero-Worshippers of Modern Times* (Philadelphia and New York, 1944).

Abegg, E., 'Nietzsches Zarathustra und der Prophet des alten Iran' (Zurich, 1945) [part of a lecture series in Geneva on the occasion of the centenary of Nietzsche's birth, 14–15 October 1944], pp. 64–82.

Aler, J. M., *Im Siegel der Form: Stefan George und Nietzsche* (Amsterdam, 1947).

Struve, W., *Die neuzeitliche Philosophie als Metaphysik der Subjektivität: Kierkegaard und Nietzsche* (Freiburg i. B. 1949).

Kamerbeek, J., 'Dilthey versus Nietzsche', *Studia philosophica* [Basle], 10 (1950), 52–84.

Maillet, A., and Roeschl, H., 'Blake et Nietzsche', in *Nietzsche (1844–1900): études et témoinages du Cinquantenaire* (Pans, 1950), pp. 143–71.

Bonifazi, C., *Christendom Attacked: A Comparison of Kierkegaard and Nietzsche* (London, 1953).

Steinacker, E., 'Nietzsche und Péguy', *Der Brenner* [Innsbruck], 18 (1954), 169–76.

Brandt, R., 'Freud and Nietzsche: a Comparison', *Revue de l'Université d'Ottawa*, 25 (1955), 225–34.

Kaufmann, Walter A., 'Nietzsche and Rilke', *Kenyon Review*, 17 (1955), 1–22.

Virtanen, R., 'Nietzsche and Corneille', *Symposium* (1957), 225–39.

Hubbard, S., *Nietzsche und Emerson* (Basle, 1958).

Cordle, T., 'Malraux and Nietzsche's "Geburt der Tragodie"', *Bucknell Review*, 8 (1959), 89–104.

244

Bibliography

Beerlin, R. F., 'Hegel und Nietzsche', *Hegel-Studien*,I (1961), 229–46.

Gaede, E., *Nietzsche et Valéry* (Paris, 1962).

Moeller, J., 'Nietzsche und die Metaphysik: Zu Heideggers Nietzscheinterpretation', *Tübinger theologische Quartalschrift*, 142 (1962), 283–310.

Pütz, Peter, *Kunst und Künstlerexistenz bei Nietzsche und Thomas Mann* (Bonn, 1963).

Boasson, Ch., 'On the Social and Legal Philosopher's Encounter with Nietzsche', *Archiv für Rechts-und Sozialphilosophie*, (1963), 447–79.

Stavrou, C. N., *Whitman and Nietzsche: A Comparative Study of their Thought* (Chapel Hill/N.C., 1964).

Heller, Erich, *The Artist's Journey into the Interior and Other Essays* (New York, 1965) [essays include 'The Importance of Nietzsche' and 'Wittgenstein and Nietzsche'].

Seidler, I., 'Das Nietzschebild Robert Musils', *Deutsche Vierteljahresschrift für Literaturwissenschaft und Geistesgeschichte*, 39 (1965), 329–49.

Hillebrand, B., *Artistik und Auftrag: Zur Kunsttheorie von Benn und Nietzsche* (Munich, 1966).

Abenheimer, K. M., 'Rilke and Nietzsche', *Philosophical Journal*, 4 (1967), 95–106.

Aspel, P., 'René Char et Nietzsche', *Liberté* [Montreal], 10 (1968), 166–82.

Boehm, R., 'Husserl und Nietzsche', in *Vom Gesichtspunkt der Phänomenologie* (The Hague, 1968).

Dyck, J. W., 'Kleist und Nietzsche: Lebensplan und Lust-Motiv', *German Life and Letters*, 21 (1968), 189–203.

La Valley, A. J., *Carlyle and the Idea of the Modern: Studies in Carlyle's Prophetic Literature and its Relation to Blake, Nietzsche, Marx and Others* (New Haven and London, 1968).

Toernqvist, Egil, 'Nietzsche and O'Neill: a Study in Affinity', *Orbis Litterarum*, 23 (1968), 97–126.

Van de Viele, J., 'Heidegger et Nietzsche', *Revue philosophique de Louvain*, 66 (1968), 435–86.

Bibliography

White, J., 'Ulysses: the Metaphysical Foundations and Grand Design', *Modern Fiction Studies*,15 (1969) S. 27–34 (deals with Nietzsche's influence on Joyce).

Boudot, P., *Nietzsche et l'au-delà de la liberté* (Paris, 1970) [discusses Nietzsche and French writers between 1930 and 1960].

Dickopp, K. H., 'Aspekte zum Verhältnis Nietzsche-Kant und ihre Bedeutung für die Interpretation des "Willens zur Macht"', *Kant-Studien*, 61 (1970), 97–111.

Heftrich, Eckhard, 'Nietzsche im Denken Heideggers', in *Durchblicke: Martin Heidegger zum 80. Geburtstag* (Frankfurt/M, 1970), pp. 331–49.

Seitter, W., 'Franz Grillparzer und Friedrich Nietzsche', *Jahrbuch der Grillparzer-Gesellschaft*, 3 (1970), 87–107.

Sondag, Y., 'Nietzsche, Schopenhauer, l'ascétisme et la psychanalyse', *Revue de philosophie de la France et de l'étranger*, 96 (1971), 348–59.

Geller, P., 'Nietzsche, Peirce et le désaveu du sujet', *Annales publiés trimestriellement par l'Universite de Toulouse-Le Mirail*, 8 (1972), 95–110.

Meyer-Wendt, H. J., *Der frühe Hofmannsthal und die Gedankenwelt Nietzsches* (Heidelberg, 1973).

Howey, Richard L., *Heidegger and Jaspers on Nietzsche*, The Hague, 1973).

Susini-Constantini, H., 'Gérard de Nerval, Frédéric Nietzsche: Une prophétie du Retour Éternel', *Cahiers internationaux de symbolisme* [Geneva] (1973) nos 24–5, 119–31.

Masao, A., 'Zen and Nietzsche', *The Eastern Buddhist* [Kyoto], 6 (1973) n. 2, 14–32.

Reboul, O., *Nietzsche critique de Kant* (Paris, 1974).

Dionne, J. R., *Pascal et Nietzsche: Étude historique et comparée* (New York, 1974).

Green, E. H., 'Blueprints for Utopia: The Political Ideas of Nietzsche and D. H. Lawrence', *Renaissance and Modern Studies* [Nottingham], 18 (1974), 141–61.

Wurzer, W. S., *Nietzsche und Spinoza* (Meisenheim, 1975).

246

Bibliography

Penzo, G., *Nietzsche nell'interpretazione heideggeriana* (Bologna, 1976).

Madera, R., *Identità e feticismo: Forma di valore e critica del soggetto, Marx e Nietzsche* (Milan, 1977).

Vattimo, Gianni, 'Nietzsche heute?' *Philosophische Rundschau*, 24 (1977), 67–91.

Weyembergh, M., *Friedrich Nietzsche und Eduard von Hartmann* (Brussels, 1977).

Clair, A., 'Énigme nietzschéenne et paradoxe kierkegaardien', *Revue de theologie et de philosophie* [Lausanne] (1977) no. 3, 196–221.

Rosenthal, B., *Die Idee des Absurden: Friedrich Nietzsche und Albert Camus* (Bonn, 1977).

Hillebrand, Bruno (ed.), *Nietzsche und die deutsche Literatur*, 2 vols (Tübingen, 1978).

Donadio, Stephen, *Nietzsche, Henry James and the Artistic Will* (London, New York and Oxford, 1978).

Behler, Ernst, 'Nietzsche's Challenge to Romantic Humanism', *Canadian Review of Comparative Literature*, 6 (1978) no. 1, 30–52.

Piga, F., *Il mito del superuomo in Nietzsche e D'Annunzio* (Florence, 1979).

Blondel, E., '"Wohin?", "Wozu?": ein Kulturproblem. Wahrheit und Leben bei Hume und Nietzsche', *Perspektiven der Philosophie*, 6 (1980), 78–89.

Assoun, P. L., *Nietzsche et Freud* (Paris, 1980).

Market, O., 'Fichte und Nietzsche', *Perspektiven der Philosophie*, 7 (1981), 119–31.

Mistry, Freny, *Nietzsche and Buddhism: Prolegomenon to a Comparative Study* (Berlin and New York, 1981).

Stack, George J., 'Nietzsche and Boscovich's Natural Philosophy', *Pacific Philosophical Quarterly*, 62 (1981), 69–87.

Schmidt B., *Der ethische Aspekt der Musik: Nietzsches 'Geburt der Tragodie' und die Wiener klassische Musik* (Würzburg, 1981).

Reckermann, A., 'Nietzsche und Pascal', *Philosophisches Jahrbuch*, 89 (1982), 325–46.

Bibliography

Bohlmann, Otto, *Yeats and Nietzsche: An Exploration of Major Nietzschean Echoes in the Writings of William Butler Yeats* (Totowa/N.J., 1982).

Bolz, N. W., 'Tod des Subjekts: Die neuere französische Philosophie im Zeichen Nietzsches', *Zeitschrift für philosophische Forschung*, 36 (1982), 444–52.

Raschel, Heinz, *Das Nietzsche-Bild im George-Kreis: Ein Beitrag zur Geschichte der deutschen Mythologeme* (Berlin and New York, 1983).

Vitello, V., *Utopia del nichilismo: Tra Nietzsche e Heidegger* (Naples, 1983).

Littek, C., *Versöhnungs-Ontologie: Zum Liebesbegriff Hölderlins und Nietzsches* (Düsseldorf, 1985).

Huchzermeyer, W., *Der Übermensch bei Friedrich Nietzsche und Sri Aurobindo* (Gladbach, 1986).

Gekle, H., *Die Tränen des Apoll: Zur Bedeutung des Dionysos in der Philosophie Ernst Blochs* (Tübingen, 1990).

d) Studies of Particular Aspects and Problems

Nietzsche and the Greeks

Wiesenthal, M., *Friedrich Nietzsche und die griechische Sophistik* (Heidelberg, 1904).

Oehler, Richard, *Friedrich Nietzsche und die Vorsokratiker* (Leipzig, 1904).

Bauer, H., 'La conception de l'hellénisme dans Goethe et dans Friedrich Nietzsche', *La revue germanique* (1908), 365–413.

Cipriani, C., *Le dottrine amoraliste di Friedrich Nietzsche e quelle dei sofisti* (Sassari, 1910).

Nestle, W. von, 'Nietzsche und die griechische Philosophie', *Neue Jahrbücher für das klassische Altertum, Geschichte und deutsche Literatur*, 29 (1912), 554–84.

Klugmann, N. und Latzarus B., *Friedrich Nietzsche et la pensée grecque* (Paris, 1920).

Howald, Ernst, *Friedrich Nietzsche und die klassische Philologie* (Gotha, 1920).

248

Bibliography

Gurlitt, Ludwig, 'Die Erkenntnis des klassischen Altertums aus dem Geist Friedrich Nietzsches', in: Max Oehler (ed.), *Den Manen Friedrich Nietzsches: Zum 75. Geburtstag von Elisabeth Förster-Nietzsche* (Munich, 1921), pp. 57–80.

Haiser, F., *Im Anfang war der Streit: Nietzsches Zarathustra und die Weltanschauung des Altertums* (Munich, 1921).

Nuesch, E., *Nietzsche et l'antiquité: Essai sur un idéal de civilisation* (Paris, 1925).

Knight, A. H. J., *Some Aspects of the Life and Work of Nietzsche, and particularly of his Connection with Greek Literature and Thought* (Cambridge, 1933).

—— 'Nietzsche and Epicurean Philosophy', *Philosophy*, 8 (1933), 431–45.

Reinhardt, K.: 'Nietzsches Klage der Ariadne', *Die Antike*, 11 (1935), 85–109.

Mis, L., 'De Nietzsche à Hugo von Hofmannsthal', *La revue germanique* (1938), 337–61 (Nietzsche's interpretation of Greek tragedy, as viewed by Hofmannsthal and Hermann Bahr).

Kerényi, K., 'Nietzsche und Ariadne', *Neue Schweizer Rundschau*, 12 (1944), 402–12.

Schlechta, Karl, *Der junge Nietzsche und das klassische Altertum* (Mainz, 1948).

Coulter, J. A., 'Nietzsche and Greek Studies', *Greek, Roman and Byzantine Studies*, 3 (1960), 46–51.

Vogt, Ernst, 'Nietzsche und der Wettkampf Homers', *Antike und Abendland*, 11 (1962), 103–13.

Duval, R., 'Le point de départ de la pensée de Nietzsche: Nietzsche et le platonisme', *Revue des sciences philosophiques et theologiques*, 53 (1969), 601–37.

Gründer, Karlfried (ed.), *Der Streit um Nietzsches 'Geburt der Tragodie': Die Schriften von E. Rohde, R. Wagner, U. v. Wilamowitz-Möllendorff* (Hildesheim, 1969).

Schmidt, Hermann J., *Nietzsche und Sokrates: Philosophische Untersuchungen zu Nietzsches Sokratesbild* (Meisenheim/Glan, 1969).

Goth, J., *Nietzsche und die Rhetorik* (Tübingen, 1970).

Ramnoux, C., *Études présocratiques* (Paris, 1970).

Bibliography

Dannhauser, Werner J., *Nietzsche's View of Socrates* (Ithaca/N.Y., 1974).

O'Flaherty, J. C., Sellner T. F., and Helm, R. M. (eds), *Studies in Nietzsche and the Classical Tradition* (Chapel Hill/NC, 1976).

Hoelscher, U., 'Die Wiedergewinnung des antiken Bodens: Nietzsches Rückgriff auf Heraklit', *Neue Hefte für Philosophie* (1979), 156–82.

Grant, G. P., 'Nietzsche and the Ancient: Philosophy and Scholarship', *Dionysius*, 3 (1979), 5–16.

Escobar, R., *Nietzsche e la filologia* (Milan, 1980).

Silk, M. S., and Stern, J. P., *Nietzsche on Tragedy* (Cambridge, 1981).

Schmid, H., *Nietzsches Gedanke der tragischen Erkenntnis* (Würzburg, 1984).

Tejera, V., *Nietzsche and Greek Thought* (Dordrecht, Boston and Lancaster, 1987).

Nietzsche and Christianity

Kaftan, J., *Das Christentum und Nietzsches Herrenmoral* (Berlin, 1897).

—— 'Aus der Werkstatt des Ubermenschen', *Deutsche Rundschau*, 32 (1905), 90–110, 237–60.

Jacobi, J., 'The Nietzschean Ideal and the Christian Ideal: Superman and Saint', *American Catholic Quarterly* (July 1916), 463–91.

Figgis, J. N., *The Will to Freedom, or the Gospel of Nietzsche and the Gospel of Christ* (New York, 1917).

De Lubac, H., *Le drame de l'humanisme athée* (Paris, 1933).

Koehler, G., *Nietzsche und der Katholizismus* (Fulda, 1937).

Wenzel, F., *Das Paulus-Bild bei Nietzsche* (Breslau, 1937).

Hauff, R. Von, *Nietzsches Stellung zur christlichen Demut* (Tübingen, 1939).

Dibelius, M., 'Der "psychologische Typus des Erlösers" bei Nietzsche', *Deutsche Vierteljahresschrift für Literaturwissenschaft und Geistesgeschichte*, 22 (1944), 61–91.

Bibliography

Jaspers, Karl, *Nietzsche und das Christentum* (Hamlin, 1946); second edn (Munich, 1952).

Buri, F., *Kreuz und Ring: Die Kreuzestheologie des jungen Luther und die Lehre von der ewigen Wiederkunft in Nietzsches 'Zarathustra'* (Berne, 1947).

Thompson, R., *Nietzsche and Christian Ethics* (New York, 1952).

Lotz, J. B., *Zwischen Seligkeit und Verdammnis* (Frankfurt/M, 1953).

Benz, E., *Nietzsches Ideen zur Geschichte des Christentums* (Leyden, 1956).

Grau, G.-G., *Christlicher Glaube und intellektuelle Redlichkeit: Eine religionsphilosophische Studie über Nietzsche* (Frankfurt/M, 1958).

Welte, B., *Nietzsches Atheismus und das Christentum* (Darmstadt, 1958).

Biser, Eugen, *'Gott ist tot': Nietzsches Destruktion des christlichen Bewußtseins* (Munich, 1962).

Wein, H., *Positives Antichristentum: Nietzsches Christusbild im Brennpunkt nachchristlicher Anthropologie* (The Hague, 1962) [very important study, not least for its presentation of broader aspects of Nietzsche's thought].

Vollmer, H., *Nietzsches Zarathustra und die Bibel* (Hamburg, 1963).

Picht, Georg, *Schuld und religiöse Erfahrung* (Freiburg i. B., 1968) [contains the essay 'Zum Problem der "Genealogie der Moral" bei Nietzsche', pp. 39–60].

Gilson, E., 'The Idea of God and the Difficulties of Atheism', *Philosophy Today*, 13 (1969), 174–205.

Kaempfert, M., *Säkularisation und neue Heiligkeit: Religiöse und religionsbezogene Sprache bei Nietzsche* (Berlin, 1971).

Valadier, P., *Nietzsche et la critique du christianisme* (Paris, 1974).

Pfeil, H., *Von Christus zu Dionysos: Nietzsches religiöse Entwicklung* (Meisenheim, 1975).

Lauret, B., *Schulderfahrung und Gottesfrage bei Nietzsche und Freud* (Munich, 1977).

Goedert, G., *Nietzsche critique des valeurs chrétiennes: souffrance et compassion* (Paris, 1977).

Valadier, P., *Jésus-Christ ou Dionysos: La loi chrétienne en confrontation avec Nietzsche* (Paris, 1979).

Bibliography

Nietzsche e l'umanesimo cristiano, special number of the journal *Aquinas*, 22 (1979) no. 3.

Blondel, Eric, *Nietzsche le cinquième Evangile?* (Paris, 1980).

—— ' "Götzen aushorchen": Versuch einer Genealogie der Genealogie. Nietzsches philosophisches Apriori und die christliche Kritik des Christentums', *Perspektiven der Philosophie*, 7 (1981), 51–72.

Steinde W., *Friedrich Nietzsche und der moderne Atheismus* (Stuttgart, 1981).

Kreß,H., *Ethische Werte und der Gottesgedanke: Probleme und Perspektiven des neuzeitlichen Wertbegriffs* (Cologne, 1990).

Nietzsche's Aesthetics

Zeitler, Julius, *Nietzsches Ästhetik* (Leipzig, 1900).

Lasserre, Pierre, *Les idées de Nietzsche sur la musique: la periode wagnérienne 1871–1876* (Paris, 1905).

Seilliere, E., *Les idées de Nietzsche sur la musique* (Paris, 1910).

Filser, Benno, *Die Ästhetik Nietzsches in der 'Geburt der Tragodie'* (Passau, 1917).

Stein, W., *Nietzsche und die bildende Kunst* (Berlin, 1925).

Baugh, H., 'Nietzsche and Music', *Musical Quarterly*, 12 (1926), 238–47.

Cysarz, Herbert, *Von Schiller zu Nietzsche* (Halle, 1928).

Guerster, E., *Nietzsche und die Musik* (Munich, 1929).

Toepfer, H., *Deutung und Wertung der Kunst bei Schopenhauer und Nietzsche* (Dresden, 1933).

Besser, K., *Die Problematik der aphoristischen Form bei Lichtenberg, Fr. Schlegel, Novalis und Nietzsche: Ein Beitrag zur Psychologie des geistigen Schaffens* (Berlin, 1935).

Diem, G., *Das Wesen der Kunst im Denken Nietzsches* (Schorndorf bei Stuttgart, 1954).

Gonzales y Reyero, A., 'L'arte nel pensiero di Friedrich Nietzsche', *Annali della Facoltà di Lettere e Filosofia dell'Università di Napoli*, 5 (1955), 233–59.

Bibliography

Grlic, D., 'L'antiesthétisme de Friedrich Nietzsche', *Praxis*, 2 (1966), 338–420.

Sojcher J., *La question et le sens: Esthétique de Nietzsche* (Paris, 1972) [an anthology with a substantial introduction].

Lambert, B., 'Les grandes théories: Nietzsche et le théâtre', *Littérature* [Paris] (1973) no. 9, 3–30.

Vattimo, Gianni, 'Arte e identità: Sull'attualità dell'estetica di Nietzsche', *Revue internationale de philosophie* [Brussels], 28 (1974), 353–90.

Bennholdt-Thomsen, A., *Nietzsches 'Also sprach Zarathustra' als literarisches Phänomen: Eine Revision* (Frankfurt/M, 1974).

Bräutigam, Bernd, *Reflexion des Schönen, schöne Reflexion: Überlegungen zur Prosa ästhetischer Theorie: Hamann, Nietzsche, Adorno* (Bonn, 1975).

Remmert, G., *Leiberleben als Ursprung der Kunst: Zur Ästhetik Friedrich Nietzsches* (Bonn, 1978).

Stern J. P., *A Study of Nietzsche* (Cambridge, 1979).

Del Caro, Adrian, *Dionysian Aesthetics: The Role of Destruction in Creation as Reflected in the Life and Works of Friedrich Nietzsche* (Frankfurt/M, Berne and Cirencester, 1981).

Further Special Studies

Gaede, Udo, *Schiller und Nietzsche als Verkünder der tragischen Kultur* (Berlin, 1908).

Riedman, M., *Nietzsche als Psychologe* (Leipzig 1911).

Rogers, A., 'Nietzsche and Democracy', *Philosophical Review*, 21 (1912), 32–50.

Bertrand, L., 'Nietzsche et la guerre', *Revue des deux mondes* (1914), 727–45.

Levenstein, A., *Nietzsche im Urteil der Arbeiterklasse* (Leipzig, 1914).

Groeper, Richard, 'Nietzsche und der Krieg', *Die Tat*, 8 (1916) no. 1, 25–38.

Brunst, G., 'Une énigme: Nietzsche et la guerre', *Mercure de France* (1919), 385–406.

Bibliography

Cunningham, G., 'Nietzsche on Democracy', *Texas Review* (1919), 185–97.

Spindler, J.: 'Die Figur des Teufels in Nietzsches "Zarathustra" und in seinem "Ecce Homo": Nietzsches Umkehr', *Preussische Jahrbücher*, 177 (1919), 54–77.

Foster, G., 'Nietzsche and the Great War', *Sewanee Review* (1920), 139–51.

Foerster, G., *Machtwille und Maschinenwelt* (Potsdam, 1930).

Becker, O., 'Nietzsches Beweis für seine Lehre von der ewigen Wiederkunft', *Blätter fur deutsche Philosophie*, 9 (1936), 368–87.

Haeuptner, Gerhard, *Die Geschichtsansicht des jungen Nietzsche: Versuch einer immanenten Kritik der zweiten Unzeitgemässen Betrachtung: 'Vom Nutzen und Nachteil der Historie für das Leben'* (Stuttgart, 1936).

Eggert-Schroeder, H., 'Nietzsches Erlebnis des großen Mittags', *Deutscher Almanach*, 8 (1937), 153–73.

Fuerstehal, A., *Maske und Scham bei Nietzsche: Ein Beitrag zur Psychologie seines Schaffens* (Basle, 1940).

Bollnow, O. F., *Das Wesen der Stimmungen* (Frankfurt/M, 1941) [contains the essays 'Rausch und Seligkeit' and 'Nietzsches Lehre vom großen Mittag'].

Hildebrandt, Kurt, 'Die Idee des Krieges bei Goethe, Hölderlin, Nietzsche', in A. Faust (ed.), *Das Bild des Krieges im deutschen Denken* (Stuttgart, 1941), vol. i, 373–409.

Spenlé, J. E., *Nietzsche et le problème européen* (Paris, 1943).

Norburn, R., 'Strange Prophet: Nietzsche and the Meaning of History', *Church Quarterly Review*, 139 (1945), 177–203.

Reverdin, H., 'Nietzsche psychologue', in *Vorträge zur Feier von Nietzsches hundertstem Geburtstag* (Zurich, 1945), 83–105.

Brunngraber, R., *Was zu kommen hat: Von Nietzsche zur Technokratie* (Vienna, 1947).

Rudensky-Brin, S. G., *Kollektivistisches in der Philosophie Nietzsches* (Basle, 1948).

Schock, H., *Nietzsches Philosophie des 'Menschlich-Allzumenschlichen': Kritische Darstellung der Aphorismen-Welt der mittleren*

Bibliography

Schaffenszeit als Versuch einer Neuorientierung des Gesamtbildes (Tübingen, 1948).

Cantoni, R., 'La figura del "Freigeist" nella filosofia di Nietzsche', *Archivio di filosofia* (1953) no. 2, 209–40.

Schlechta, Karl, *Nietzsches großer Mittag* (Frankfurt/M, 1954).

Sonns, S., *Das Gewissen in der Philosophie Nietzsches* (Winterthur, 1955).

Allemann, Beda, *Ironie und Dichtung* (Pfullingen, 1956) [contains a chapter on Nietzsche, pp. 98–118].

Stambaugh, Joan, *Untersuchungen zum Problem der Zeit bei Nietzsche* (The Hague, 1959).

Vogel, Martin, *Apollinisch und Dionysisch: Geschichte eines genialen Irrtums* (Regensburg, 1966).

Arendt, D., 'Der Nihilismus: Ursprung und Geschichte im Spiegel der Forschungsliteratur seit 1945', *Deutsche Vierteljahresschrift für Literaturwissenschaft und Geistesgeschichte*, 43 (1969), 344–66.

Bulhof, Ilse N., *Apollos Wiederkehr: Eine Untersuchung der Rolle des Kreises in Nietzsches Denken über Geschichte und Zeit* (The Hague, 1969).

Dupuy, R. J., *Politique de Nietzsche* (Paris, 1969) [a selection of texts with an introduction].

Raub, M., 'Die Einsamkeit Zarathustras: Eine Untersuchung des 4. Teils von Friedrich Nietzsches "Zarathustra"', *Zeitschrift für Religions-und Geistesgeschichte*, 21 (1969) no. 2, 55–72.

Sandvoss, E., *Hitler und Nietzsche* (Göttingen, 1969).

Bueb, B., *Nietzsches Kritik der praktischen Vernunft* (Stuttgart, 1970).

O'Flaherty, J. C., 'Eros and Creativity in Nietzsche's "Birth of Tragedy"', in *Studies in German Literature of the 19th and 20th Centuries* (Chapel Hill/NC, 1970).

Philonenko, A., 'Mélancholie et consolation chez Nietzsche', *Revue de métaphysique et de morale*, 70 (1971), 77–98.

Stambaugh, Joan, *Nietzsche's Thought of Eternal Return* (Baltimore, 1972).

Röttges, Heinz, *Nietzsche und die Dialektik der Aufklärung* (Berlin and New York, 1972).

Bibliography

Brose, K., *Geschichtsphilosophische Strukturen im Werk Nietzsches* (Berne and Frankfurt/M, 1973).

Funke, M., *Ideologiekritik und ihre Ideologie bei Nietzsche* (Stuttgart-Bad Cannstatt, 1974).

Hammer, F., *Leib und Geschlecht: Philosophische Perspektiven von Nietzsche bis Merleau-Ponty und phänomenologisch-systematischer Aufriß* (Bonn, 1974).

Dauer, D. W., 'Nietzsche and the Concept of Time', in *The Study of Time* (Berlin and New York, 1975), pp. 81–97.

Rodingen, H., *Aussage und Anweisung: Zwei Auslegungs-und Verständigungsmuster dargestellt an Texten von Leibniz und Nietzsche* (Meisenheim, 1975).

Schipperges, H., *Am Leitfaden des Leibes: Zur Anthropologik und Therapeutik Friedrich Nietzsches* (Stuttgart, 1975).

Paronis, M., *'Also sprach Zarathustra': die Ironie Nietzsches als Gestaltungsprinzip* (Bonn, 1976).

Grimm, Rüdiger H., *Nietzsche's Theory of Knowledge* (Berlin and New York, 1977).

Bertin, G. M., *Nietzsche, l'inattuale idea pedagogica* (Florence, 1977).

Goyard-Fabre, S., *Nietzsche et la question politique* (Paris, 1977).

Malet, N., 'L'homme et la femme dans la philosophie de Nietzsche', *Revue de métaphysique et de morale*, 82 (1977), 38–63.

Chassard, P., *Nietzsche: Finalisme et histoire* (Paris, 1977).

Balmer, H. P., *Freiheit statt Theologie: Ein Grundgedanke von Nietzsche* (Freiburg i. B., 1977).

Gianarolo, P., 'Le rêve dans la pensée de Nietzsche', *Revue de l'Enseignement Philosophique*, 28 (1977–78) no. 5, 11–32.

Escobar, R., *Nietzsche e la filosofia politica del XIX secolo* (Milan, 1978).

Pütz, Peter, 'Der Mythos bei Nietzsche', in Helmut Koopmann (ed.), *Mythos und Mythologie in der Literatur des 19. Jahrhunderts* (Frankfurt/M, 1979), pp. 251–62.

Henke, D., *Gott und Grammatik: Nietzsches Kritik der Religion* (Pfullingen, 1981).

Gerhardt, W., 'Zum Begriff der Macht bei Nietzsche', *Perspektiven der Philosophie*, 7 (1981), 73–101.

256

Bibliography

Masini, F., 'Il divino come "seconda innocenza" in Friedrich Nietzsche', *Paradigmi*, 1 (1983), 57–74.

Alfieri, L., *Apollo tra gli schiavi: La filosofia sociale e politica di Nietzsche (1869–1876)* (Milan, 1984).

Warren, Mark, *Nietzsche and Political Thought* (Cambridge/Mass. and London, 1988).

Stauth, George, and Bryan S. Turner, *Nietzsche's Dance: Resentment, Reciprocity and Resistance in Social Life* (Oxford and New York, 1988).

Taurek, B. H. F., *Nietzsche und der Faschismus: Eine Studie über Nietzsches politische Philosophie und ihre Folgen*, Hamburg, 1989.

Brose, K., *Sklavenmoral: Nietzsches Sozialphilosophie* (Bonn, 1990).

Commentaries

Naumann, G., *Zarathustra-Kommentar*, 4 vols (Leipzig, 1899–1901).

Gramzow, O., *Kurzer Kommentar zum Zarathustra* (Charlottenburg, 1907).

Weichelt, H., *Friedrich Nietzsche: 'Also sprach Zarathustra', erklärt und gewürdigt* (Leipzig, 1910).

Messer, A., *Erläuterungen zu Nietzsches 'Zarathustra'* (Stuttgart, 1922).

Heller, P., *'Von den ersten und letzten Dingen': Studien und Kommentar zu einer Aphorismenreihe von Friedrich Nietzsche*, Berlin 1972 (deals with aphorisms 1–34 of *Human, All Too Human*).

Index

Index

Index

Index

Index

Index

Index

Cultural Memory | *in the Present*

Reinhart Koselleck, *Timing History, Spacing Concepts: The Practice of Conceptual History*

Niklas Luhmann, *The Reality of the Mass Media*

Hubert Damisch, *A Childhood Memory by Piero della Francesca*

Hubert Damisch, *A Theory of /Cloud/: Toward a History of Painting*

Jean-Luc Nancy, *The Speculative Remark: (One of Hegel's bon mots)*

Jean-François Lyotard, *Soundproof Room: Malraux's Anti-Aesthetics*

Jan Patočka, *Plato and Europe*

Hubert Damisch, *Skyline: The Narcissistic City*

Isabel Hoving, *In Praise of New Travelers: Reading Caribbean Migrant Women Writers*

Richard Rand, ed., *Futures: Of Jacques Derrida*

William Rasch, *Niklas Luhmann's Modernity: The Paradoxes of Differentiation*

Jacques Derrida and Anne Dufourmantelle, *Of Hospitality*

Jean-François Lyotard, *The Confession of Augustine*

Kaja Silverman, *World Spectators*

Samuel Weber, *Institution and Interpretation: Expanded Edition*

Jeffrey S. Librett, *The Rhetoric of Cultural Dialogue: Jews and Germans in the Epoch of Emancipation*

Ulrich Baer, *Remnants of Song: Trauma and the Experience of Modernity in Charles Baudelaire and Paul Celan*

Samuel C. Wheeler III, *Deconstruction as Analytic Philosophy*

David S. Ferris, *Silent Urns: Romanticism, Hellenism, Modernity*

Rodolphe Gasché, *Of Minimal Things: Studies on the Notion of Relation*

Sarah Winter, *Freud and the Institution of Psychoanalytic Knowledge*

Samuel Weber, *The Legend of Freud: Expanded Edition*

Aris Fioretos, ed., *The Solid Letter: Readings of Friedrich Hölderlin*

J. Hillis Miller / Manuel Asensi, *Black Holes / J. Hillis Miller; or, Boustrophedonic Reading*

Miryam Sas, *Fault Lines: Cultural Memory and Japanese Surrealism*

Peter Schwenger, *Fantasm and Fiction: On Textual Envisioning*

Didier Maleuvre, *Museum Memories: History, Technology, Art*

Jacques Derrida, *Monolingualism of the Other; or, The Prosthesis of Origin*

Andrew Baruch Wachtel, *Making a Nation, Breaking a Nation: Literature and Cultural Politics in Yugoslavia*